PRAISE FOR *THE CREATIVE THINKING HANDBOOK*

'A really inspiring and pragmatic guide to innovation and creativity – key drivers of great businesses.'
Peter Estlin, Lord Mayor of the City of London

'As always, Chris Griffiths thinks ahead. He also thinks, up, down, around the back and under! Here, he shares this art with us and prepares us to think creatively for ourselves on challenges we can't even perceive of yet. It's a must-read.'
Sharon Curry, Executive Leadership Coach, Mind Map, Creativity and Innovation Instructor

'Chris Griffiths delivers the perfect, practical recipe book for driving creativity and innovation into action.'
Stuart Miller, Chief Executive Officer, MindMapUSA

'As technology evolves to the point that it becomes a commodity, individuals and organizations must compete by unlocking human potential and inspiration. This book could not be better timed. Chris Griffiths gives us a powerful, hands-on approach to tap into our creative flow and become masters in our chosen field. An essential resource for anyone looking to "be different" and create at their highest capacity.'
Jan Mühlfeit, Executive Coach/Mentor, former Chairman of Microsoft Europe, author of *The Positive Leader*

'If you want your innovation to become part of everyday practice, this book is for you. Very accessible, with a structure that lays out a pathway to sustainable growth.'
Bill Lowe, Leadership and Learning Writer and Trainer, Executive Consultant at Kestrel Education

'There are many reasons why innovation has an increasingly important role to play in the modern workplace, but there are few practical guides on how to establish robust systems and processes to deliver it. In this insightful book, Chris Griffiths provides a comprehensive suite of tools that will provide any business with a great track to run on when implementing innovation with their teams.'
David Jones, Financial Services Professional

'Essential reading for any HR professional, manager or CEO looking to extend the boundaries of what is possible in their organization. This book challenges readers' assumptions about their thinking and the traps we must avoid if we are to develop our creative thinking abilities.'
Keith Usher, Managing Director, Insight Learning Organisation

'In times of industrial revolutions like the digital revolution today, it is simply key to think not only differently, but creatively. Chris Griffiths provides a very useful toolkit.'
Steffen Niehues, C-Level Executive, Software

'A great read; thoroughly enjoyable and providing inspirational insight into thinking that will change the way you approach your own.'
Andy Hayward, Director, Infinity BTS Ltd

'If you don't want to wait for ever for ideas to occur, then Chris Griffiths can tell you how to generate useful ideas right when you need them most.'
Pavan Bhattad, Pavan Bhattad Institute of Thinking

'Simply a must-read if you want to innovate and grow your business.'
Matteo Salvo, bestselling author on learning strategies and memory techniques, MINDPERFORMANCE

'Chris Griffiths has been inspiring me since our first meeting. He taught me not to over-glorify creativity. He gave me the keys to human thinking, and they opened the doors to real creativity.'
Karl Mortier, Educational Professional

'Another great read from Chris Griffiths. Through his experience and insights, he is not only inspiring organizations about really being innovative but showing the way. I hope more organizations take on board Chris' thinking.'
Richard Bradley, Managing Director, Master Trainer Institute, Geneva, Switzerland

The Creative Thinking Handbook

Your step-by-step guide to problem solving in business

Chris Griffiths with Melina Costi

KoganPage

First published in Great Britain and the United States in 2019 by Kogan Page Limited

2nd Floor, 45 Gee Street	122 W 27th St, 10th Floor	4737/23 Ansari Road
London	New York, NY 10001	Daryaganj
EC1V 3RS	USA	New Delhi 110002
United Kingdom		India

www.koganpage.com

© Chris Griffiths with Melina Costi, 2019

The right of Chris Griffiths and Melina Costi to be identified as the authors of this work has been asserted by them in accordance with the Copyright, Designs and Patents Act 1988.

ISBNs

Hardback	978 0 7494 9813 9
Paperback	978 0 7494 8466 8
Ebook	978 0 7494 8467 5

British Library Cataloguing-in-Publication Data

A CIP record for this book is available from the British Library.

Library of Congress Cataloging-in-Publication Data

Names: Griffiths, Chris, author. | Conti, Melina, author.
Title: The creative thinking handbook : your step-by-step guide to problem
  solving in business / Chris Griffiths and Melina Conti.
Description: 1 Edition. | New York : Kogan Page Ltd, [2019] | Includes
  bibliographical references.
Identifiers: LCCN 2018052641| ISBN 9780749484668 (pbk. : alk. paper) | ISBN
  9780749498139 (hardback : alk. paper) | ISBN 9780749484675 (ebook)
Subjects: LCSH: Creative ability in business. | Creative thinking. | Thought
  and thinking. | Problem solving.
Classification: LCC HD53 .G747 2019 | DDC 658.4/03–dc23 LC record available at
  https://lccn.loc.gov/2018052641]

Typeset by Integra Software Services, Pondicherry
Print production managed by Jellyfish
Printed and bound by CPI Group (UK) Ltd, Croydon CR0 4YY

CONTENTS

Downloadable templates and resources

This is a practical handbook that focuses on the application of creative thinking processes and tools. It comes with a selection of canvas templates and checklists to download and use, either for working alone or in teams. Each template has all the components you need to help capture your ideas and thoughts as you progress through the stages of the Solution Finder.

These resources can be downloaded and printed free of charge from **www.thinking.space**

ABOUT THE AUTHORS

Chris Griffiths

Chris Griffiths, the founder and CEO of OpenGenius, has helped thousands of people worldwide drive business growth using highly practical innovation processes, including teams and individuals from Fortune 500 and FTSE 100 companies, the United Nations, governments, the European Commission and Nobel Laureates. He is a pioneer in combining creative thinking strategies with technology to enhance productivity and is behind the iMindMap and DropTask apps, now utilized by over two million people worldwide.

Chris has over 28 years' experience in setting up and leading successful businesses that have ranked in the Deloitte European Fast 50 and *The Sunday Times* Fast-track 100. He sold his first company at the age of 26. He is a bestselling author on creativity and innovative thinking skills; *Grasp the Solution* reached number 2 on the Amazon UK Business Chart and *Mind Maps for Business*, which he co-authored, ranked number 5.

Chris was responsible for the creation of a Licensed Instructor Course in Mind Mapping, setting up a worldwide network of over 1,000 instructors. Along with his wife, Gaile, he is on a mission to promote innovative and entrepreneurial thinking from the grass roots up through the Inspire Genius Foundation. His latest development, Tec Marina, provides a creative hub for innovative growth stage companies in a converted 20,000 square foot warehouse in Penarth Marina, Wales.

Melina Costi

Melina Costi is a professional business writer and copy editor with a background in marketing management. She is co-author of *The Positive Leader* (with Jan Mühlfeit, former Microsoft Europe Chairman) and *Grasp the Solution*, which reached number 2 on the Amazon UK business chart.

Melina holds a first class BSc (Hons) degree in Business Studies from City University, London. She is also an accredited indexer and member of the Society of Indexers. Besides her work in publishing, Melina provides academic support services for adult students with learning difficulties and disabilities.

ACKNOWLEDGEMENTS

I'd like to thank the following exceptional minds who've helped this book come together:

First, the OpenGenius team for their magical creative touch, sterling efforts and readiness to 'think differently' day in day out. It's an enormous pleasure to work with you all. Additional special thanks to my co-author, Melina Costi, for her research, insights, edits and care with the material, not to mention her unwavering commitment to bringing this book to life. Melina has a magic with words that very few possess and I feel honoured to have worked with her over many years.

I owe a huge debt to the many Licensed Instructors in Mind Mapping and Applied Innovation, and Partners across the globe who have willingly and enthusiastically provided their input and tested many of my ideas across a spectrum of environments. Through their sound advice and feedback the material in this book was able to take on a concrete form. Thanks also to my treasured clients, customers and to all those who have provided feedback and support.

At Kogan Page, my heartfelt gratitude goes to our commissioning editor Rebecca Bush for her unstinting excitement about the project, savvy editing and extensive guidance through every draft. And to the rest of the publishing team, thanks for making it all possible.

I must also pay tribute to all the authors, researchers and creativity experts referenced in this book whose illuminating insights have laid a firm foundation for understanding our mental barriers. Their groundbreaking work continues to impact businesses and individuals far and wide and offers great promise that we can all blaze our own creative paths of success.

Finally, I will be forever grateful to my family – my wife Gaile and my two amazing children, Alex and Abbie, for their patience and infinite encouragement throughout this journey. Thank you for gracing my life and making it special every single day.

Chris Griffiths

FOREWORD

The challenge is the same. Whether you are an entrepreneur working to create a new business, a team member in a small company striving to grow, or a manager in a large company facing the challenges of a rapidly changing market, sustained creativity in the face of difficult and unfamiliar problems is the 'magic sauce' that underpins success. Yet despite its importance, the companies and individuals I work with seem to spend remarkably little time thinking and talking about creativity (at least the less-successful ones). In fact, it seems as if there is a tacit agreement in many companies that creativity is something you either have or don't and, in any case, it is a dark art that can't be explained or improved.

Yet there is extensive evidence that this is not true. Much is known about creativity and it is clear that people and teams *can* learn to be more creative. Thinking about creativity in the correct way, and learning new ways of approaching problem solving, has real and positive impacts on the level of creativity that results. It is unfortunate that the most common approach in companies is to try and hire creativity in the form of consultants and advisors (or, more recently, 'millennials'). But when these routes don't solve the creativity drought, companies are often left wondering if there isn't a better way?

Indeed, there is! In *The Creative Thinking Handbook*, Chris Griffiths and Melina Costi have produced a repeatable system that enables people to open their minds and conquer their professional challenges, using the power of creative thinking. They show us how creativity can be equally imaginative and logical, and how this traditionally 'soft' skill can be systematically channelled for hard results. This is the solution for anyone who wants to increase their creativity, their ability to solve problems creatively, and, as a result, their ability to succeed in a rapidly changing world.

This book is highly practical in that it takes the reader through the mental preparation to be an effective creative problem solver from start to finish. Through self-assessment using the Decision Radar profiling tool, you can gain an insight into the way you think and develop a fundamental understanding of the thinking errors that are holding you back. With this background knowledge in place, you are given a proactive four-step process – the

Solution Finder – to meet business challenges head on and to better seize new opportunities. During the process, readers can choose from a selection of tools and techniques to help them achieve the right outcome for the stage they are at.

Chris's unique approach to creativity is as powerful as it is practical, embodying more than 30 years' experience in the field. An acclaimed speaker, Chris coaches and trains individuals and businesses to think better and maximize their creative output. People from all over the world have engaged in the OpenGenius Applied Innovation training course which takes participants through the four-step process shown in this book to tackle their real-life business challenges. *The Creative Thinking Handbook* is packed full of thought-provoking examples, concepts, downloadable templates and methodologies that have been thoroughly road-tested in these workshops, on top of drawing from the latest scientific research on how we think.

As someone who teaches innovation and works extensively with growing companies, I must congratulate Chris Griffiths on the tremendous service he has provided by writing this book. His broad experience with thousands of individuals and companies has put him in a unique position to provide a structured and concrete guide to being more creative. The simple and highly practical approach he provides will allow anyone to be more creative and provide the crucial ingredient to innovative problem solving by giving us the confidence and tools to succeed. Following its simple steps will not only help to kickstart people's creativity, but used faithfully and habitually, will enable managers, professionals and entrepreneurs to create and embed a culture of continuous and radical innovation in their organizations.

Professor Nelson Phillips
Abu Dhabi Chamber Chair in Innovation and Strategy
Imperial College London

Professor Phillips is Abu Dhabi Chamber Chair in Innovation and Strategy at Imperial College London. He teaches courses in strategy, organizational behaviour, innovation, and leadership at undergraduate and graduate level, and is active in executive education, including facilitation and course leadership of the Elite Accelerator Programme at the London Stock Exchange.

Introduction

Why do we need new ideas, really?

One can resist the invasion of armies; one cannot resist the invasion of ideas.
– VICTOR HUGO, French poet and novelist, in *Histoire d'un Crime*

Knowledge is no longer power

How many times have you heard that 'knowledge is power'? There was an era when possessing information and being an expert in your field gave you prime advantage. Your unique mass of experience, professional training and knowledge put you ahead of the game and gave you your 'edge'. Now, not so much.

What's becoming apparent in the fast and furious cycling of today's world is that what used to work before no longer works today, and existing knowledge, while still useful, is not enough to thrive. Compare life to how it was 30 years ago – today we eat differently (convenience foods, multicultural cuisine), we communicate differently (mobile phones, e-mail, social networks), we shop differently (online, huge one-stop supermarkets), we work differently (sophisticated machinery and technology, new jobs such as 'app developers'), we even learn and study differently (virtual learning environments, interactive whiteboards, internet research). The list goes on. In just three short decades, we're living in a different world!

What does this mean? It means that no matter how smart or talented we are, we must be able to adapt and evolve – both as businesses and as individuals. The dilemma is that while everything around us is on the move, much of our present way of thinking is stagnant. Most of the time we manoeuvre through our work domain following the assumptions, patterns and belief systems that we've carefully honed over our years of expertise, responding to challenges and opportunities using standardized strategies that worked for us before. After all, we're paid to have all the answers. However, 21st-century business problems contain too many variables and unknowns to be answered with existing knowledge alone. The tried-and-tested solutions of the past won't cut it when it comes to solving present and future challenges. We need creative thinking to find new and interesting ways to crack them. Consequently, **creativity is the new power.** Success is no longer about what we know, but what we can *create*.

When the time is ripe to explore the unknown and generate new ideas, our conventional thinking habits let us down. They box us in by focusing on what we already know, rather than bringing something entirely new to the table. Eventually, they turn into thinking 'errors' because they stop us searching for inventive ways to accomplish our goals. The following exercise will show you how easy and natural it is to base your thinking on past programming (aka 'knowledge'). Try it now.

ACTIVITY
Months of the year

Recite the months of the year as fast as you can. I'm guessing you were probably able to do it in less than five seconds.
Now list the months again, this time alphabetically.
Not so easy now, is it?

SOURCE *Think Better* (Hurson, 2008)

To see the answer, head to page 225. With the normal pattern, you can list the months quickly without problem. But without it, you have to really think about the information. You're forced to break the usual pattern and look at the situation afresh. In doing that, the information becomes more dynamic and you can broaden your thinking to construct a completely new pattern.

Thinking is the hardest work there is, which is probably why so few engage in it.

– HENRY FORD, American industrialist and founder
of the Ford Motor Company

The entire focus of this book is to get you thinking differently and I'm going to ask you to do some thinking as you work through it. Throughout the chapters, there are methodologies, exercises and tools that will take you out of your comfort zone, but they serve a very important purpose – to help you master your biases and think clearly, constructively and creatively. You'll be asking questions to which you won't already have immediate answers, so I suggest you remove your 'expert' cap before you continue. It's worth the effort. Thinking differently is the key to unlocking the best, most innovative answers to your business challenges, so you're not just 'getting stuff done' but 'getting it done better'.

Create or die!

According to research by Yale School of Management professor Richard Foster, the average life expectancy of a company listed in the S&P 500 Index dropped from 61 years in 1958 to just 18 years by 2012 (Innosight, 2012). Foster also estimated that, at the current churn rate, 75 per cent of top US firms will be replaced by companies we haven't even heard of by 2027. In the UK, it's a similar story. Of the 100 companies listed in the FTSE 100 in 1984, only 24 were still in that position in 2012.

There's a stark lesson in these figures. If companies aren't constantly looking to innovate and reinvent themselves, they risk being caught off guard by new entrants and falling by the wayside. The large organizations whose power previously rested on their command of scientific knowledge and expertise are on a losing path. There's a maxim that goes, 'If you keep doing what you've always done, you'll keep getting what you've always got.' Again, this is no longer true. In the new economy, if you aren't moving forward, you're not just standing still, you're being left *way* behind. Remember Blockbuster, Compaq, Blackberry and HMV? These are companies that once dazzled with promise but have long since gone to rust. It's easy to follow in their footsteps if you fail to see the opportunities around you.

Today's businesses require a constant flow of new ideas, angles and solutions to stay abreast of rapid change and uncertainty. Creative insights are needed to solve industry challenges in new and useful ways, and to make bold leaps into uncharted territory. There are still professionals and businesses out there that believe creativity has no real substance. They see it as decoration – something pink and fluffy to beautify the look of a product or garnish a company's reputation. In this, they're inherently mistaken. Creativity can, and indeed should, be as focused and targeted as any other key operation in the business, from HR to Finance to Product Development. I like to call this rigorous and forward-thinking approach **applied creativity**.

Through applied creativity, you can find new ideas about the causes of problems, ideas to help you solve those problems, ideas to make common executive decisions, and ideas about where you will go next. Knowledge is still important. It's a crucial pillar of the creative process; you need knowledge to help you connect information and evaluate ideas. But its value is limited without creative application. Creativity allows you to discover new knowledge and fresh ideas, and these ideas are what will change the status quo. Just like Google changed the way we access information, Netflix changed the way we watch TV and Twitter changed the way we interact with others. Regardless of size or scope, producing novel ideas is what will help you break new ground in your corner of the world.

Ideas help you answer all sorts of questions, such as:

- How can we retain more customers/clients?
- What could be causing problem W?
- How can we streamline our business processes?
- What opportunities are available to us this year?
- How can we improve our performance in Department X?
- How can I solve problem Y?
- What new markets can we enter?
- How can we take advantage of this change in legislation?
- What extra features can we add to product Z?
- How can I motivate my team?

Bit by bit, the power of creativity is coming to recognition. In its 'The Future of Jobs' report published in 2016, the World Economic Forum identified complex problem solving, critical thinking and creativity as the top three crucial workplace skills needed to thrive by 2020, stating: 'With the avalanche of new products, new technologies and new ways of working, workers are going to have to become more creative in order to benefit from these changes' (Gray, 2016).

Adobe surveyed 1,000 full-time, college-educated professionals and found creativity to be an integral part of modern work, with more than 85 per cent agreeing that creative thinking is critical for problem solving in their career (Adobe, 2012). Nine out of ten workers agree that creativity is required for economic growth, and 96 per cent believe it is valuable to society. Yet, 32 per cent don't feel comfortable thinking creatively in their career and a huge chunk (78 per cent) wish they had more creative ability.

The creativity gap

82% of surveyed companies believe there is a strong connection between creativity and business results

BUT

61% of senior managers do not see their companies as creative

Only 11% agree that their current practices are aligned with creative working

10% felt their practices were the opposite of what creative companies do

SOURCE 'The Creative Dividend' (Adobe, 2014)

We lose our creativity with age

As children, we were all far more creative than we are today. This premise has been tested many times over the years. For example, 1,600 five-year-olds were given a creativity test used by NASA to select innovative engineers and scientists in 1969. Of these children, a staggering 98 per cent scored in the 'highly creative' range. Five years later, these same children (now 10 years old) were re-tested and only 30 per cent were still rated 'highly creative'. Another five years later, when the children were 15 years old, just 12 per cent of them were ranked in this category. More revealing, however, was that 250,000 adults over the age of 25 also took the same test and a paltry 2 per cent of them scored in the highly creative range (see Figure 0.1). Given that you're reading this book, I'm guessing you want to be part of that 2 per cent!

What does this study prove? In the words of innovation author Stephen Shapiro (2003), 'Creativity is therefore not learned, but rather unlearned.' Creativity is a quality that can be universally found in all of us as young children, but it dies out rapidly as we reach adulthood. As a little kid, you probably had no problem using your imagination. So, what happened? Consider the questions that follow Figure 0.1.

Figure 0.1   NASA creativity test

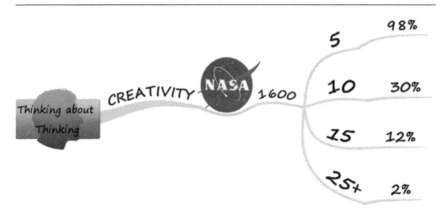

Q1. How many hours did you spend learning maths at school?
Most people who've gone through the standard school system would say
about 5,000+ hours. Was it the same for you? How much of that was valuable time? How much do you remember now?

Q2. How many hours did you spend learning creativity?
A few? None? Most of us learn this outside of the education system. Did
you ever take an Innovation 101 class?

At school we have countless limits set on us by our teachers. The educational system focuses on training our minds for storing and analysing information instead of developing our power to generate new ideas and bring
them into being. We're taught to memorize the right answers and use other
people's solutions and knowledge, and at the same time we're 'untaught' to
find our own answers, solutions and knowledge. It doesn't take long for us
to learn that mistakes are bad, either. A fear of being wrong frightens even
the bravest of us out of expressing ourselves in ways that are mildly unconventional or different. By the time we enter the world of business, we're so
used to putting constraints around our thinking that it becomes institution-
alized very quickly.

  Young kids can come up with strikingly original solutions to problems
because they aren't bound by the rigid conventions and methodologies of
adulthood. They don't have the same mental restrictions as us poor adults.
Pablo Picasso, the Spanish artist and painter, illustrated this point perfectly
when he said, 'It took me four years to paint like Raphael but a lifetime to
paint like a child.' That mindset of always being open, excited and curious
to look at different things is what exposes children to new ideas. Instead of

being constrained by boundaries, their thinking is boundless; instead of conforming, they are creating.

Because of this loss of creativity over time, it's common for people to believe that they're 'just not the creative type'. This line of thinking is crushing as it leads them to doubt whether there's any point even trying to think or act creatively – creativity is for artists, designers, musicians and mad bohemian types, not for us straight-faced professionals. Some of us aren't very sporty, but if we start a training regime and take care of our diet, then in a few months we would be much fitter and healthier. By the same token, we don't actually lose our creative capacity as we get older; this is a false impression. It just gets out of shape through lack of use because of our misguided belief that it doesn't have any practical application. Like a muscle that's never exercised, creativity withers through neglect. By relearning how to play and adopting an active pursuit of creativity and mental improvement, we can all rediscover and re-experience the magic of creativity that we knew as children. Imagine what you could achieve if you could go back to your creativity levels at five years old!

Think without the box

Some people say creativity is about thinking *outside* the box, others that it's about being creative *inside* the box. But what if there is no box? If you can realize what the box is and remove it, you can unlock unlimited streams of creativity. The box represents your existing assumptions, habits, biases and default thinking routes. Apple threw away the box when they asked themselves, 'What if we developed a mobile phone without a keypad?' This was a magic moment for Apple, and the unprecedented success of the iPhone, with its huge touchscreen and sleek, sexy design, soon toppled the global market leader Nokia from the top spot. At the time, every other manufacturer had overlooked the emergence of touchscreen technology. They couldn't break free from existing assumptions about phone design and judged that consumers would continue to prefer physical keypads. If, like me, you've attended your fair share of brainstorming sessions, you'll know from experience that discarding the box is not an easy thing to do. Let's look at a typical scenario.

Brainstorming blunders

The morning meeting with your colleagues kicks off well. You start generating some ideas and gradually get into a moderate flow. There are the practical 'no-brainer' ideas, the crazy 'out there' ideas and all sorts of varied and interesting ideas in between. Things look promising. But then what happens? Any number of things can occur to knock you and other team members off your creative stride. Usually, the ideas will dry up and fizzle out. Or they become that little bit too wacky for your liking, so you decide to stick to the 'safe', less risky options. *'Let's keep doing what we're doing, only do it better and faster!'*

Or

'Let's go with the same design but re-package it in purple this time.'

Perhaps you or other members of the team automatically begin nit-picking and analysing the ideas, taking your attention away from creating any new ones.

'Someone's already done that.'
'Our customers won't like it.'
'It's not our style.'
'But how will that make money?'
'We did it last year.'
'It's a great idea but we can't afford it.'

Or maybe you fall prey to a fearful, extra-negative outlook which blocks your ability to see the potential in certain ideas and causes you to kill everyone's buzz.

'That would never work.'
'It's against our policy.'
'Sounds hard.'
'Nothing like that has ever been done in the industry before. It would be a complete waste of time.'

Sometimes you get lucky and the right idea comes bounding in early during the process. There's no point carrying on with the session. You've already got your perfect solution… or have you?

You start taking action on your idea only to find that you didn't think it through properly and it simply won't work in reality. You blindly neglected to give any other suggestions a chance and now you're stuck with seeing the bad idea through, otherwise you'll have wasted all that precious time and energy. Whichever way, the box has turned up to block your creativity; you need to knock it out of the way and get back on the road to innovation. No box means your mind can remain fully open as the process unfolds.

'Minds are like parachutes. They function only when open'

As with a parachute, if your mind is kept closed when you're trying to be innovative, sooner rather than later you'll come crashing down. To open your mind, you need to know what locks are on it. An open mind, free of any locks, is fundamental to creativity, particularly at the beginning of ideation. There are a surprising number of mental locks and restrictions that you'll need to watch out for and I'll be describing the most common ones in Part One. In Part Two, you will learn positive strategies to reduce their impact and make better decisions. Sometimes knowing what not to do is just as important as knowing what to do.

Creativity and innovation – what's the difference?

Although most of us have an intuitive understanding of what it means to be creative, there's still a great deal of uncertainty when it comes to defining this notoriously tricky concept. Before flexing your creative muscles, it's worth getting clear on what creativity really means. Despite a plethora of definitions on the web, the challenge is to identify a common definition you and your team can all understand and get on board with. A shared definition puts everyone on the same page and helps to set the creative direction for the business.

Feel free to use my definition of **creativity**:

> The incubator and cultivator of new ideas, which are born from existing knowledge and combined to form a new neural pathway in the brain, leading to a personal original thought.

It might not be the most glamorous definition around, but it describes the nature of how creativity is expressed in a way that people can easily engage with. Creativity is about connecting things in your mind until you come across an idea that is original and useful. Steve Jobs, the late co-founder of Apple, referred to the same principle as 'connecting the dots'.

Creativity and innovation are often used interchangeably, but there is a significant difference. **Innovation** is:

> The marriage of creative thinking and sound logic, which when applied together, create a new and potentially better solution or direction for one to explore and deliver.

Innovation is the whole package – creative and logical thinking combined to produce something meaningful and take ideas forward. In this sense, innovation is a connected process in which many activities come together to bring an idea to fruition. An innovation can be any idea that creates change and gets you moving closer to your goal. It doesn't have to be a supersonic development of historic importance, like the microchip, the printing press or the motor car. These transformational ideas are what Harvard business professor Clayton Christensen (1997) calls 'disruptive innovations' in his classic book *The Innovator's Dilemma*. An innovation can be incremental and still offer great value, such as a tiny improvement to customer service or inventory management processes. No matter if it's already been done elsewhere, if an idea is new to your business, then it still counts as an innovation. Together, such small changes add up to make a huge difference.

Applied creativity

While we know creative thinking and problem solving is hugely important to our success in business, few of us know how it comes about or how to put it into practice. As you'll soon discover, being creative is more than just rallying a bunch of people round to play the odd brainstorming game and jot down ideas on sticky notes or flipcharts. Think of the most innovative brands out there: Amazon, Apple, Disney, Google, Microsoft, Samsung, Starbucks, Tesla, Toyota, Virgin. And now consider the creative 'geniuses' you admire: James Dyson, Elon Musk, Richard Branson, Steve Jobs, Thomas Edison, Rihanna. For these companies and individuals, creativity is not merely the result of free-form improvisation. Far from being a stroke of luck, there are deliberate methods, structures and mindsets involved in generating new ideas. For instance, the guiding principle at the heart of Google's innovation process is '10x thinking' – trying to improve something by 10 times, not just 10 per cent. The Google X division was established to focus on breakthrough ideas and major technological advances that would change the landscape of the world, such as self-driving cars. The company likes to call these 'moonshot' projects.

CASE STUDY   Nintendo leaves luck to heaven

Like Google, Nintendo believes in having a crack at new things rather than trying to replicate its competitors' success. The name Nintendo means 'leave luck to heaven' and the company does just that by embracing a blue-ocean strategy to create new market spaces where it can swim freely in uncontested waters, far away from its competition in the gaming industry. A blue-ocean strategy is a marketing approach where, rather than viciously battling it out with rivals in an overcrowded market sector (ie the bloody 'red ocean'), you seek out 'blue oceans' of new market space where you can generate an innovative leap in value for consumers, often while reducing costs and unnecessary features. It's this mentality that has seen Nintendo's latest offering, the Switch, make headlines as the first hybrid console that can be utilized as a home gaming centre or a portable handheld device. The Nintendo Switch has been a smashing success, setting records in the United States and Japan as the fastest-selling console and beating even the PlayStation 2 in terms of early adoption (Kuchera, 2018).

Structure enables creativity to grow. Unending, chaotic creativity is almost as bad as no creativity at all. To change the way we do things, we need to start by changing the way we think. We do this by putting a strategy around our thinking processes. Just like a business creates strategies, systems and processes to facilitate its success, our thinking needs a proactive and purposeful strategy through which we can bring about the results we want. This is where the **Solution Finder** process comes in (you'll learn all about this in Part Two). This systematic approach adds order and logic to creativity, so it becomes something practical and concrete rather than an airy-fairy notion.

How to use this book

The Creative Thinking Handbook is divided into three parts. It can be read and applied from cover to cover during a live project or challenge. Whether working solo or in collaboration with others, you can move effortlessly and dynamically through the problem-solving process. Alternatively, you can dip in and out of the stages or sections that will help you the most. Depending on the challenge, not all steps may be immediately relevant, but reading them all will provide you with a background appreciation of the entire process and help to inspire creativity as you go about your day-to-day work.

Part One gives an insight into your thinking and sets the scene for what's to come. You'll begin by taking the Decision Radar test in Chapter 1 to assess and identify the 'risk areas' in your thinking, before getting to grips with the common thinking errors in Chapters 2, 3 and 4.

Figure 0.2   The Solution Finder process

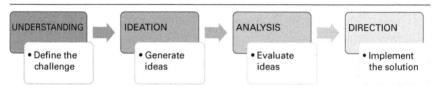

Part Two is the crux of the book – the Solution Finder (Figure 0.2), which is a pragmatic strategy devised to provide focused direction for your creative problem solving and decision making. Chapter by chapter, you'll be guided through the four steps to help you create the right mindset and atmosphere to uncover fresh approaches for real-life problems and projects, no matter how big or messy. From defining the challenge and generating lots of ideas, through to evaluating those ideas and setting your goals and action plans, each step features customized tools and techniques to assist you in overcoming your biases. It also comes with downloadable canvas templates and checklists to use in your individual or group creative sessions.

Part Three offers an opportunity to revisit the Decision Radar to see how far you've come after implementing the lessons in this book. Reflect on your improved skills and celebrate your progress, while also taking note of the areas you want to keep working on. Finally, we'll look at how you can commit to thinking differently as part of a lifelong strategy, so you can continue to drive creativity and innovation in your business and beyond.

You will learn how to:

- Assess your thinking to identify 'risk areas'
- Understand the context for better thinking
- Gain clarity on a business problem, challenge or opportunity
- Generate multiple ideas to any kind of problem
- Engage yourself and others in the creative process

- Look beyond the obvious ideas
- Explore fresh perspectives and opportunities
- Choose the 'best' ideas to develop
- Get past foolish and outdated assumptions
- Put a halt to hasty judgement
- Bring more objectivity into the decision-making process
- Combine tools and techniques for more powerful problem solving
- Break the problem–reaction loop
- Let go of fear and learn from mistakes
- Develop confidence in the quality of your solutions
- Avoid analysis paralysis
- Take on more helpful thinking habits, attitudes and beliefs
- Become more creative in your thinking over time
- Embed a creative culture into your organization

Whenever you're stuck on a decision, need a new idea or want to bring about positive change, it is my sincere hope that *The Creative Thinking Handbook* will inspire and guide you on your way.

Are you ready to get started?

References

Adobe (2012) [accessed 21 February 2018] Creativity and Education: Why It Matters [Online] www.adobe.com/aboutadobe/pressroom/pdfs/Adobe_Creativity_and_Education_Why_It_Matters_study.pdf

Adobe (2014) [accessed 21 February 2018] The Creative Dividend: How Creativity Impacts Business Results [Online] https://landing.adobe.com/dam/downloads/whitepapers/55563.en.creative-dividends.pdf

Clayton, CM (1997) *The Innovator's Dilemma: When new technologies cause great firms to fail*, Harvard Business Review Press, Boston, MA

Gray, A (2016) [accessed 21 February 2018] The 10 skills You Need to Thrive in the Fourth Industrial Revolution, *World Economic Forum*, 19 January [Online] www.weforum.org/agenda/2016/01/the-10-skills-you-need-to-thrive-in-the-fourth-industrial-revolution

Hurson, T (2008) *Think Better: An innovator's guide to productive thinking*, McGraw-Hill Professional, New York

Innosight (2012) [accessed 21 February 2018] Creative Destruction Whips Through Corporate America [Online] www.innosight.com/wp-content/uploads/2016/08/creative-destruction-whips-through-corporate-america_final2015.pdf

Kuchera, B (2018) [accessed 22 February 2018] Why the Nintendo Switch Is Selling So Well (update), Polygon, 31 January [Online] https://www.polygon.com/2018/1/4/16849672/nintendo-switch-sales-numbers-success-price-mario-zelda

Shapiro, S (2003) Unleashing the innovator, *Control*, 3, pp 19–21

Part One
Thinking About Your Thinking

01
The Decision Radar

The brain is a wonderful organ. It starts working the moment you get up in the morning, and doesn't stop until you get to the office.

— attributed to ROBERT FROST

Mind-numbing patterns

The quote above might well be said in jest, but it communicates a crucial point. Most of us go through our lives without being aware of the thinking processes behind the decisions we make or activities we perform. We operate on autopilot – we wake up in the morning, get dressed, journey to work, and go about our daily tasks without giving it much thought.

This is because the human mind works on pattern and rule recognition. The brain is bombarded with oodles of information all the time. If it tried to evaluate each and every individual bit of data in real time, it would shut down. So, to cope with this, the brain groups information into patterns or rules and then operates on these high-level sets of data, rather than concerning itself with low-level details. Look at language, for example. When you're learning to talk and read, you have to create patterns for letters, words and sentences. Over time these patterns become well established and neatly logged into your brain. So now, as you're reading these pages, you don't have to stop and think about what you're processing, you just put together words and sentences into recognizable patterns.

Our default patterns can be very useful and practical most of the time. They make it easier to get things done, particularly dull and boring things. When you get dressed in the morning, you don't consciously think about the sequence of how you'll put on your clothes. Once you've chosen what to wear, you don't have to make any decisions at all about getting dressed; you just do it. You automatically follow your getting-dressed pattern. In the same way, you follow your going-to-work pattern and brushing-your-teeth pattern.

As you can expect, this automatic thinking and behaviour is ideal for routine work tasks as it puts us in the right frame to tackle things quickly and efficiently. For instance, we might have found an approach that works exceptionally well for dealing with awkward customers and will use it time and time again with great success. We don't have to waste our energy reinventing the wheel each time we encounter that same problem. Our routine patterns allow us to get on with the business of living... But what about the business of succeeding?

While these pre-programmed actions save us valuable time and effort, they can also make us blind to other opportunities. As our mind recognizes and stores patterns, they become entrenched and difficult to change, so we remain stuck on one path.

Try solving this number task.

ACTIVITY
The equation

Look at this equation:

Figure 1.1   The equation

$$2 + 7 - 118 = 129$$

As you can see, it's incorrect. How can you make this equation correct by adding a single straight line? Have a go now.

For the answer, see page 225.

Did you find a way to correct the equation? Were you surprised that there's actually more than one way to do it?

That's the interesting thing about your routine mental patterns. They would have you thinking that there's only one right answer, and only one optimal way of finding that answer. For any challenge, there are countless possible solutions and paths. If you struggled with this, it's probably because your mind unconsciously imposed a 'number-solving pattern' that had you approaching the task from only one direction. While it would appear to be a mathematical problem, the answer itself is *visual*. You need to shift your mental focus away from the figures to look at the problem as a whole, and then you can see the answer/s.

The message is clear – if we want to become wow-the-world innovative, we sometimes have to interrupt our patterns or even go against them completely. In creative terms, too much routine amounts to insanity, which has been memorably defined as 'doing the same thing over and over again and expecting different results'. As our work climate changes rapidly and we stumble upon new kinds of challenges, we need our thinking to become more switched on and proactive so that we can seek out different ways to get results. Thus, the real skill to creativity is being able to think with purpose.

Metacognition

Metacognition plays a governing role in creating successful innovation. This is commonly understood to mean the act of 'thinking about thinking', but it goes far beyond this. Metacognition is the ability to control one's cognitive processes and has been linked in several studies to intelligence (Borkowski, Carr and Pressely, 1987; Brown, 1987; Sternberg, 1984, 1986a, 1986b). According to Sternberg (1986b: 24), the underlying purpose of metacognition is 'figuring out how to do a particular task or set of tasks, and then making sure that the task or set of tasks are done correctly'. These executive processes involve planning, evaluating and monitoring problem-solving actions. Sternberg suggests that the ability to self-regulate cognitive resources, such as deciding how and when a task should be accomplished, is key to intelligence (Hendrick, 2014).

Thus, more than anything, metacognition is the act of applying a strategy around your thinking to get the results you want (Griffiths and Costi, 2011). In this sense, it represents the highest order of thinking possible. The following are questions that I often pose to my audiences during workshops or conferences. What would your answer be to each one?

Q. Do you think about your diet?

Q. Do you think about your fitness?

Q. Do you think about your appearance?

Q. Do you think about your thinking?

If you're like most people, your answer to the first three questions is likely to be an immediate 'Yes'. It's only when we reach the last question that the response is apt to be quite different! At best, the answer is 'Sometimes'.

More often than not, it's a flat 'No'. This is precisely the problem – we rarely, if ever, think about our thinking.

When it comes to different areas of your life such as your health and appearance, you probably put in place strategies and processes to manage them. For instance, you might design a meal plan or exercise programme to help you reach your ideal weight and fitness level. But I would stake a decent-sized bet that you hardly ever do the same with your mind. Surely it makes sense to manage your thinking just as you would other areas of your life. Applying a strategy is key to overcoming your natural, automatic tendencies, so you don't succumb to 'active inertia', that is, reverting to the same old responses whenever a new threat comes along. But, before you can apply a strategy, you need to get to grips with the thinking errors that keep you trapped in old habits and patterns.

If not checked, thinking errors can paralyse your creative thinking. To understand this better, imagine that you're running a sprint as you would normally, with two arms and legs working freely. Then visualize that you're running with your left hand tied to your left foot. Would you be half as effective or less than half as effective as before?

You would be much less than half as effective, of course. While you're still using half of your running resources, that is, one arm and one leg, the reduction in your power and efficiency is far greater than 50 per cent. It's closer to a deterioration of 99 per cent because the distribution of your body weight has changed massively, increasing the chances of you tripping over and falling flat on your face! This type of restriction is exactly what we do to ourselves when trying to implement new strategies and ideas. We put so many limitations on our ability to think, the result is that we often stop ourselves going anywhere.

Put your thinking under the radar

Before I show you how to eradicate thinking errors and construct a strategy around your thinking, you need to learn more about how you and your colleagues make decisions. Our purposefully designed **Decision Radar** profiling tool will help you identify the strengths and weaknesses in your thinking, giving you the groundwork from which you can increase your personal capacity to think more productively and nurture a balanced decision-making environment for you and your team (Figure 1.2).

Figure 1.2   The Decision Radar

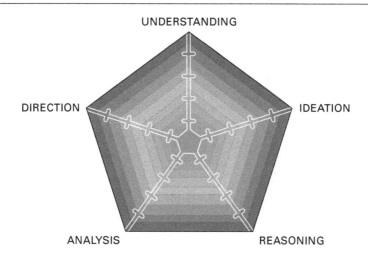

The tool consists of a series of multiple choice questions to assess your decision-making skills according to five factors:

- **UNDERSTANDING.** The ability to define and understand a problem or challenge.

- **IDEATION.** Generative thinking that facilitates the formation of new ideas.

- **REASONING.** The mental powers concerned with forming conclusions by using sound judgement and good sense by thinking about something in a logical, objective and sensible way (ie your overall thinking habits).

- **ANALYSIS.** The ability to sort, screen and select the alternative that has the best chance of providing a successful outcome based on defined criteria.

- **DIRECTION.** The ability to take a decision that's been made and deliver a successful outcome.

Think about the way you approach situations and problems, then take the test. Answer the questions honestly, without thinking too hard about your responses. Allow up to 20 minutes to complete the assessment. Take the Decision Radar evaluation here: **https://decisionradar.opengenius.com/**

After completing the assessment, you will be given a score evaluation according to the five factors, each corresponding to a particular colour gradient on the radar. The closer to green (on the outside ring), the better, while

Figure 1.3   The Decision Radar – example profile

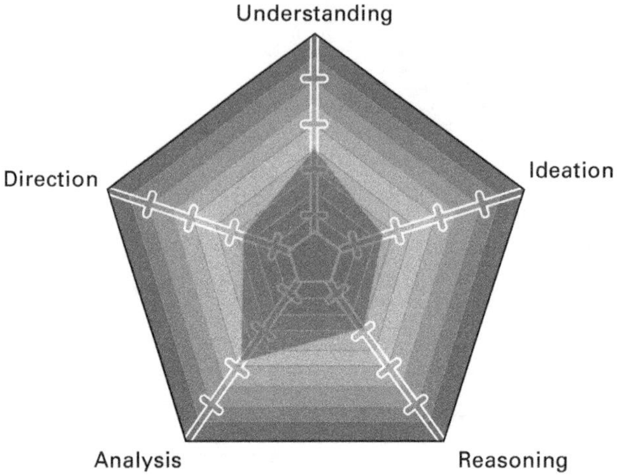

Understanding	49%
Ideation	33%
Reasoning	38%
Analysis	58%
Direction	34%

Test date:
21 February 2018 17.07

scores in the red (on the inside ring) indicate areas for strong improvement. Note: The images in this book are not shown in colour, but you will be able to see the distinctive colours of the Decision Radar on screen and in any printouts. Your radar will reflect the way you make decisions in a professional environment and may look something like the example in Figure 1.3.

From the example, we can see that this individual has relatively low scores for Ideation (33%), Reasoning (38%) and Direction (34%), indicating that their skill is noticeably less developed in these areas. With this information at the ready, it's easy to determine which aspects of their thinking process call for the strongest attention. The radar pinpoints exactly where they need to target their efforts, and they would benefit by spending some extra time on the associated chapters in the book.

Take action on your results

Based on the results of your Decision Radar profile, you'll be able to clearly determine the strongest and weakest areas in your thinking. Notice which facets you have already developed, and which ones need adjusting.

It's not enough just knowing about your thinking, however. You also need to know what to do about it. Note that your results are not fixed. The brain can be trained and retrained for better outcomes. A 2010 McKinsey study of more than 1,000 major business investments showed that when organizations worked at reducing the effect of bias in their decision-making processes, they achieved returns up to seven percentage points higher (Lovallo and Sibony, 2010). Good thinking practices can make a concrete difference, as can an innovation focus. In a landmark study over an 11-year period, Harvard Business School professors John Kotter and James Heskett found that the net income for firms with an adaptive, innovation-focused culture increased by 756 per cent compared to 1 per cent for those who had not developed a philosophy of thinking creatively (Kotter and Heskett, 1992).

Take heed of the advice given by the Decision Radar to help you minimize your risk areas. The coming chapters will provide you with further knowledge and the right techniques to neutralize these risks. If working collaboratively, consider how you can achieve greater balance as a team, so you can implement your most innovative ideas together. Once you've read the book and applied the Solution Finder process, do this assessment again to check on how your thinking has progressed.

Key takeaways

- At home and in the workplace, we all learn to rely on routine patterns and rules to guide our behaviour and be efficient. Sadly, these old patterns fail to serve us when we need to think differently; for instance, we might only see the obvious way of looking at a problem or stick to comfortable, familiar ways of finding solutions.

- Becoming fitter and healthier isn't something that happens by chance; it requires strategy, as does your thinking if you're going to increase your creative capacity for coming up with better ideas.

- Metacognition is more than 'thinking about thinking'. It's the act of putting a strategy around your thinking to help you accomplish your goals.

- Take the Decision Radar test to discover your personal thinking profile. Identify your strengths and weaknesses and find out how to handle them.

References

Borkowski, J, Carr, M and Pressely, M (1987) 'Spontaneous' strategy use: perspectives from metacognitive theory, *Intelligence*, **11** (1), pp 61–75

Brown, AL (1987) Metacognition, executive control, self-regulation, and other more mysterious mechanisms, in *Metacognition, Motivation, and*

Understanding, ed FE Weinert and RH Kluwe, pp 65–116, Lawrence Erlbaum Associates, Hillsdale, NJ

Griffiths, C and Costi, M (2011) *Grasp the Solution: How to find the best answers to everyday challenges*, Proactive Press, Cardiff

Hendrick, C (2014) [accessed 12 March 2018] Metacognition: An Overview [Blog], *Wellington Learning and Research Centre*, 22 September [Online] http://learning.wellingtoncollege.org.uk/resources/metacognition-an-overview/

Kotter, JP and Heskett, JL (1992) *Corporate Culture and Performance*, Free Press, New York

Lovallo, D and Sibony, O (2010) [accessed 21 February 2018] The case for behavioral strategy, *McKinsey Quarterly*, March [Online] www.mckinsey.com/business-functions/strategy-and-corporate-finance/our-insights/the-case-for-behavioral-strategy

Sternberg, RJ (1984) What should intelligence tests test? Implications for a triarchic theory of intelligence for intelligence testing, *Educational Researcher*, **13** (1), pp 5–15

Sternberg, RJ (1986a) Inside intelligence, *American Scientist*, **74** (2), pp 137–143

Sternberg, RJ (1986b) *Intelligence Applied: Understanding and increasing your intellectual skills*, Harcourt Brace Jovanovich, New York

02
Common thinking errors

Selective thinking

Killing creativity and smart decisions

If your brainstorming isn't succeeding, if you're not getting enough ideas or you're not getting the right ideas, chances are you're stuck in an unhelpful or corrupt thinking pattern. No doubt you and others in your team are largely unaware of this. Our minds can do amazing things, but under certain circumstances they can also let us down badly. There's plenty of evidence in the field of psychology that indicates how we all have glitches in our thinking when making decisions or solving problems. Behavioural science has openly acknowledged that not only are we sometimes irrational, but we are predictably irrational! Nobel Prize winner Daniel Kahneman has done a great job of bringing many of our thinking faults, heuristics and biases to light in his outstanding book *Thinking, Fast and Slow* (Kahneman, 2011).

In the next three chapters, I'll be using exercises, questions and games to uncover the flaws lurking in your mind and really bring home the error of your thinking ways. As you learn about the different types of thinking errors, ask yourself whether you've had these or similar thoughts and experiences. Try to recall any occasions where your mental mistakes may have prevented you from successfully solving a problem.

Our thinking errors tend to fall into one of three camps of thinking:

- **SELECTIVE thinking:** The tendency to validate certain ideas and discount others (eg favouring our 'pet' ideas).
- **REACTIVE thinking:** The tendency to react to existing influences, events or ideas, often too quickly.

- **ASSUMPTIVE thinking:** The tendency to accept a belief, convention or idea as true, often with no proof (usually based on past experience or 'common knowledge').

Selective, Reactive and Assumptive are all very useful kinds of thinking when used at the right time. But used at the wrong time – namely, when you need to think expansively and generate soaring ideas – they can hold you back quite drastically. For instance, reacting to situations and making decisions quickly is essential for physical survival and for dodging dangerous situations. It's not so productive, however, when you've got to make a big strategic decision and need to explore your options in depth.

That's the idea!

Nothing is more dangerous than an idea when it's the only one we have.
                                    – EMILE CHARTIER, French philosopher

If I were to pick out the single aspect of human thinking that causes the most harm in the brainstorming and decision-making process, it would have to be selective thinking. When people come up with what they think is a great option or decision, what do they do? They immediately look to justify it. As human beings, we rarely seek to prove ourselves wrong. But being able to find disconfirming evidence is just as (if not more!) important than seeking confirming evidence if we're to make the right decisions about which new product to launch or new market to enter. Failing to do this can very easily lead to some lousy choices and costly mistakes. Much like a filter on a camera lens that only allows in certain kinds of light, selective thinking leads us to accept or reject ideas almost immediately based on whether or not they fit into our existing paradigms.

CASE STUDY   We don't buy books for information

A 2009 meta-analysis study published by the American Psychological Association reviewed several research reports in the area of confirmation bias (a form of selective thinking). It concluded that people were almost two times more likely to seek information that supported their existing view than to seek information that contradicted their current view (Hart *et al*, 2009).

Think about it. What do we choose to read? Books written by people we agree with. During the 2008 US presidential election, Valdis Krebs at orgnet.com analysed purchasing trends on Amazon. He found that people who already supported Obama were the same people buying books that painted him in a positive light and, vice versa, people who already disliked Obama were the ones buying books showing him in a negative light (McRaney, 2010). Kreb's research highlights an interesting fact – we don't buy books for the information, but for the confirmation.

We can fall victim to different types of selective thinking:

Selective attention. You see what you expect to see. When you watch football, how often do you think the referee is biased against your team?

Selective recall. You only remember the things you want to. We have a weaker memory than we think. Have you noticed how two people can recount the same event differently?

- You: 'Remember that lovely road trip we took to the seaside last year?'
- Your partner: 'Oh *that* trip? It wasn't lovely, it was awful...'

Each of you could argue to the death that you were right, but in both cases, your recall of the event is selective.

Selective observation. You accept certain pieces of information that support your position, while ignoring the counter arguments. Or more simply, you count the hits and forget the misses. With selective observation, you can prove anything you want if you spend enough time on it. Doctors, accountants and politicians tend to get caught up in this.

The bias that binds

There are countless ways that selective thinking can creep into our minds, cloud our judgement and put a stop to our creativity.

1. Ignoring the facts

One of the main signs of selective thinking is ignoring the evidence that's right in front of you. By the 1920s, the Ford Motor Company was producing more than 60 per cent of all the motor vehicles in the United States and over half in the entire world. Henry Ford's Model T was a huge success – it was the car for the common man and seemed to have a personality of its own. However, as the 1920s progressed, the desires and expectations of consumers began to change. Consumers had more money and leisure time, and the automobile was no longer just an appliance to get them from A to B, it was a status symbol. There was ample evidence of these changes at the time; consumers wanted more colours, more variety, more customization. But Henry denied these changes. He was so in love with his product that he chose to ignore the facts and lost sight of his market (Tedlow, 2010). Indeed, Henry was famously quoted as saying: 'Any customer can have a car painted any color that he wants as long as it is black.' And he was insistent on keeping costs and prices down by offering limited features. Between 1924 and 1925, the market was growing but Ford's share declined from 54 to 45 per cent. Henry even went as far as to fire an executive who dared to deliver a seven-page report in 1926 which warned of the dire situation!

In the meantime, General Motors was on a roll – it began to offer customers cars in a variety of colours with added features. They also extended credit to make their cars more affordable and differentiated by leading the customer through the product line as he aged and his income increased. Unlike Ford's 'universal car' strategy, the General Motors strategy was 'a car for every purse and purpose'.

Henry Ford's blindness resulted from his conviction that he knew what customers wanted and his attachment to his own product/idea. In the end, he had to shut down his main plant for almost a year to retool and redesign his model. This left the field clear for General Motors to seize market leadership and opened up a market for Chrysler. While Ford was able to make a comeback with the new Model A, the company never managed to reclaim the market dominance they once had.

2. The 'right' answer

Time for another exercise.

ACTIVITY
Drop the block

Look at the picture opposite, which shows a person holding a block of wood. What do you think will happen to the piece of wood when the person lets go of it?

Figure 2.1   Person holding a block of wood

For the answer, see page 226 in the appendix.

How did you do?

Predictably, most people answer that the block of wood will fall down to the floor. While this answer is correct and appropriate given the laws of gravity, it's not the only one (Brainstorming.co.uk, 2011). This puzzle highlights how easy it is to give the most obvious answer first, based on your existing knowledge, and to ignore other possibilities that don't 'fit'.

In the 'Drop the block' exercise, we see how selective thinking causes us to stop thinking when we've found our answer. Nothing unusual about this – it's all very normal. For years, our education systems and workplace environments have been geared towards teaching us to find the one right answer, the one key idea or proposal. And in the process, we're *untaught* how to explore many possibilities for approaching problems creatively. One-answer-thinking has become deeply ingrained into our mental processes. Yet this doesn't fit the reality of life and business. Most situations have more than one right answer. In the activity above, each of the answers were correct – it just depended on your point of view. A business decision is the same. There are many right answers for it, but we just tend to stop with the one 'sure thing' that most fits our point of view. We take away our flexibility when we do this, and that only hampers our chances of creating success in a world that's constantly changing. In today's high-speed society, every right idea eventually becomes the wrong one!

3. Attached to a pet idea

Just as you shouldn't stop at one answer, you would be well warned against getting too attached to your pet idea. This is the absolute 'genius' idea that you came up with early while brainstorming and which you continue to cling to during the rest of the decision-making process, even though it's no longer looking all that clever in the big scheme of things.

You don't need me to tell you why this is a menace to your creativity. When you get attached to the first great idea that pops into your head, whether it's a hunch, formula, product or strategy, you find it difficult to see any other possible solutions. The whole creative process ceases to be dynamic and you become stuck in wishful thinking. Instead of your mind running free, it becomes imprisoned by that one idea you refuse to let go of.

For nearly a century, no company was as successful at commercializing the camera as Kodak. Some of their breakthroughs included the Brownie camera in 1900, Kodachrome colour film and the easy-load Instamatic camera. What they couldn't imagine was how quickly and violently their products would be made irrelevant by new digital competitors. They were so attached to their film-based lines that they stood by while progress in digital photography and printing, software, file sharing and third-party apps revolutionized their market. Kodak has since tried to expand into pharmaceuticals, memory chips, healthcare imaging and document management, but has never quite been able to return to its former glory. By 2010, its stock price was 96 per cent below the peak it hit in 1997 (Newman, 2010).

Kodak made the classic mistake of becoming too attached to their pet idea – film. This hurt them badly because they failed to see that there were other ideas out there that could work far better. But this doesn't mean that you should discount your favourite idea. Do some exploration and fact-finding to make sure it's the correct one first.

4. Duped by expectations

Have a go at this activity.

ACTIVITY
I love Paris

Take a look at this image:

Figure 2.2 I Love Paris

What does it say? 'I love Paris in the Springtime'
   Does it?
   Or does it say: 'I love Paris in the the Springtime!'
   Your brain didn't expect to see the word 'the' twice, and skipped over it.
So, you were duped by your own expectations.

Selective thinking is very much in league with our expectations – we see what we expect to see. An interesting study on this was carried out by Lidwien van de Wijngaert at the University of Twente in Enschede, Netherlands, with colleagues from Utrecht University (Simonite, 2009). He showed 60 people the same video clip on the same standard-definition television. Before showing the clip, he told half of them to expect clearer, sharper pictures thanks to high-definition (HD) technology. He backed this up by putting up posters, handing out flyers and connecting an extra-thick cable to the screen. The other half were correctly told to expect normal DVD images. Afterwards, the 60 people were asked to complete a questionnaire.

Lo and behold, the people who had been led to expect HD reported seeing higher-quality images. They simply could not tell that they were watching a conventional TV. Consequently, Lidwien van de Wijngaert was able to confirm that: 'Participants were unable to discriminate properly between digital and high-definition signals.' They saw what they expected to see! Another example of how selective thinking gives you selective vision.

5. Loss aversion

Ready for another quick riddle?

ACTIVITY
Toss the coin

Let's imagine I'm going to toss a coin. If you lose, you must pay me £100. What is the minimum amount that you would need to win to make this bet attractive?

A sensible response would obviously be an answer above £100. However, if you're risk neutral you should be willing to play for £100. No more, no less. When behavioural finance expert James Montier conducted this test on 600 fund managers using US dollars, the response was generally much higher than $100, averaging just over $200 (Montier, 2010). This is very telling; the fund managers felt that they needed to win twice the amount they might lose before they'd consider this a good bet.

Overall, people hate losses somewhere between two and two-and-a-half times as much as they enjoy equivalent gains; a concept known as *loss aversion*. This term was introduced in 1979 by behavioural economists Daniel Kahneman and Amos Tversky, and it explains a lot of strange things, such as why threats usually overtake opportunities when it comes to our motivation, why we're often slow to sell investments that have lost value, and why most of the time we do nothing. Because we give less psychological weight to the 'gains' we could make than the 'losses' we might suffer, we opt for inaction instead of action.

Loss aversion crops up all the time in business. Changes to the organizational status quo will usually involve both gains and losses to some degree. The problem we have here is that selective thinking often tips the balance more towards the avoidance of the negative aspects. The current baseline (or status quo) is taken as a reference point, and any change from that baseline is seen as a loss.

New situations always appear dicey. If you want to start a business you have to face up to the potential loss of a steady and predictable income, and this is what stops most people from getting started in the first place. But the gains could well be greater than you imagined. Like confirmation bias, loss aversion is another selective thinking trap. It likes to 'stick' you exactly where you are... doing nothing and going nowhere. Check your habits. Is loss aversion holding you back from actively seeking and creating opportunities? Are you exaggerating the riskiness of certain moves and underestimating the benefits?

Key takeaways

Selective thinking – you pay more attention to information that supports what you already believe or want to be true, while at the same time snubbing information that would challenge your current thinking. This type of thinking error leads you to:

- Go into denial and ignore blatant facts. You avoid asking tough questions and discount new information that might put your favourite ideas or theories to the test (confirmation bias).

- Stop at the first 'right' answer and so miss out on a multitude of possible answers you could find if you bothered to look.

- Get overly attached to pet ideas, even if they don't turn out to be all that great.

- Be made a fool of by your own expectations. You interpret the future based on what you expect to happen – and are caught off guard by what actually happens!

- Avoid taking risks owing to fear of losing (loss aversion). Rather than being driven by what you can gain, you're more worried about what you might lose. As a result, you sidestep exciting opportunities and rebuff innovative suggestions.

References

Brainstorming.co.uk (2011) [accessed 23 February 2018] Creative Thinking Puzzle 2 – the 'Drop the Block' Problem, *Infinite Innovations* [Online] http://www.brainstorming.co.uk/puzzles/dropblock.html

Hart, W, Albarraccin, D, Eagly, AH *et al* (2009) Feeling validated versus being correct: a meta-analysis of selective exposure to information, *Psychological Bulletin*, **135** (4), pp 555–88

Kahneman, D (2011) *Thinking, Fast and Slow*, Allen Lane, London

Montier, J (2010) *The Little Book of Behavioural Investing: How not to be your own worst enemy*, John Wiley & Sons, Hoboken, NJ

McRaney, D (2010) [accessed 23 February 2018] Confirmation Bias, *You Are Not So Smart*, 23 June [Online] https://youarenotsosmart.com/2010/06/23/confirmation-bias

Newman, R (2010) [accessed 26 February 2018] 10 Great Companies That Lost Their Edge, *US News*, 19 August [Online] https://money.usnews.com/money/blogs/flowchart/2010/08/19/10-great-companies-that-lost-their-edge

Simonite, T (2009) [accessed 23 February 2018] Think Yourself a Better Picture, *New Scientist*, 7 October [Online] https://www.newscientist.com/article/dn17930-think-yourself-a-better-picture/

Tedlow, RS (2010) *Denial: Why business leaders fail to look facts in the face – and what to do about it*, Penguin, New York

03
Common thinking errors

Reactive thinking

Quick, let's do something! True to the subject of this chapter, let's jump right into an exercise.

ACTIVITY

Cognitive reflection test

Answer the following three questions:

1 A bat and a ball together cost £1.10 in total. The bat costs £1 more than the ball. How much does the ball cost?

2 If it takes five minutes for five machines to make five widgets, how long would it take 100 machines to make 100 widgets?

3 In a lake there is a patch of lily pads. Every day the patch doubles in size. If it takes 48 days for the patch to cover the entire lake, how long will it take to cover half the lake?

How did you find these questions? Relatively easy? Difficult?

Before I give you the answers, it might interest you to know that out of 3,500 people given this test, only 17 per cent managed to get all three questions right, and more alarmingly, 33 per cent got none of them right. There's a clear reason for this. Each of these questions has an obvious, but unfortunately incorrect answer, and a not-so-obvious answer which is correct.

Take question no. 1. The obvious and immediate answer to this would be £0.10. Is that what you got? If so, you didn't think long and hard enough. The correct answer is £0.05. With a little time, you can work it out. The bat costs £1 more than the ball, so let's remove that from the equation: £1.10 − £1.00 = £0.10. £0.10 is then divided by two because there are two items (1 bat and 1 ball) = £0.05. If the ball cost £0.10 then the bat would only be £0.90 more than the ball, not £1 more. It follows, therefore, that one bat costs £1.05 and one ball costs £0.05. Coming at it from another angle: £1.10 − £0.05 = £1.05. £1.05 is one pound more than £0.05.

In question no. 2, the gut reaction is often to say 100 minutes. Look at the question more carefully and you'll realize that if it takes five machines five minutes to produce five widgets, then the output is one widget per machine for every five minutes. So, the answer is that it would take 100 machines **five minutes** to make 100 widgets.

Lastly, with question no. 3, most people will respond with an answer of 24 days (half of 48 days). But just think, if the patch doubles in size each day, the day before it covers the entire lake it must have covered half the lake, so the correct answer is actually **47 days**.

This three-question test is known as the Cognitive Reflection Test (CRT) and it was designed by Yale professor Shane Frederick (formerly of Massachusetts Institute of Technology, MIT) to reveal the type of thinking process you predominately use: an emotional, reactive one or a conscious, reflective and logical one (Frederick, 2005). As simple as it seems, this test is much more powerful at working this out than any IQ test or SAT score. Judging by the number of wrong answers given, a hefty portion of us are prone to decision making using 'quick and dirty' mental shortcuts rather than a slower, more deliberate, more rational way of processing information.

System 1 vs System 2

According to Nobel Prize-winning psychologist Daniel Kahneman (2011), there are two cognitive systems that drive the way we think and make decisions. System 1 is fast, instinctive and emotional; System 2 is slower, more thoughtful and methodical.

System 1 is our default option, so all information goes here first for processing. It's automatic and effortless, and uses mental shortcuts (heuristics), key situational characteristics, associated ideas and memories to deal with tons of information simultaneously. As it works so fast, it gives answers that are approximately (rather than precisely) correct. Being able to detect that one object is more distant than another and completing the phrase 'bread and...' are examples of System 1 thinking in action. As you can probably gather, this system is especially helpful in familiar situations when time is tight and immediate action is called for.

System 2, on the other hand, is much more disciplined and attempts to follow a deductive and systematic approach to problem solving. It allows us to deal with complex or abstract concepts, to plan ahead, to consider options carefully, and to review and revise things in light of new information. Like any logical process, it requires a deliberate effort and can only handle one step at a time, so it's a slower but much more precise way of dealing with information. This system is engaged when you're parking in a narrow space, or filling out a tax form, for example. Overall, it's useful when you find yourself in an unfamiliar or high-stakes situation and have more time to work things out. What's great about this system is that it can correct or override the automatic judgements made by System 1 if it detects that your instinctive response is wrong.

It can be useful to distinguish these systems as **reactive thinking** (System 1) and **proactive thinking** (System 2). Most of us like to think that we operate with our conscious, reasoning self when we're making decisions (System 2). The reality, however, is that System 1 handles far more of our actions than we would care to admit. Instead of thinking deeply, we react instantly to events, tasks or external influences, often in pre-programmed ways.

Think about it. What's the first thing you do in the morning when you get to work? Like most of us, you probably check your e-mails. What then? You immediately jerk into action by typing out your responses to the important ones; that is, you start the day by reacting quickly to what's in front of you.

Reacting to your e-mails like a robot answering commands means that you're not giving yourself time to think things through, to gather more information, to be innovative or flexible in how you answer. What this proves is that we almost always trust our initial reaction, and only every now and then do we bring in System 2 to review the decision. It just stays running in low mode in the background until we decide to call it in. A major pitfall of reactive thinking shows its face during meetings and group brainstorming sessions. Watch out for reactive language and hasty judgements when working with others (see Table 3.1).

Table 3.1 Watch for reactive language

Reactive	Proactive
I must…	I prefer…
I have to…	I have alternatives…
We always do…	We can do this, or that…
If only…	I will…
I can't…	I can choose…
Nothing I can do…	I'll look at the options…

CASE STUDY   Snap judgements for Snapchat

When Stanford University students Evan Spiegel and Robert Murphy first presented their idea of an app for sharing time-limited photos and videos as part of a university assignment, it was instantly ridiculed. Thankfully, they were undeterred by the negative reaction of their fellow students and continued to build on the idea. Two years later, Snapchat was valued at $3 billion (McKeown, 2014).

The need for speed

It's true that reactive functioning is incredibly useful and makes a powerful contribution to our day-to-day output. These days most of us are crazy busy. We need reactive thinking (System 1) to act as our autopilot and help us take quick and practical shortcuts as we whiz through the patterns of life. It's great for helping us perform the regular and commonplace activities in our lives and putting situations to bed swiftly when there's high time pressure. By thinking reactively, we conserve our (much needed!) energy and free up valuable time for other things.

But here's the problem. Thanks to our 'always on' digital culture and haphazard economy, we feel the need to run our lives faster and faster. Each day we scurry from task to task and cram our calendars to the brim. There are deadlines to meet, e-mails to exchange, obligations to fulfil, papers to file, phone calls to answer and meetings to attend – no wonder we're all frazzled! It's tempting to think that being busy means being productive; that if we deal with stuff as soon as it arises, we're making great progress. But in rushing to get through these tasks, we're not giving them the attention and depth of thought they might need, which can be lethal to our creativity. To reach peak levels of performance we need to be *proactive*, not reactive. No one can deny that speedy reactions are often necessary in business, but we have to be aware of the hazards.

Did you know?

Working without any rest periods throughout the day could impact your productivity and focus by as much as 75 per cent (Ciotti, 2012).

Consider the following question:

Q. If you were running a marathon, how effective do you think you'd be if you spent most of it sprinting?

Unless you possess incredible, super-athletic powers, you're probably going to burn out pretty quickly. If you try to run a marathon at a sprinter's pace all the way through without any breaks, your batteries will likely go flat before you even reach the halfway mark. The same applies in business. If you focus all your energy on full-time 'inbox monitor' duty, or contending with every short-term crisis that comes your way, before too long your productivity will plummet. Speed is important at certain times, but at the wrong times it's a massive inhibitor.

According to performance psychologist Tony Schwartz, people who try to push on through the workday without any periods of rest and rejuvenation can easily zone out and lose focus, meaning that they're only reaching 25 per cent of their potential output across the day (Ciotti, 2012). Life (and business) is a marathon, but it's a marathon run in a *series of sprints*. Although staying constantly in motion can make you feel like you're racing ahead, the reality is that you're more likely to be stuck in one place running non-essential errands. Human beings are not designed to run on continuous high speed for long periods of time – allowing intermittent breaks for renewal gives you time to incubate ideas for your most mission-critical projects and leads to more sustainable productivity in the long run. Working on the basis of sprint–rest, sprint–rest, then sprint again, enhances not only your energy levels but your inspiration levels. So, make sure you carve out a few blank spaces in your calendar for those must-attend important meetings – with yourself.

In the heat of the moment

Reactive thinking comes with several systematic flaws, some of which can be downright dangerous. Here are a few problem areas you might be familiar with.

1. First-mover disadvantage

A quick question. You're in third place. You pass the person in second place. Where are you now?

...If you answered 'first place', think again. You would be second!

This leads us onto another, more complex question. Is it best to be first to do something or a fast second?

It's widely claimed that the first company to launch a new product or enter a new market has an inherent competitive advantage over later entrants. Have you heard of the **first-mover advantage**? By getting in there first, we can establish ourselves as a leader in that particular field and erect barriers to deter competitors. This is what System 1 would have us thinking and doing – acting on an idea or opportunity while it's still hot. However, the first-mover advantage concept may be more myth than reality. The fact is that pioneering a new product or industry breakthrough is a huge and costly venture; it takes a lot to educate and prime consumers for your innovation, and to establish distribution, brand and marketing strength. And while you're doing it, you allow competitors to learn from your mistakes and increase their game.

There are lots of examples out there that prove that it's rare for the first mover to really capture a market. For instance, the tablet PC was first introduced by Microsoft in 2001 but has been dramatically eclipsed by the Apple iPad and others in recent years. The first search engine was established by Overture (now part of Yahoo) but is now lagging far behind the omnipresent Google. The first social networking site Friendster was launched in 2002 but was later overlooked in favour of Facebook and Twitter. The first disposable nappies (diapers) brand wasn't Pampers by Proctor & Gamble, it was Chux diapers (developed by Johnson & Johnson). Hydrox was the first cookie to consist of white cream sandwiched between two dark biscuits in 1908, four years before Oreo, yet Oreo has now achieved iconic status.

Being 'first' does not guarantee success. First movers tend to launch prematurely without fully understanding the market situation, customer problems and objections, and with average features in a product, not out-standing ones. The race to be first into a market can be destructive, as it's based on guesswork and compromise. Remember, business is a marathon in a series of sprints, not a single sprint, so slow down and take a break:

- Think more before you act on that amazing opportunity, event or idea.

- Engage your System 2 and take the time to thoroughly consider your options and reach a well-reasoned conclusion.

- Exercise a degree of patience to make sure you have the right mix of product, promotion, price and place in the bag.

As Google, Apple and others have proved, sometimes being a fast second is a better idea.

2. Who let the dogs out?

Bizarrely, the very compulsion that makes us want to be a first mover is the same one that leads us to copy others. There's a simple analogy for this. One dog barks and before you know it all the other dogs in the neighbourhood are barking. This is how the competitive corporate world works. No sooner has someone launched a new product or adopted a certain management programme than everyone else follows suit. This is not to say that imitating others is wrong; the previous section proves that being a fast follower can have more rewarding outcomes than being a first mover. However, that only works if you take the time to think things through.

Often, we mindlessly copy what others are doing – such as buying an item of clothing purely because it's all the rage for that season, and not be-cause it suits us or our purposes. There's no conscious thought process around the decision. Likewise, when we're faced with a minor problem, we jump to try to fix it because of the classic 'fight or flight' response. Our ap-proach is tactical, not strategic, and our view is short range, not long term.

From this position it becomes difficult to implement innovation in any planned way, as our energy and resources are tied up in reacting to what other players in the field are up to. It's a never-ending problem–reaction loop.

3. No, the customer isn't always right

Marketing and PR departments generally have no concept of reactive thinking. One of the traditional rules that many businesses faithfully abide by takes the form of either 'Listen to your customers' or 'The customer is always right'. It's important to understand what drives your customers and the reasons for their actions, of course – listening to your customers and their problems is a no-brainer if you want to provide first-rate customer service and make desirable, sought-after improvements to your product. However, sticking to this rule religiously can prove fatal as it locks you into reactive mode.

Every year, companies spend millions trying to understand customer needs in a bid to innovate quickly and outdo competitors. But the process is loaded with risk; often customer research is done badly and hardly ever leads to full-blown, break-new-ground innovation. We all know about products that were launched on the back of extensive consumer research, but which bombed in the marketplace. Remember the New Coke fiasco?

CASE STUDY   New Coke nightmare

Customer surveys and questionnaires about new products and ideas can often fail. Reacting to the growing popularity of Pepsi, Coca-Cola shot themselves in the foot with the release of New Coke in 1985. The company conducted all manner of consumer taste tests, surveys and focus groups which showed a preference for the new formula. Testers agreed it didn't just taste better than the old Coke, it also tasted better than Pepsi. However, all the time, money and skill poured into consumer research failed to reveal the depth of people's emotional attachment to the original formula, and the value of brand loyalty in their buying decisions. When New Coke was released and old Coke was taken out of circulation, customers were outraged that their much-loved brand had been changed. Needless to say, performance failed to live up to expectations and results were tragic. Coca-Cola made the wise decision to reinstitute the old Coke as Coke Classic, and eventually recovered its leading market position. Company President Donald R Keough admitted, 'We did not understand the deep emotions of so many of our customers for Coca-Cola' (Ross, 2005). There's a lesson here. What consumers say they like doesn't always reflect what they will buy.

Nowadays, it's the done thing for businesses to ask customers what features they want to see in their product and then deliver on those features as a priority. This is by no means wrong. In fact, it's essential for making good, honest, gainful tweaks to your product. At OpenGenius, we always listen to what customers have to say when weighing up potential features for upgrades of our software products. But the problem with listening to your customers is that they can't tell you about a need that they don't even know they have. And seldom will they admit that they're willing to pay more for a premium product.

Some of the most successful products and services of recent years aren't the reactive outcome of customer surveys or suggestions to crowdsourcing websites. They're the result of the foresight and proactive drive of determined innovators. One example of this is First Direct, which stormed into the banking market in 1989, pioneering the UK's first 24/7 telephone banking service. This was inspired by the awareness that a growing number of people didn't have time to visit their bank branch and that younger customers wanted greater control and flexibility in how they managed their finances (Gower, 2015). Before then, anyone wanting to carry out any type of banking transaction had to physically queue up at a high street branch to be seen by someone behind the counter. The launch was a brave endeavour and was mocked by rival banks, financial services experts and the media. Given how entrenched the retail banking industry was, sceptics could not understand how anything could substitute for the face-to-face customer service that was given at a branch. First Direct had identified a need that customers had not really been aware of. Until customers experienced telephone banking and the simplicity it offered, they would never have known it was the solution they wanted. These days, with the addition of internet banking, it's hard to imagine that there used to be only the one option for banking of visiting a local branch. Fast forward 29 years and First Direct is the one laughing all the way to the bank, with over 1.37 million customers and enviable figures of customer satisfaction. In 2017, it once again topped a poll carried out by consumer body Which? for the best brand in customer service (Ingrams, 2017).

CASE STUDY   Facebook ignores its customers

Facebook offers another example of non-reactive thinking. The social network site wasn't designed to meet any apparent customer need. LinkedIn and MySpace were already active players in the market and the entry of yet another social network service didn't seem anything to write home about. But look at what has happened: Facebook has gone on to achieve unparalleled success, and as of the fourth quarter of 2017 it was reported to have 2.2 billion monthly active users, making it the most popular social networking site in the world (Statista, 2018).

Ignoring its customers is something Facebook does very well. It frequently makes the news by upsetting customers with unwanted changes, for example replacing profiles with a 'timeline' structure. And only once in a blue moon will it take on board customer suggestions. Mark Zuckerberg, the brains behind Facebook, is even tipped to have said, 'The most disruptive companies don't listen to their customers' (Thomas, 2009). Consider this. If Facebook listened to its customers, we would end up with strict privacy settings, no advertising, more fiddly functions and arguably a less 'social' and more unwieldy tool.

If First Direct and Facebook had depended on their customers to tell them what they wanted or needed, they might well have ended up as followers in their field, rather than leaders. But a word of warning – don't ignore your customers completely. Once you've launched a breakthrough innovation such as a new product or service, you can be sure that your competitors will soon be hot on your heels. The only way to stay on top is through continual innovation and incremental improvements that keep your customers happy. So, look carefully at what your customers need and want, but instead of listening to what they say, *watch what they actually do*. This will give you more concrete information to base your decisions on than anything that comes out of their mouths.

No matter what your product or service is, it's in your interest to make sure your work gets examined by customers, either in usability labs or in the customer's own environment. A nifty shortcut or concept that you're super proud of might be completely overlooked or disregarded by the customer. Or they might struggle to make sense of a task or process that you assumed would be obvious. Seeing how customers use your product will reset your expectations on what they really need and focus your attention on solving the real problems they have (Berkun, 1999). A chance to 'walk in your customer's shoes' can be a humbling experience that will shift you into thinking more proactively and making better decisions about what you're offering.

Letting information overload you

Information overload is a symptom of our desire to not focus on what's important. It's a choice.

— BRIAN SOLIS, American industry analyst

Try your hand at these scrambled letter puzzles.

ACTIVITY
Scrambled letters

1. SSUEPVEERNMALRTKRTEST
Cross out 10 letters in the above line so that the remaining 11 letters spell out a well-known English word. The word must be spelt in the correct sequence.

2. SBAIXNLETATNERSA
Do the same with this line, but this time only crossing out six letters to spell a common word without changing the order of the letters.
    Check your answers on page 227.

Were these easy enough for you? If so, then you've demonstrated an excellent capacity to cut through visual noise and get to the core of a problem. Finding the solution is a cinch after that.

Too much of a good thing?

Information is a wonderful thing. It's a huge source of inspiration for business people looking for new ideas, fresh approaches and support for decision making. And never before has there been so much of it. Thanks to the amazing developments of the digital age, we have information all around us on a 24/7, all-you-can-eat basis. For the most part, this is awesome because we can find what we need to know, when we need to know it. But as legions of us in the workplace are discovering, you can have too much of a good thing. Too many websites to visit, too many notifications, reports to read, links to click, videos to watch, news stories to read… and let's not forget all those e-mails waiting in your inbox. It's hard to keep a straight head while being bombarded by a relentless flood of data, which soon plunges you into 'information overload'. According to a 2017 Institute of Practitioners in

Advertising (IPA) Touchpoints report, UK adults are spending eight hours a day consuming some sort of media (IPA, 2017). In practice, that means that half of our waking life is spent receiving information, mostly electronically.

Data: what happens every minute?

- 15,220,700 texts sent
- 3,607,080 Google search queries
- 456,000 tweets on Twitter
- 154,200 calls made on Skype
- 4,146,600 video views on YouTube
- 527,760 photos shared on Snapchat
- 103,447,520 spam e-mails sent
- 69,444 hours of video streamed on Netflix
- 74,220 posts published on Tumblr
- 600 new page edits on Wikipedia
- 13 new songs added on Spotify
- 46,740 photos posted to Instagram
- 120+ new LinkedIn accounts created
- $258,751 worth of sales made on Amazon

SOURCE Information collated by marketing data company Domo in 2017, https://www.domo.com/learn/data-never-sleeps-5

Drowning in data

The impact of this onslaught of information is alarming. Unrelenting torrents of data flood our minds, taking focus and resource away from where it's needed – our 'real' work. When we're bombarded with information, we feel pressure to act on it straight away – to think reactively. What happens then? We end up making the wrong decisions because we haven't taken time to think about the information rationally and objectively. And it gets worse. Information overload also crushes our ability to generate ideas. Wading through it absorbs our time and takes up most of our mind space, so we have hardly any left for thinking creatively. How many hours have you lost searching through reams of irrelevant data to find that crucial piece of information you're looking for?

The knowledge worker's day

25% – Information overload
19% – Content creation
19% – Reading content
17% – Meetings/phone calls/social interaction
10% – Search and research
5% – Personal time
5% – Thought and reflection

SOURCE Basex survey findings (2010), http://www.basexblog.com/2010/11/04/our-findings/

As you go about your working day, every bit of information you come across presents you with a three-pronged choice:

1 Reply immediately

2 Factor it into an imminent decision

3 Ignore it entirely

In a bid to keep up with all the information you're bombarded with, your brain instinctively goes with the first option. It's wired to respond instantly and automatically, and it will do this even if it's making bad decisions. This is because the more information that keeps pouring in, the more your brain struggles with what it should keep for future reference, and what it can get rid of. Your working memory can only hold about seven items of information; after that, it's a real conscious effort to work out what should be shuttled into your long-term memory – a similar effort to studying for exams. The way around this is to make your judgements quickly, but as we've already discussed, a quick decision is rarely the best decision. Whenever you have a task that needs your full attention, it's best to eliminate as many superfluous pieces of information or distractions as possible. By simplifying the way you look at everything, you're more likely to introduce a source of creativity to the process and set up the conditions to make the right choices.

CASE STUDY   IKEA – design thinking

The Swedish DIY furniture phenomenon IKEA was able to crank up its store sales and profit almost overnight by breaking a reactive pattern and simplifying a shopping process that could be overwhelming for most people (Hurson, 2008). Instead of going down the usual route and selling through traditional outlets, IKEA's concept was to offer customers a supermarket for its stylish furniture. Customers walked in, picked up their shopping trolleys and browsed through a carefully designed, user-friendly maze of aisles, easily finding and picking up the goods they needed. They then wheeled their often jam-packed trolleys through supermarket-style checkout counters to make their payments. This unique system worked amazingly well and became a source of real and sustainable differentiation. Today, IKEA is the largest and most profitable furniture company in the world.

Key takeaways

Most of us are prone to decision making using an emotional, reactive approach (System 1: Reactive thinking) rather than a deliberate and rational one (System 2: Proactive thinking). Too much reliance on reactive thinking tips us into:

- Acting on an idea in the heat of the moment because we want to be a 'first mover'. Recent history shows that being first into a market or to launch a new product doesn't guarantee success, and can even be destructive (note: business is a marathon run in a series of sprints, not a single sprint).
- Mindlessly copying what others are doing rather than consciously creating our own futures. We become followers, not leaders!
- An over-reliance on 'listening to our customers'. This cheats us into making reactive so-so changes and improvements, and we miss out on designing those breakthrough innovations. Most of the time, customers don't know what they want until we show it to them.
- Non-stop access to information is on the one side wonderful and on the other utterly overwhelming. Before we know it, we're in a stressed-out frenzy trying to keep our head above the flood of e-mails, reports,

projects, blog posts, updates and sundry that add up to information overload. Watch out for the tendency to react instantly and automatically to information. A quick decision is seldom the best decision.

References

Berkun, S (1999) [accessed 28 February 2018] The Power of the Usability Lab [Blog], *Microsoft*, Nov/Dec [Online] https://msdn.microsoft.com/en-us/library/ms993288.aspx

Ciotti, G (2012) [accessed 25 February 2018] Why Better Energy Management is the Key to Peak Productivity [Blog], *Lifehacker*, 29 February [Online] https://lifehacker.com/5955819/why-better-energy-management-is-the-key-to-peak-productivity

Frederick, S (2005) Cognitive reflection and decision making, *Journal of Economic Perspectives*, **19** (4), pp 24–42

Gower, L (2015) *The Innovation Workout: The 10 tried-and-tested steps that will build your creativity and innovation skills*, Pearson, Harlow

Hurson, T (2008) *Think Better: An innovator's guide to productive thinking*, McGraw-Hill Professional, New York

Ingrams, S (2017) [accessed 14 March 2018] Which? Reveals 2017's Best and Worst Brands for Customer Service, *Which?*, 25 August [Online] https://www.which.co.uk/news/2017/08/which-reveals-2017s-best-and-worst-brands-for-customer-service/

IPA (2017) [accessed 1 March 2018] Adults Spend Almost 8 Hours Each Day Consuming Media, 21 September [Online] http://www.ipa.co.uk/news/adults-spend-almost-8-hours-each-day-consuming-media#.Wpg0mkx2uhc

Kahneman, D (2011) *Thinking, Fast and Slow*, Allen Lane, London

McKeown, M (2014) *The Innovation Book: How to manage ideas and execution for outstanding results*, FT Publishing, Harlow

Ross, ME (2005) [accessed 28 February 2018] It Seemed Like a Good Idea at the Time, *NBCNews.com*, 22 April [Online] http://www.nbcnews.com/id/7209828/ns/us_news/t/it-seemed-good-idea-time/#.WpaXu0x2uhd

Statista (2018) [accessed 28 February 2018] Number of Monthly Active Facebook Users Worldwide as of 4th Quarter 2017 (in millions) [Online] https://www.statista.com/statistics/264810/number-of-monthly-active-facebook-users-worldwide/

Thomas, O (2009) [accessed 28 February 2018] Even Facebook Employees Hate the Redesign [Blog], *Gawker*, 20 March [Online] http://gawker.com/5177341/even-facebook-employees-hate-the-redesign

04
Common thinking errors

Assumptive thinking

Begin challenging your own assumptions. Your assumptions are your windows on the world. Scrub them off every once in a while, or the light won't come in.

– ALAN ALDA, American actor, commencement speech
at Connecticut College (1980)

They're everywhere!

Assumptions are everywhere. We make them all the time and in almost every situation. Whenever we approach a business problem, whether simple or complex, we attach assumptions to it before we try to solve it.

What's an assumption? It's a belief, convention or idea we accept to be true, often with no proof. And we all have lots of them – they've been drilled into us over the course of a lifetime by our parents, teachers, workplaces and society in general. In business, our assumptions are the things that we implicitly believe about our customers, products, processes, markets, team-mates, industries, ourselves, etc.

Some typical assumptions might be:

- Work only takes place in the office.
- Our company needs to have a diverse range of business to survive.
- This is the best way to organize our distribution – it has never let us down.
- Our largest clients are our most important clients.
- I'm not creative.

- Our customers are all young people.

- We should only hire people who fit in well with our team.

An assumption is like a mental shotgun. It makes it easy to find quick, sharp answers to questions without imposing too much hard work on your brain. Instead of wasting hours generating and scrutinizing a million possibilities, you can visit your storehouse of assumptions and pick out an off-the-shelf solution. You've got a basis for action almost immediately.

A lot of the time our assumptions are spot-on. For instance, most people who act friendly are, in fact, friendly. And young men are far more likely than elderly women to drive aggressively (Kahneman, 2011). But assumptions can be our worst enemy as well as our best friend. The danger comes when we take them for granted.

There's a great saying that goes, 'When you assume you make an **ass** of **u** and me.' What's striking about assumptions is that they lead us to think we know more than we do. When we encounter a situation similar to one we've experienced before, we assume it will have a similar result and don't bother exploring alternative options. This can be a serious roadblock, especially during those times when we need to be creative. Like a noise that drowns out other sounds, assumptions limit our perceptions and keep us retreading the same old path of ideas instead of branching off into new terrain. The reality is that innovation comes from doing things differently, not from firmly sticking to 'rules of thumb' that worked in the past. Before we unleash our creative energy on finding killer ideas, we need to challenge the assumptions we're making and throw away the ones that have gone off.

Challenging assumptions

If you're feeling constrained by your unquestioned assumptions and conventions, then you need to tackle them head-on to uncover the paradigm-breaking ideas you've been missing.

How can you challenge your assumptions? First, recognize that you're bound to have assumptions in the first place. Second, use a conscious process or technique to help you separate facts from falsities on a regular basis or whenever you're problem solving. Let's have a go at challenging an assumption together, using the following three-step method.

Step 1. State your problem

Before you start pouncing on your assumptions, you need to clearly state the problem you want to solve or opportunity you want to crack. Let's take the following as an example: '**Set up a restaurant business.**'

Step 2. Map out your assumptions

Next, you need to map out or list all the assumptions, boundaries and ground rules you're holding about that situation. This might be a stupidly obvious step, but how often do you actually make your assumptions explicit like this? Take a magnifying glass to your problem and examine all the different elements of it closely. What seems so blindingly absolute or watertight that you wouldn't even think to question it?

Typical assumptions (Creating Minds, nd) might be that:

- It's impossible to do something because of constraints such as time and cost.
- Something works because of certain rules and conditions that are in place.
- People believe, think or need certain things.

In our restaurant scenario, some of our assumptions in setting up a successful restaurant could be that it has to have:

- A menu
- Food
- Staff

ACTIVITY
Restaurant

Figure 4.1   Restaurant

Restaurant = Menu + Food + Staff

Step 3. Challenge each assumption

Finally, you need to challenge each of the assumptions to see if they're correct or can be done away with. Ask questions to get to the bottom of things and trigger new lines of thought. For instance:

- What would happen if we deliberately broke this rule?
- Why do we do it this way?
- Why might this assumption be false?

This is such a simple but illuminating exercise. I don't think you can ever realize just how many unwarranted assumptions you have until you make the effort to confront them. Going back to our restaurant example, how could we challenge each assumption and uncover new options?

Do we need to have a menu?

Maybe not. There are lots of alternatives we could consider:

- Customers could bring dish ideas for the chef to cook.
- The waiter could inform customers of the dishes available.
- It could be a buffet restaurant or a restaurant that offers only a set meal.
- There could be a list of ingredients from which to create recipes.

Do we need to offer food?

While this question might seem pointless at first, when you think about it more deeply it can throw up lots of ideas. For instance, people could bring their own food and pay a service charge for the location. Or we could offer another type of product such as:

- Drinks only
- Adventure experiences
- Bring your own
- Cat café
- Laughter club
- Willy Wonka meal chewing gum
- Culture café

- Food for thought
- An oxygen lounge – try different flavoured oxygen
- A software restaurant… or any other kind of restaurant

This question challenges the definition of what a restaurant is.

Do we need to have staff?

Again, not necessarily:

- The restaurant could operate via vending machines or a self-service counter.
- Customers could serve other customers.
- Robot waiters could replace traditional service.
- Customers could cook their own food.

In Japan, you can find a vending machine restaurant that doesn't require any staff at all, aptly named Jihanki Shokudo (or Automat Diner in English). Also, more and more self-service stands and kiosks are popping up inside companies to cater for office workers (Jiji Press, 2017).

Do you see where I'm going with this? By questioning and re-examining our assumptions, we've picked up a whole series of new perspectives on our challenge. This fires us up to create more original ideas. It doesn't matter if the new ideas are odd or silly. Remember, we're aiming to be as creative as possible, so we have to be able to push past our usual boundaries. And I mean really push. Don't hold back. Be brutal and force each assumption to fight for its life.

Creativity, as has been said, consists largely of rearranging what we know in order to find out what we do not know. Hence, to think creatively, we must be able to look afresh at what we normally take for granted.

– GEORGE KNELLER, author of *The Art and Science of Creativity* (1965)

Bad assumptive moves

There are several ways that assumptions can ruin our thinking. Here are just a few.

1. Assumptions aren't hard facts

Treating an assumption as a 'fact' can be dangerous. If a claim or belief sounds plausible enough and we have no obvious reason to doubt it, we tend to assume that it's right. And there's the problem – assumptions can be so powerful that they make us accept things that even the tiniest investigation would show to be false.

Researchers at Cardiff University looked at 2,000 news stories from the four 'quality press' (what used to be known as broadsheet) British newspapers (*Times*, *Telegraph*, *Guardian* and *Independent*) and found that 80 per cent were wholly, mainly or partially based on second-hand material, and the key facts had been checked in only 12 per cent of them (Davies, 2008). What this means is that most of the news we read is based on unchecked assumptions, not first-hand facts.

Like in the media world, assumptions become so prevalent in businesses that they become true in everyone's minds: 'Our customers expect us to have a local presence', or 'We have to launch a new range of products every year to keep up with competitors'. Whether these assumptions are valid or not doesn't usually come into question. They often become widely accepted falsehoods.

2. Self-imposed limits

If you were to ask an accountant for a great idea, you'd get a solution based around numbers. Ask a designer and you'd get a solution that involves visuals. Get my drift? It's pretty clear that we are a product of our experience. After all, we've all walked our own unique path in life. The danger of this is that when it's time to think creatively, we impose limits on ourselves. These limits are usually false because they're based on assumptions that we have due to our particular specialization or role. They cause us to stay within the confines of what we know – our comfort zone.

One of my favourite examples concerns Xerox Corporation and Apple. Back in the 1970s, scientists at Xerox's Palo Alto Research Center (PARC) in California had pioneered many of the fundamental components behind the personal computer, such as the graphical user interface and mouse device. However, not many people are aware of this because Xerox (a high-margin copier business at the time) failed to commercialize its innovations effectively, and consequently made one of the greatest mistakes in corporate history (Wessel, 2012). Steve Jobs, co-founder of Apple, saw rudimentary versions of the technologies being demonstrated while on a visit to the facility in 1979. He immediately spotted their potential in making computers appealing to the masses and adopted the concepts in developing the Apple Macintosh. Well, you know how the story goes from there. The Mac became the first commercially successful operating system that featured a graphical user interface (with windows and menus) and mouse. It went on to transform the way people interact with computers.

What does this tell us? The poor Xerox researchers and managers hadn't fully realized the promise their technology held to revolutionize personal computing because they were grounded in assumptions based on their specialism – making new and better copiers. If they had forced themselves to look past their self-imposed limitations, they could have seen lots of other possibilities. As Jobs said years later, 'If Xerox had known what it had and had taken advantage of its real opportunities, it could have been as big as IBM plus Microsoft plus Xerox combined – and the largest high-technology company in the world' (Gladwell, 2011).

ACTIVITY
Assumption-busting questions

Have another go at checking your assumptions by answering the following questions:

1 A writer with an audience of millions insisted that he was never to be interrupted while writing. After the day when he actually was interrupted, he never wrote again. Why? (Rogers and Sheehan, 1960)

2 If you have a long line, how can you make it short without changing its length?

Now skip to page 228 at the end of this chapter for the answers. How did you do? Did your line of thinking help you find the answers? Or were you completely off the mark?

These simple exercises prove how easy it is for your mind to make interpretations based on immediate assumptions, and to consider only answers that tie in with those assumptions. As with selective thinking, once your mind is committed to a particular direction of thought it's hard to make a detour or diversion. And the hidden nature of assumptions makes it especially difficult to even realize that you've taken a wrong turn.

3. Out-of-date thinking

There's an interesting tale told by British philosopher Bertrand Russell. It's about a farmer and his turkey. While living on the farm, the turkey noted that every day the farmer would greet him at sunrise with a bucket of grain. This led him to make the conclusion: 'I am always fed at sunrise'. It therefore came as a huge shock when on Christmas morning, instead of getting fed, he got his throat cut.

What's the moral of this story? You can't always deduct the truth from past experience. The history or frequency of an event is *not* proof that it will continue in the future. Although in business it might make sense to base expectations of what's to come on what's gone on before, past performance is by no means any guarantee of future returns.

Take the *Encyclopaedia Britannica* for example. Over 240 years, it built a successful franchise selling thick tomes of knowledge and established a ubiquitous reputation for 'scholarly excellence'. However, it was forced to reinvent itself after being blindsided by digital sources such as Wikipedia, which offered greater speed and convenience. Its long history and time-honoured conventions couldn't protect it from what the future had in store. In order to survive disruptive change, the company had to challenge every assumption they held about their business model and go fully digital. This was a bold move for the former print publisher, enabling it to reach millions more people with its high-quality curated content (Sword, 2016).

Long-standing assumptions keep you stuck on 'business as usual' when you need to be thinking much bigger than that. In many ways they lead to intellectual laziness. If you're planning a marketing campaign, you might already think you have a good sense of what your consumers want and how to make them want more of it. But the chances are this 'tried and (supposedly) true' knowledge could be undermining your ability to think differently and innovatively: a case of good assumptions gone bad. I'm not saying that we should forget about our past altogether – that would be just as foolish as having faulty assumptions. But it's well worth reminding ourselves regularly that nothing strictly follows from it.

The folly of assumptions

Check out some of these assumptions made by well-known people throughout history:

- *'Everything that can be invented has been invented.'* Charles Duell, Commissioner, US Office of Patents, 1899

- *'I think there is a world market for about five computers.'* Thomas Watson, founder of IBM, 1943

- *'It will be years – not in my time – before a woman will become Prime Minister.'* Margaret Thatcher, future UK Prime Minister, 1969

- *'Man will not fly for 50 years.'* Wilbur Wright, American aviation pioneer, to his brother Orville (their first successful flight was in 1903)

- *'640 kilobytes ought to be enough for anybody.'* Bill Gates, founder of Microsoft (talking about computer memory in 1981)

- *'Television won't last because people will soon get tired of staring at a plywood box every night.'* Darryl Zanuck, movie producer, 20th Century Fox, 1946

Rules are made to be broken

Have a go at this exercise.

ACTIVITY
The tricky grid

Look at the grid below. Can you circle exactly four of these numbers so that the total is 12?

Figure 4.2   The tricky grid

For the answer, see page 228.

Did you get it? If you struggled with this, it's probably because your mind unconsciously imposed the rule that the grid can only be approached from one direction. But this assumption is only imaginary, and so to solve the puzzle you literally need to turn it on its head. In creative problem solving, pretty much anything goes.

Rule-following is something we learn very early on as children: 'Don't colour outside the lines', 'Copy this from the blackboard', 'Be quiet in class'. Over the years, we carry on building up our set of rules based on what we believe to be best for ourselves and others, and what authority figures tell us. In the corporate world arbitrary rules such as 'The customer is always right' and 'The board always sets the direction for the organization' are reinforced to the point of becoming sacred. As a result, we become comfortable with rules and don't think to challenge them. But the major problem with rules, as with assumptions, is that they often continue to live well beyond the circumstances they were designed for in the first place.

A good example is the QWERTY keyboard used today on desktop and laptop computers. Do you know how this layout came about? It was invented by Sholes & Co, a leading manufacturer of typewriters, back in the 1870s. The idea behind the configuration was to slow down the speed of typing because the typewriter keys would jam together if the operator went too fast. By positioning the most commonly used letters – e, a, i and o – away from the index fingers of the hands, the speed of typing was reduced. Operators would have to use their relatively weaker fingers to press them, and this solved the problem of keys sticking together.

Since that time, however, keyboard technology has come on in leaps and bounds and computers can now go much faster than human operators. Yet despite new and quicker layouts being available, we're still stuck with the outdated QWERTY rule. Isn't this ridiculous? Once a rule gets in place, it's tricky to eliminate it even though the original reason for it has disappeared. So, the real challenge with creative thinking is not just generating ideas, but escaping from the ones that no longer work for us.

Let's say you're looking for ways to improve the productivity of your business. Your rules might be:

1 We use external coaches to train our workforce and motivate teams to do better.
2 We always communicate with clients by telephone.
3 The research and development department creates new products.
4 We work on one major project before beginning another.

What happens when you break the rules?

1 Line managers have the key responsibility to train and incentivize their team, leading to better communication and closer relationships.

2 We use alternative methods of speaking to clients, including e-mail, social media and personal visits.

3 We involve other departments in the product development process, including customer service, technical support, production and finance. As a result, we develop more robust solutions.

4 We work on a wide range of projects at any one time, which is more stimulating for workers.

Over the years, I've worked with several large companies whose rigid rules and bureaucracies have held them back from adapting to the changing dynamics of their marketplace. Obeying the rules has worked so well for them in the past that they're beyond reproach; they're untouchable. People are scared to question them. It's hard to make innovation happen in this sort of environment. If rules are never open to investigation or challenge, then how can you ever break new ground? How can you see the merits of other approaches when you're not free to look for them?

If you don't ask, 'Why this?' often enough, someone else will ask, 'Why you?'
                                        – TOM HIRSHFIELD, American research physicist

Losing out to newcomers

Businesses can trundle on for decades, even centuries, within invisible restrictions that are accepted without questioning. Often it takes the shock of a newcomer entering the industry and blatantly flouting the rules that brings home just how pointless they were.

Richard Branson demonstrated this perfectly when he launched Virgin Atlantic, flying in the face of British Airways, American Airlines and Pan Am. These established players all stuck to the same rules – first-class passengers enjoyed a top-notch service, business passengers received adequate service, and economy passengers got basic, 'no-frills' treatment. What did Branson do? He eliminated first class and instead gave first-class service to business passengers. He also introduced innovative perks such as free drinks for economy passengers, videos in headrests and limousine service to the airport, altogether transforming a somewhat stale industry.

Lots of established companies are so anchored in the rules and bureaucracies that keep them operating that they just never have enough time in the day to be creative. When there's a problem, they opt to 'work around' it, adding new process steps or approval layers instead of finding a quality solution to put things right. After a while, they don't even remember where the new rules came from! Newcomers, on the other hand, enter an industry with a fresh perspective and a clean slate, so they aren't scared to do what everybody else doesn't. They change the ground rules of the markets they enter. For instance, Japanese automobile manufacturers opted to make small, fuel-efficient cars; something the incumbent Americans wouldn't consider at the time. The US manufacturers stuck with their strategy of releasing large, high-powered vehicles and lost out on an entire market segment. Like new entrants, reputable organizations shouldn't be scared to ask the question, 'What would happen if we broke the rules?'

CASE STUDY   The Body Shop – challenging the norms

Anita Roddick, founder of The Body Shop retail chain, achieved phenomenal success by going against the grain in the cosmetics retail industry. She broke just about every rule in the book from the moment she first conceived the idea of selling natural, non-animal-tested cosmetics in 1976. At the time, most pharmacies and beauty chains were sterile places that sold toiletries, cosmetics, perfumes and medicinal creams in expensive, pretty packaging. Roddick did the opposite by bottling her products in cheap plastic containers with plain, hand-printed labels, and encouraged her customers to bring back the containers for refills. Not only did this save money but it fostered a natural, earthy image for the products and made them all the more appealing to environmentally conscious consumers.

As the brand became more and more successful, Roddick continued to flout the rules. For instance, she never advertised, even when the first shops were being opened in the United States. And to this day the company still puts ideals before profit. In a world where the bottom line is the be-all and end-all, The Body Shop stands out as forging an impressive path to a new socially responsible and compassionate reality.

Key takeaways

Assumptive thinking is the tendency to accept a belief, convention or idea as true, often with no proof. Flawed assumptions are one of the worst barriers to innovation. They're invisible, chronic and insidious, and we're all ruled by them in one situation or another. How do they hold us back?

- They lead us to think we know all the facts when we really don't. Assumptions such as 'We have to launch a new range of products every year to keep up with competitors' should be checked for validity.

- They cause us to become trapped by our own self-imposed limits and specializations, for example Xerox's failure to capture the personal computing market by limiting itself to making better copiers.

- Rules, like assumptions, keep us stuck in outdated patterns. The more entrenched the rule is, the greater the chance that it's no longer valid. Sometimes, we need to shake up or reverse our existing patterns to stand out from everyone else.

References

Creating Minds (nd) [accessed 1 March 2018] Assumption-Busting, *CreatingMinds.org* [Online] http://creatingminds.org/tools/assumption_busting. htm

Davies, N (2008) [accessed 1 March 2018] Our Media Have Become Mass Producers of Distortion, *The Guardian*, 4 February [Online] https://www. theguardian.com/commentisfree/2008/feb/04/comment.pressandpublishing

Jiji Press (2017) [accessed 1 March 2018] Self-Service Convenience Store Stands and Kiosks Popping up Inside Companies, *The Japan Times*, 10 August [Online] https://www.japantimes.co.jp/news/2017/08/10/business/corporate-business/ self-service-convenience-store-stands-kiosks-popping-inside-companies/#. Wpfcgkx2uhc

Gladwell, M (2011) [accessed 1 March 2018] Creation Myth: Xerox PARC, Apple, and the Truth About Innovation, *The New Yorker*, 16 May [online] https:// www.newyorker.com/magazine/2011/05/16/creation-myth

Kahneman, D (2011) *Thinking, Fast and Slow*, Allen Lane, London

Kneller, GF (1965) *The Art and Science of Creativity*, Holt, Rinehart and Winston, New York

Rogers, A and Sheehan, RG (1960) [accessed 1 March 2018] *How Come – Again?* Doubleday, Garden City, NY

Sword, A (2016) [accessed 18 October 2018] Encyclopaedia Britannica: How a Print Company Embraced Disruptive Innovation in Publishing, *Computer Business Review* [Online] https://www.cbronline.com/cloud/encyclopaedia-britannica-how-a-print-company-embraced-disruptive-innovation-in-publishing-4898586/

Wessel, M (2012) Big Companies Can't Innovate Halfway, *Harvard Business Review*, 4 October [Online] https://hbr.org/2012/10/big-companies-cant-innovate-halfway

Part Two
The Solution Finder

05
The context for creative problem solving

Creativity can solve almost any problem... the defeat of habit by originality, overcomes everything.

– GEORGE LOIS, American art director, designer and author

Are you market-driven or market-driving?

Today, many companies and entrepreneurs pride themselves on being market-driven. They seek to understand the specific characteristics of the market through exhaustive research and then react to those characteristics. This is a classic 'think within the box' approach and makes little attempt to satisfy latent customer needs or reshape market behaviours and preferences. When you are market-driven, you are letting your past make your decisions. As strategic marketer Andrew Stein (2012) highlights, 'How can you project a forward-looking vision, envisioning a new and different future, if you are driving while looking backwards?' Selective, reactive and assumptive thinking all result in us being market-driven, not the market-driver.

Market drivers are visionary risk-takers and consistently surprise customers by predicting the products and services they need. They see opportunities where others do not to deliver a leap in customer value (Kumar, Scheer and Kotler, 2000). Instead of a reactive business strategy, they are proactive and agile, unhindered by conventional thinking and industry rules. Noteworthy examples include FedEx, Amazon, The Body Shop, IKEA, Starbucks, Wal-Mart and Swatch. You cannot be both market-driving and market-driven – it's an oxymoron. See Table 5.1 for the key differences.

Table 5.1   Market-driving vs market-driven

Market-driving	Market-driven
Disruptive	Reactive
Innovative	Incremental
Creative	Insignificant
Value	Features
Agile	Rigid
Competitive	Tentative
Decisive	Unsure
Clear	Confused
Dynamic	Static

SOURCE A Stein, SteinVox.com, 2012

How to become a market-driver

To become a market-driver, you must first commit to overcoming the barriers of traditional thinking. In a selective, reactive or assumptive work climate, the problem-solving process usually only happens in response to a crisis or the consequences of bog-standard market research. This seldom allows for opportunity seeking. Taking charge of selective, reactive and assumptive thinking leaves you better placed to deliver more creative and useful outcomes in any situation. How? Through a *process* that forces your brain to break out of its usual patterns; this is essential for setting up a fertile and productive environment. Remember that a process helps with **metacognition** – the act of 'thinking about thinking'. When facing a challenge, you get the best results by applying a strategy around your thinking to call on the right skills at the right time.

A winning process

It's time that we stop seeing creativity as a one-off festival of experimentation and wild thinking. As I like to say, innovation is a *process* not an event. One killer idea is not enough. Long-term success is built on a conveyor belt of creative ideas – one new thing after another, so you keep moving forward into the future instead of staying stuck in the past. If you keep innovating, as an individual, as a team and as an organization, you dramatically increase your chances of winning... and that's what the business game is all about. Because innovation is a process, it's crucial to build a system around your creative practices so you can continue to make useful advances and break boundaries in your field. Yes, some innovations are the result of accidents or mistakes, but a formal process is still necessary to transform those errors and unexpected insights into something practical for the real world.

Think about a casino and all the different games you can play. All casino games have a winning process and the odds are stacked in favour of the house. Their approach to securing a good outcome is by a laser-like focus on process. It's exactly the same with your thinking. A good process makes your thinking mindful and deliberate, dramatically improving your ability to find robust new opportunities, reason with greater clarity, and problem solve more effectively. As much as we would love for there to be magic shortcuts for creativity, focusing on quick outcomes can create all sorts of problems and lead us to compromise on our options. Think of the first-mover disadvantage described in Chapter 3 on reactive thinking; rushing to get short-term results won't serve you well when competitors who have had more time to prepare make an entrance into the market. Next time you're faced with a problem, opportunity or challenge, don't act right away. Think first. Map your journey before you go exploring.

Your creative process must have enough structure to enable you and your team to develop and progress ideas, while still remaining flexible. Anything too rigid will suck the enthusiasm, and indeed the creativity, out of people. In this part of the book (Part Two), I'll be introducing you to the **Solution Finder** (Figure 5.1), an approach I developed for applied creativity and in-novation, and one which I regularly teach in my training courses and work-shops. The name is a bit of a giveaway, but if you're under any doubt about what the Solution Finder does, it's essentially a framework for finding inven-tive solutions to problems or challenges. Based on four simple steps, the aim of the Solution Finder is to help you create the right mindset and atmosphere

Figure 5.1   The Solution Finder

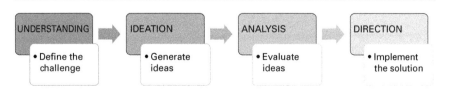

to unleash the creative thinking power of your team and make the best decisions to drive your organization forward. The Solution Finder will not only kickstart your creativity when you need a boost, but used faithfully and habitually, it will enable you to create and embed a culture of true innovation in your organization.

Step 1. Understanding – Define the challenge. Explore the issue fully; try to understand what's causing the problem and outline precisely what you need to deal with.

Step 2. Ideation – Generate ideas. Use creative thinking tools to spark an abundance of ideas to potentially solve the problem/challenge.

Step 3. Analysis – Evaluate those ideas. Sort, screen and select your best idea(s) using a 'whole brain' approach. Make the decision.

Step 4. Direction – Implement the solution. Strengthen, improve and refine your solution as far as possible. Gather acceptance and set your goals. Then create your plan and put it into action!

Divergent and convergent thinking

As with any good thinking system, the Solution Finder is influenced by Guilford's (1967) notion of divergent and convergent thinking:

Divergent thinking: An expansive, free-flowing activity that extends us away from the original subject in all directions. It cracks our minds wide open to consider all possibilities and ideas, even those that are zany or off-the-wall. Divergent thinking is viewed as 'soft' and is associated with things like:

Metaphor, creative, dream, humour, visual, emotions, visualization, ambiguity, play, imaginative, approximate, generative, fantasy, spontaneous, intuition, analogy, hunch, random, unconscious, general.

Convergent thinking: The mental activity that guides us towards making a correct and informed decision. It enables us to examine how different concepts fit and focuses our thoughts sharply on one target. Convergent thinking is a 'hard' thought process, characterized by words like:

Reason, logic, precision, consistency, critical, facts, rational, deliberate, work, exact, reality, direct, conscious, focused, sequence, number, analysis, linear, specific.

Divergent thinking is generative, while convergent thinking is analytical and selective. Both types of thinking play a valuable role during the creative process, but only at different stages. There are three main phases in the development of new ideas (Figure 5.2):

1 **Generative/imaginative stage:** We generate a vast range of possible options, eg through brainstorming. For many, this is the fun and creative stage where you are free to expand your mind, manipulate problems, test assumptions, break the rules and think up tons of ideas. This phase is DIVERGENT – you allow your thoughts to diverge or go in different directions. It should be facilitated well to ensure that early judgement and editing does not stop any new idea in its tracks.

2 **Analytical/practical stage:** We analyse these options and gather information with the aim of converging to a single solution. This involves whittling down feasible solutions and considering practicalities (costs, resources, timings, etc). This phase is CONVERGENT – the idea is to force your thoughts to converge, to make them come together to a single point. Only then can you progress to the selective/action phase where you can implement the solution you plumped for.

3 **Selective/action stage:** We build up and reinforce our chosen solution and begin to take it forward. This involves generating recommendations, setting goals, testing the solution and preparing to carry it into action.

Figure 5.2   The order of creative thinking

Now consider how you go about the creative process. Be honest with yourself. Do you follow this order of thinking? For the bulk of us who are mainly analytical thinkers, it can be awkward to be wildly divergent in our thinking without making a real, strenuous effort. That's because convergent thinking is our normal state. Often, we allow 'hard' thought patterns such as analysis and judgement to come in far too early, infiltrating the imaginative phase. This narrows our thinking ahead of time, causing us to kill off ideas that might seem ludicrous or offbeat too quickly: 'That's silly' or 'That won't work'. Given a chance, these might have turned out to be our best, brightest ideas, but we've rejected them at the outset. It's like we can't help ourselves.

Logic and analysis are super-important tools, we need them to help us sort, screen and select from ideas and avoid the errors of erratic thinking. But an excessive reliance on them, especially during ideation, can short-circuit the whole creative process. You can't drive a car in first gear and reverse at the same time. Likewise, you can't create and evaluate simultaneously – you'll wreck your mental gears. You must diverge and converge in the correct order. Innovation author Paul Sloane (2010) describes how scientists Crick and Watson used divergent thinking as an initial stage to help them consider an array of possible patterns and arrangements in their discovery of the structure of DNA in 1953. They followed this with convergent thinking to zero in on the one correct answer – the double helix. The Solution Finder is set up to override the instinct to narrow down your thoughts too soon and to make problem solving a more fluent process, helping you first *diverge* your thinking to produce lots and lots of ideas, and then *converge* your thinking towards the solutions with the most potential. By following the clear steps, you can stay organized while looking for the inspired answers that will make you successful.

Innovation is not the product of logical thought, although the result is tied to logical structure.

– ALBERT EINSTEIN, Nobel Prize-winning theoretical physicist

Left and right brains unite!

Even during the 'practical' idea-evaluation stage of decision making, we have to be careful not to allow our analytical side to take over. When we focus heavily on logic, judgement and criticism, our hard, left-brain cortical skills (words, numbers, analysis, listing, language and logic) become overly dominant and skew our thinking. It's vital to engage other softer, right-brain cortical skills (rhythm, feeling, colour, shape, maps, imagination, daydreaming) to balance things out and draw upon our full mental strength. Note that this also means using *emotion*, *intuition* and *gut feeling* to fuel our interpretation of the situation and help us judge our options.

While this concept of left- and right-brain thinking has been widely discredited in recent years, much of Roger Sperry's Nobel Prize-winning work in this area still holds true. Researchers have validated that the two major hemispheres of the brain (left and right) do indeed operate differently in terms of mental processing. But what is perhaps most interesting is that both sides become active in a complementary and cohesive fashion when certain activities are engaged (Hellige, 2001). Thus, to achieve the best ideas and decisions it's not just a case of 'either/or', left-brain/right-brain thinking. We need both our analytical and generative faculties working harmoniously together. We need 'whole brain' thinking.

Judgement jeopardy

We usually spend the overwhelming majority of our time at work thinking logically and critically. So, it's no surprise that when we're summoned into an impromptu brainstorming session, our critical side is still all revved up in full working mode. No matter how useful judgement and analysis are in decision making, they're hopeless at coming up with creative solutions to problems. The whole point of a brainstorming session is to take 'time out' from logic so we can get as many ideas as we can, no matter how wild or outrageous. We're practical every other moment of the day, so why can't we take an hour or two to be totally illogical? Give budding ideas a chance and you may learn something new. Instead of knocking them down, you should be thinking, 'What's interesting and innovative about this idea?' and 'Can this lead to another creative idea?' See the creative merit in every single idea thrown out by your team. Now is not the time or the place to be sorting them into piles of good or bad, useful and useless. Remember, every time you stop to evaluate, you stop creating. You'll have plenty of time to mentally road-test ideas and work out which ones make the grade for your company later on.

What if it's the other way round and it's your own inner critic that's putting a jam on things? Self-doubt gets to us all at some point or another. We often fall victim to negative thinking when it comes to our own ideas: 'Will people really want this?', 'Isn't there too much competition?', 'Why waste time on something that's going to fail?' We need to counteract this natural pessimistic bias to allow new ideas to come sauntering in. In Table 5.2, I outline seven types of negative thinking that impair creative performance. Do you suffer from any of these?

Table 5.2   Negative thinking

1 Black or white thinking	Extreme thinking: Things are either good or bad, right or wrong. You either love or hate an idea – there are no shades of grey or middle ground. During brainstorming, this leads you to believe that a less-than-perfect-answer can't be right. – *'If I'm not a winner, I'm a loser.'*
2 Comparative thinking	Performance is judged only by comparison with other people. – *'John always has the best ideas. Compared to him, I never come up with anything useful.'*
3 Overgeneralization	Coming to a general conclusion based on a single event or piece of evidence. If something went wrong once, you expect it to happen again and again instead of looking at the situation afresh. Characterized by the use of 'always', 'never', 'everybody', 'the world is'… – *'We won't get the project done on time. This is what always happens.'*
4 Mind-reading	Believing you can tell what other people are thinking about you or your ideas, and assuming that it's negative. – *'She thinks my idea is too far-out. She feels threatened by it.'*
5 Labelling	We attach a description to ourselves, other people, or events and then assume any similar or related labels also apply. – *'That idea I just suggested was terrible. I'm useless at being creative.'*
6 Catastrophizing	Overestimating the chances of disaster. Expecting something unbearable or intolerable to happen. – *'I'm going to make a fool of myself and people will laugh at me.'*
7 Fortune telling	You *know* how something is going to turn out, so you don't bother putting yourself in the situation. Making negative predictions discourages you from experimenting and taking positive risks. – *'There's no use going for that idea. I know it won't work out.'*

The Creativity toolkit

The only way to build your creative confidence is through doing and practice. But it can be unnerving staring at a blank page and waiting for inspiration to strike. It helps to give creativity a guide to work from. There are thousands of creative thinking and problem-solving tools out there that can help trigger new connections and make sense of all the data available for effective analysis and decision making. However, techniques by themselves are insufficient to spark more creative behaviour – they cannot be used to 'force' creativity out of people (Cook, 1998). Techniques are most useful when an appropriate context has been created. This is the purpose of the Decision Radar and Solution Finder, which together produce the right circumstances to allow people's inherent creative talent to emerge. The Solution Finder contains my own favourite methods, based on years of live testing in solo and group environments. The tools are all user-friendly and have been specially chosen for their suitability at each stage, depending on whether divergent or convergent thinking is required. A wide menu of choices is offered, so that you can match the tools to your particular problem or opportunity. What's more, they can inject a great deal of fun into your problem-solving sessions (always a bonus!).

Canvas templates and checklists

Handy templates and checklists are included to help you navigate each stage of the Solution Finder. At various points, you can complete the relevant canvases to immediately make sense of your learning while working on a real-life challenge.

All the resources in this book can be downloaded from **www.thinking. space**

References

Cook, P (1998) The creativity advantage – is your organization the leader of the pack? *Industrial and Commercial Training*, 30 (5), pp 179–84

Guilford, JP (1967) *The Nature of Human Intelligence*, McGraw-Hill, New York

Hellige, JB (2001) *Hemispheric Asymmetry: What's right and what's left*, Harvard University Press, Cambridge, MA

Kumar, N, Scheer, L and Kotler, P (2000) From market driven to market driving, *European Management Journal*, **18** (2), pp 129–42

Sloane, P (2010) *How to be a Brilliant Thinker: Exercise your mind and find creative solutions*, Kogan Page, London

Stein, A (2012) [accessed 6 March 2018] 9 Differences Between Market-Driving and Market-Driven Companies [Blog], *SteinVox*, 31 October [Online] http://steinvox.com/blog/9-differences-between-market-driving-and-market-driven-companies/

06
The Solution Finder Step 1: Understanding

The greatest challenge to any thinker is stating the problem in a way that will allow a solution.

> – attributed to BERTRAND RUSSELL, British philosopher and logician

Define the challenge

When you were at school, do you remember being told to make sure that you read the question in the exam properly before answering? The same advice applies to problem solving. Normally, when faced with a problem our first instinct is to go looking for a solution; the sooner we put it to bed the better. However, what we should really be doing is looking harder at the problem. Instead of rushing headlong into finding solutions, invest time in defining your problem correctly. The way you define your problem sets the principal direction for all your creative sweats and struggles. It influences the line of thought you follow and has a powerful effect on the ideas you entertain, so it's important to get it right.

Individuals and businesses that I work with seem to have mind-blowing realizations when they try out this activity – but it's the stage of the problem-solving process that most of us tend to skip. We think we know what the problem is and don't want to waste any time dilly-dallying. When we have a marvellous solution or idea, we just want to get it out there. It's frustrating having to stop and reflect on every aspect of our problem first. However, what we fail to twig is that our understanding of the problem may be too fuzzy and vague. If we don't understand and articulate our challenge early on, we may find out later down the line that the problem we're trying to tackle is not actually the right problem – just the most obvious. Or, we may even be trying to solve a symptom of the problem, not the problem itself.

New opportunities abound in business and taking enthusiastic action to launch a new idea is all well and good, but our efforts will be a complete waste if they are misguided. Innovation is not about making any idea happen purely for the sake of novelty or as a quick fix. Change needs to be *relevant* and *purposeful* in that it brings you or your organization closer to achieving your goals. Ask yourself: 'Why are we doing this in the first place?' If this isn't startlingly apparent, then make it so. In any creative process, the quality of your output always depends on the quality of your input. This first stage is therefore essential in helping you get clarity on what you're innovating for. It also:

- Prevents you making hasty judgements and jumping to the wrong conclusions.
- Helps you check and challenge your assumptions.
- Gives you better insight into the underlying causes of the problem – why does the problem exist?
- Enables you to identify priorities so you can target your efforts more accurately.

At the start of a thinking project, take time by yourself and with your colleagues to accurately define and understand your challenge – whether it's to solve a problem, disrupt the marketplace, offer a better way of doing things, deal with an immediate threat or exploit a recent opportunity that's opened up.

Each goal or problem needs its own special treatment in terms of the people involved and the data brought to bear on it. Look at the challenge from different angles so that you develop a total view of what you're dealing with. Gather information about the facts and feelings involved. Once this is done, you'll have set the scene to invite better, more meaningful ideas for the issue or goal at hand.

CASE STUDY   The wrong problem

Problems and challenges can take on a vast number of shapes and sizes. They may represent shortcomings ('repeat sales are falling', 'our budget has been reduced') or goals ('design an up-to-date product', 'regain market share'). They can be broad or specific, internal or external, and can vary from a relatively minor hiccup to a major switch in operational focus.

In heaps of organizations, people will spend hours finding solutions to issues that are trivial, or in some cases non-existent. Why? Because selective, reactive or assumptive thinking leads them down that path. They're solving what they think the problem or opportunity is, and wasting valuable time, energy and resources doing so.

Jonah Lehrer (2012), author of *Imagine: How Creativity Works*, highlights a striking example of this kind of unproductive approach. Proctor & Gamble was faced with a problem – it needed a new floor cleaner for mopping floors. A group of its best scientists (with more PhDs than any other company in the United States at the time) were given the task of designing one. Now, this wasn't an easy problem. While it was possible to make a stronger floor cleaner, it would have the unwelcome side effect of stripping off wood varnish and irritating delicate skin. After years of exhausting and unsuccessful research and development, the problem was outsourced to design firm Continuum. The first thing Continuum did was to take nine months to observe people mopping the floors in their own homes. They took detailed notes and set up video cameras in living rooms. It was a tedious process, but it revealed just how much of a messy ordeal mopping as a cleaning method is. Then... an interesting discovery was made when some coffee grounds were spilt on the kitchen floor of one of the subjects. Instead of reaching for the mop, she reached for a paper towel, wet it and wiped the floor by hand. The towel was then tossed.

This led to the revelation that they were trying to solve the **wrong problem**. They didn't need a new floor cleaner; they needed a quick and easy spot-cleaning tool that people could throw away. The result was the invention of the Swiffer – a disposable paper towel attached to a mop handle.

What can you take away from this? Before you try to find solutions, stop to consider whether you're solving the right problem.

What's the problem?

Most entrepreneurs and business professionals must make decisions that require problem solving in any number of areas in their career or organization. Table 6.1 lists some question prompts for describing typical challenges that call for creative thinking.

Table 6.1   Typical challenges that call for creative thinking

What...	How can I...
What would I like to accomplish?	How can I make more efficient use of my time?
What isn't working correctly?	How can I resolve a conflict at work?
What standards/objectives aren't being achieved?	How can I enhance client relationships?
What is the mission of our organization?	How can I motivate myself and/or my team?
What will improve our customer retention rates?	How can we design better products/ services?
What changes/ideas would I like to introduce?	How can we remove bottlenecks in the system?
What systems of control are needed?	How can we cut costs through more efficient production methods?
What profitable opportunities are there in the market?	How can we attract more customers to our business?
What can we organize better?	How can I best train people for their jobs?
What steps can we take to counteract the decline in our retail sales?	How can I reduce stress in my job?
What have I never done that I would like to do?	How can we run this department better?

The Understanding toolkit

INPUT

Presented challenge

PROCESS

Examine the brief and define the challenge in detail

TOOLS

Define and Understand Canvas

5W1H Canvas

Changing Perspectives Canvas

OUTPUT

Challenge clearly defined

The creative process begins with the challenge that you have identified. In Step 1 of the Solution Finder, you are given practical tools to help you get a laser-like focus on your problem, goal, project or situation. Make sure you record all your problem-defining activity as you work through this stage and keep your notes in one place for easy reference. Download the canvases for this step here: **www.thinking.space**

Define and Understand Canvas

The purpose of this first canvas is to urge you and your team to immerse yourselves in the problem for better understanding of the context. Examine your goals and thoughts, frame and reframe the challenge and check your assumptions.

1. Identify your challenge and desired outcomes

State your goal, challenge, project or wish as concisely as you can. Use invitational stem language (phrases or questions that invite exploration) to open your mind for divergent thinking on the problem, such as 'It would be great if...' or 'How might we...?'. This prevents you closing in on the problem prematurely. Outline your ideal outcomes as well as acceptable outcomes. If you had unlimited time and resources, what would you like to achieve? What are the criteria for success? What would be a 'good enough' result? Determine the positive consequences you would expect as a result of taking action. This sets the target and direction for your problem-solving activity.

2. Describe opinions and obstacles

Next, note down your initial opinions and thoughts regarding the challenge you face. Why do things need to change? How does this problem make

Figure 6.1 Define and Understand Canvas

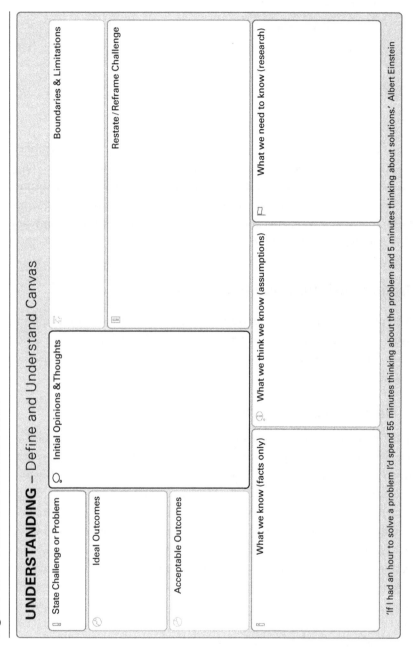

UNDERSTANDING – Define and Understand Canvas

State Challenge or Problem

Initial Opinions & Thoughts

Boundaries & Limitations

Ideal Outcomes

Restate / Reframe Challenge

Acceptable Outcomes

What we know (facts only)

What we think we know (assumptions)

What we need to know (research)

'If I had an hour to solve a problem I'd spend 55 minutes thinking about the problem and 5 minutes thinking about solutions.' Albert Einstein

you feel? Is it even necessary to seek new ideas? What does your gut tell you? What is annoying or upsetting about the problem? At this stage, be sure to record only opinions and viewpoints, not ideas. Set aside any ideas that crop up to revisit in the next step of the Solution Finder (Ideation). Consider any boundaries or limitations there are in connection with your challenge. For instance, is there a lack of support? Do you have the right level of influence to address the challenge? This thinking forms the groundwork from which you can gather data and further sharpen awareness of the problem.

3. Reframe the challenge

Now play around with the wording of your problem statement. Your first impression of the problem is by no means the only one. Reframe the challenge in multiple ways to alter the focus and find the most beneficial direction. Each time you rephrase the problem, you shift to a new starting point from which you can look at the information available to you afresh. You can use this tactic to transform a negative view into a positive one to bring more energy to your problem solving. Let's look at an example. If you were a line manager and approached your colleague with the statement:

'We're going to look at ways to increase your productivity'

what do you think would happen? Well, not only would your colleague feel terrible about their current performance, but you would stifle their ability to come up with unusual ideas. They would get stuck looking at all sorts of ways to 'work harder'. However, if you rephrased the statement to:

'We're going to look at how we can make your job easier'

what would this do? You would have simplified the problem, as well as putting a positive spin on something that would have been viewed as negative. In the end, the problem is still the same, but the feelings and viewpoints associated with it are different, so you can respond to it more directly and creatively. It's a particularly useful method for lifting morale after something has gone wrong at work or for viewing a problem as an opportunity (Cotton, 2016).

Reframing also helps to **simplify** a problem to stimulate new thinking. When we're overburdened with a problem, we can get stuck in complexity. This often happens when we feel we know a problem inside out – we've spent plenty of time on it and have gone through the whole convoluted process of dismantling it, searching it and verifying that it's the correct one. The good news about this is that we know exactly what the problem is. The not so good news is that we have so much information that we end up knowing *too much*. We've piled up lots of reasons for and against doing things, and we've got myriad approaches we could take. So, what happens? The push and pull of so many conflicting thoughts eventually leads to a mental jam and our ideas stop flowing. We can bring things back to basics by reframing the problem. Essentially, this involves removing all the 'bells and whistles' to get to the very core of things.

CASE STUDY   LEGO goes back to basics

Seeing your challenge or mission in a clear light is one of the best ways of finding creative solutions. During the 1990s, brand extensions into software games, children's clothing, lifestyle accessories, theme parks and television shows had fragmented the LEGO brand in the eyes of consumers, and by the end of 2003 the iconic toy manufacturer stood on the verge of bankruptcy. While no one could accuse LEGO of not being innovative (as a matter of fact, there was a great deal of hyper-innovation going on), it had clearly lost its way. It was by getting back to basics and refocusing on its core purpose – bricks and building as a system of play – that LEGO was able to successfully right its course and 'rebuild' its fortunes (Robertson, 2013).

4. Uncover assumptions

The Define and Understand Canvas incorporates an Assumptions Matrix (Souter, 2007) to help you understand your problem better and challenge any near-invisible assumptions. In the left-hand column (What we know), list all the **facts** about the problem. These must be completely true and verifiable. If you can't back up a certain point, it must belong in the second column of **assumptions** (What we think we know). This is what you think you know but can't actually prove or haven't been able to prove. While going through this process, you might uncover areas of ignorance that are relevant to your challenge. This is information you need to know, so put it in column 3 for **research** (What we need to know).

At the end you should have a clear idea of what you know, what you think you know and what you need to know. When you're trying to unscramble a problem, stick to the facts and seek out the information you need so you're not working in the dark.

5W1H Canvas

This tool is all about gathering data to help you get to grips with the 'real' problem – handy if your challenge is abstract or ambiguous. A smart way to do this is to use the universal question prompts: What? Why? Where? Who? When? and How? Collecting information and approaching the problem from different angles can often turn up some unusual perspectives and insights. This method is valuable for complex problems that carry a lot of information as it helps you interrogate and extrapolate the most important stuff.

We run the company by questions, not by answers.

– ERIC SCHMIDT, former Chairman and CEO of Google

WHAT? What are the **facts**? Look at both hard data such as statistics, history and time factors, and soft data such as opinions, human factors, attitudes and behaviours. What have you already tried to solve the problem? What worked and what didn't? What are you trying to achieve? Sketch out your **goal** or purpose. Are you trying to 'understand customers better' or 'win a government contract', for example?

WHY? If you have kids then you'll be familiar with those maddening occasions when they repeatedly ask 'why?' What your four-year-old already knows is that asking 'why?' is a great way of learning and gaining a deeper understanding of an issue, yet we stop doing it as adults because we think it's immature or that we already know all the answers. Ask the question 'why?' at least five times until you get to the bottom of a problem or goal. This is a great way to ensure that you're addressing the root cause and not just a symptom. The concept of 'Five Whys' was popularized by leading Japanese car manufacturer Toyota as a management tool, based on a story of a welding machine robot that had broken down during a demonstration (Ohno, 2006). Here's an example:

1 Why did we lose client XYZ this month?
Because we didn't finish the job on time... again.

2 Why didn't we finish the job on time?
Because we didn't have enough skilled workers allocated to the project.

Figure 6.2 5W1H Canvas

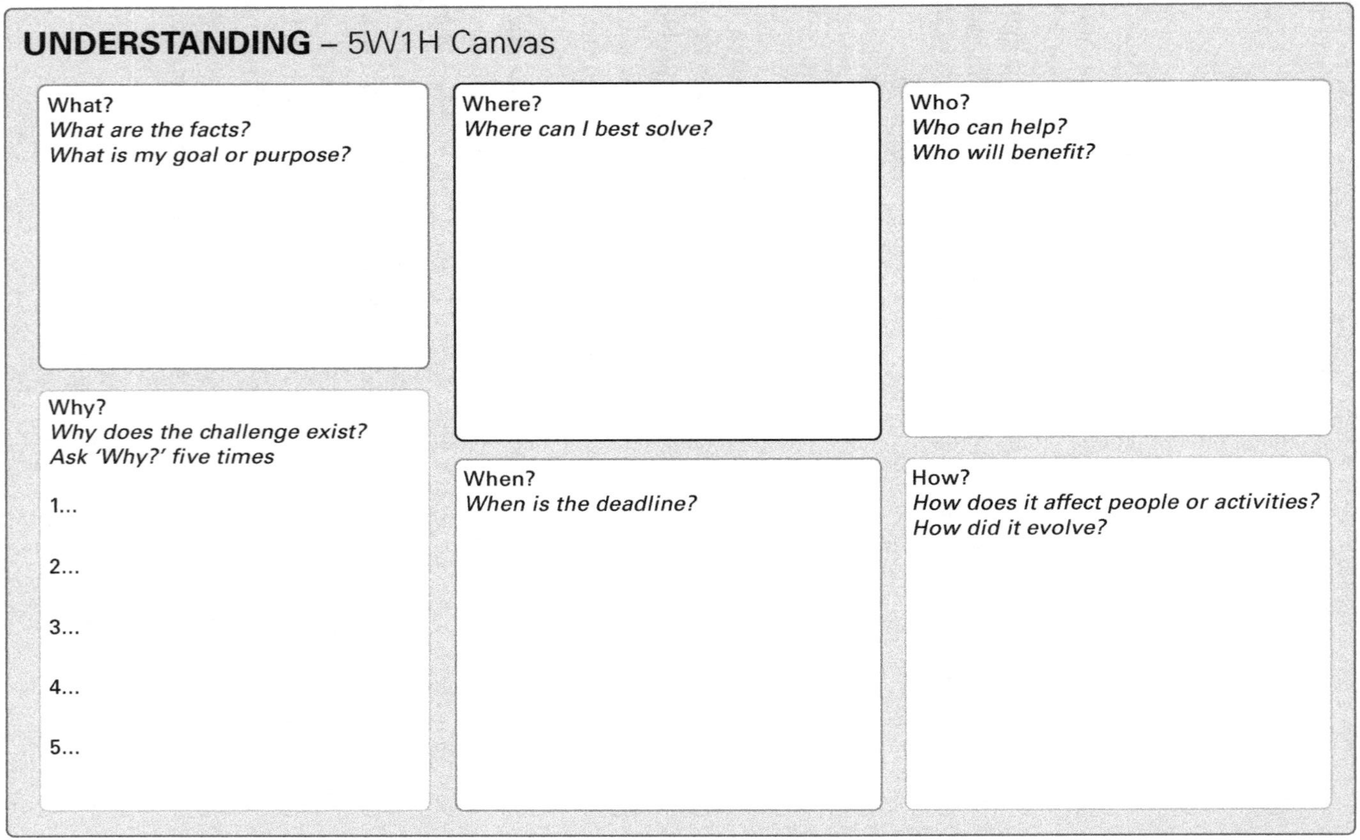

UNDERSTANDING – 5W1H Canvas

What?
What are the facts?
What is my goal or purpose?

Where?
Where can I best solve?

Who?
Who can help?
Who will benefit?

Why?
Why does the challenge exist?
Ask 'Why?' five times

1...

2...

3...

4...

5...

When?
When is the deadline?

How?
How does it affect people or activities?
How did it evolve?

3 Why didn't we have enough skilled workers allocated to the project?
Because we don't have enough workers with the necessary training for this type of specialist work.

4 Why don't our workers have the necessary training?
Because we don't have enough budget to offer specialist training.

5 Why isn't there enough budget for training?
Because training isn't a company priority.

And here we have the root cause! You don't have to stop at five levels, by the way, you can keep drilling until you have built as full a picture as possible of the underlying causes of the problem.

WHERE? Where can you resolve the problem? Where can you find additional help? Locate the best place or environment for working things out or putting your solution into effect. Your challenge might be something that can be sorted out easily enough at the office or in a specific department such as Production or Customer Services. Or it could be better served at specific branches, shop locations or even a client's office.

WHO? Who can help to solve the problem? Who benefits most from the problem being solved? Identify the person or people who can be involved in the solution, both directly and indirectly. For example, if there's an issue with poor customer service in a supermarket chain, the responsibility for carrying out the solution falls mostly on the shop service counter staff as they're in direct contact with the customer, and on the supervisors who manage them. Indirectly, it could involve lots of others too. For instance, key members of the head office who can help research and develop better customer service initiatives to roll out across the company, and maybe HR personnel to provide support for dealing with low staff morale.

WHEN? When do you need to have a solution ready? Strictly speaking, what's your deadline? This is a key question because it helps you work out a timeframe for the rest of your problem solving. If your challenge is to develop a new marketing campaign or product line, when do you plan on launching it? Your decision here will feed into your action planning, helping you build in time for earlier tasks and keep on track.

HOW? How does the problem or challenge influence people or activities? Explore the impact of the problem on specific tasks, departments, resources, products or tools. How did the problem evolve and how long has it been a concern?

CASE STUDY Airbnb – locate the problem, disrupt the market

Airbnb is an excellent example of how focusing on a problem can bring about an innovative answer. The idea for Airbnb, a website that allows people to list and rent short-term accommodation in residential properties all over the world, initially came about as an alternative to the problem of fully booked hotels (Salter, 2012). Founders Brian Chesky and Joe Gebbia saw an opportunity to earn some extra income by renting out their spare floor space when a major design conference came to their home city of San Francisco in 2007. They realized that there was a huge demand for no-frills lodging and soon knocked up a website enabling people to advertise their rooms for overnight guests, taking a cut of between 9 and 15 per cent per booking. Just a decade later, the company was valued at $31 billion (Statista, 2018).

Changing Perspectives Canvas

A unique way to explore your problem and shed your mental constraints is to temporarily pretend you're someone else. When it comes to problem analysis, your perspective or standpoint provides just one singular view of the situation, one that's likely to give you similar outcomes to those you've experienced in the past when solving problems. The simple act of borrowing another person's point of reference can make a huge difference in how creatively you approach things, as it forces you to break the pattern of your usual approach. Different people with varied backgrounds, experiences, professions and interests all look at things in different ways. How would a reality TV star view your problem? A nurse? An eight-year-old child? A bus driver? You can escape your narrow vision and open up a whole new world simply by mentally borrowing their perspectives and looking at the problem through fresh eyes. It's a very playful approach and will easily liven up any lacklustre meeting. Here's how to do it.

Step 1. Identify different points of reference

Use a random selection of people in different roles, circumstances or professions. You can include people affected by the problem, such as colleagues, customers or partners, but it's far better to use people unrelated to the problem – Sir Alan Sugar, your sister, a farmer, or someone you admire, for

Figure 6.3 Changing Perspectives Canvas

UNDERSTANDING – Changing Perspectives Canvas

State challenge or problem	What would I do if I had no fear?

How would the following people you identify find a solution to the challenge?

Person 1 _____

Person 2 _____

Person 3 _____

Person 4 _____

What do I need to do differently to find the solution?

What do I want to say about how I handled this challenge one year from now?

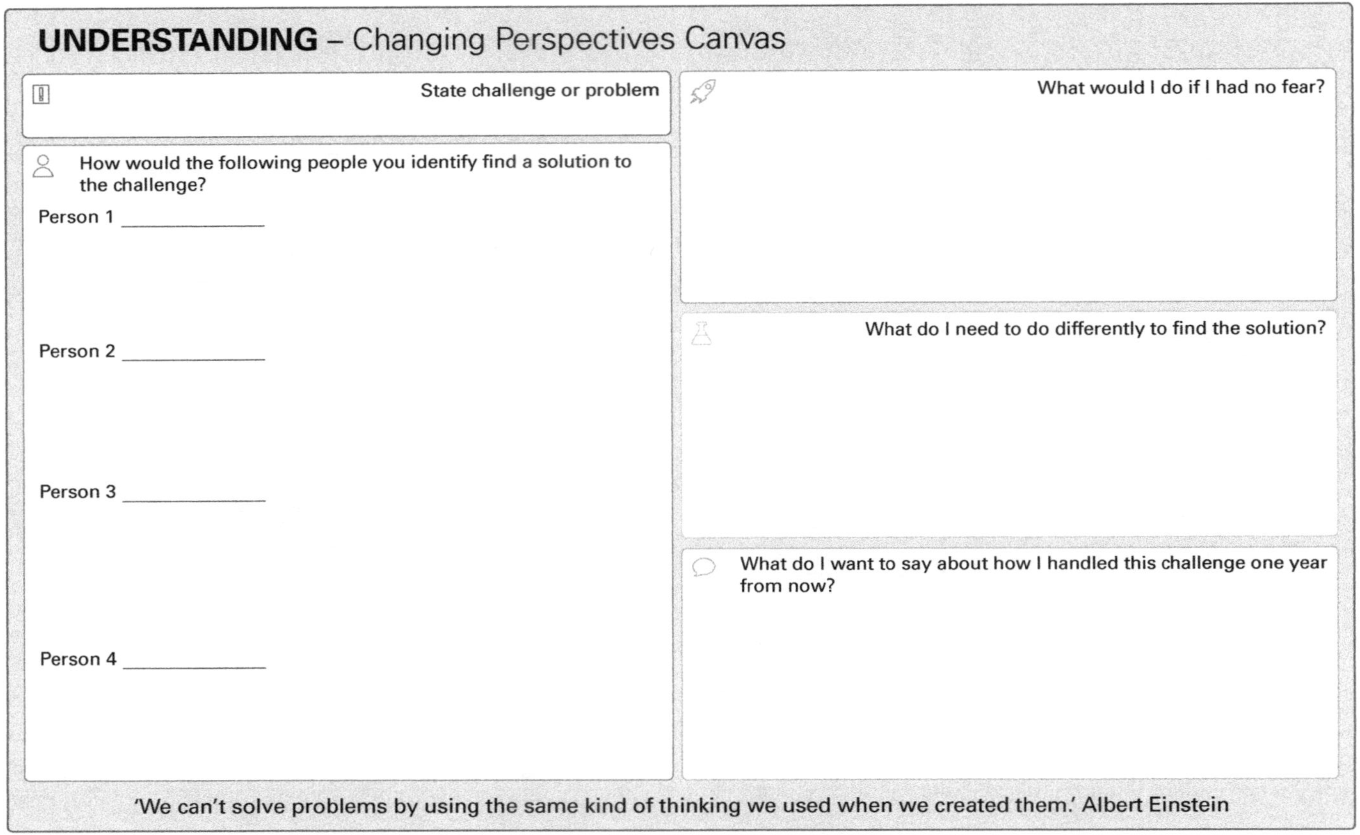

'We can't solve problems by using the same kind of thinking we used when we created them.' Albert Einstein

example. You can even use archetypes like those Carl Jung describes (Hero, Lover, Sage, Magician, Outlaw, etc), fairy-tale characters like Snow White or even superheroes like Superman. The more assorted the choice, the better, as you get a much broader base for generating solutions. Table 6.2 offers a sample of perspectives you could explore.

While some perspectives will work better than others, all will stretch your thinking to offer valid ideas. I recommend you pick at least four different characters to role play. Try to keep them unrelated to each other for a more comprehensive take on the issue.

Step 2. Explore each viewpoint

Next, consider how each of these people would view your particular challenge. Put yourself in their shoes – their mindset or environment – and imagine how they would think about it or describe it. Try asking the following questions:

- What would be the important factors to them?
- What aspect of the issue might they focus on?
- How would they describe the problem?
- How would their description differ from mine?
- Would they even see a problem at all?

Table 6.2 Examples of perspectives

Mother/Father	Poet	Flight attendant
Clown	Librarian	Child
Racing-car driver	Spiderman	Hairdresser
Doctor	Minister	Kim Kardashian
Accountant	Musician	Leonardo da Vinci
Stand-up comedian	Retired person	Sales manager
Homer Simpson	Teacher	Scientist
A dog	Queen Elizabeth	Will Smith
Napoleon	Bill Gates	The Hulk
Football player	Chef	Detective
The Dalai Lama	Pilot	Cinderella
Reporter/Journalist	Burglar	Politician

List the thoughts from each perspective on your canvas worksheet. For instance, what do you think your father would say about your problem? What would a clown say? Entirely different, even nutty or laughable explanations might come up. A priest might look to explore the deeper spiritual meaning of an issue, while a lawyer would examine the evidence for opposing sides of an argument before deciding on how to present a case. If possible, talk directly to some of these people and record what they say on your canvas. Notice the similarities and differences in how each person would approach the problem.

Another way to change your perspective is to contemplate your challenge using an alternative outlook. Ask yourself these three things:

- What would I do if I had no fear?

- What do I need to do differently to find the solution?

- What do I want to say about how I handled this challenge one year from now?

This deeper line of thinking forces you to zero in on the core of what you want to achieve and why. Again, record your responses.

Step 3. Collate initial thoughts and ideas

Reflecting on these perspectives, jot down any rough ideas that come to mind for solving your challenge. How would these people tackle the challenge? What ideas or approaches might they have? What actions would they take? Can these ideas work for your situation? Doing this will help you draw out lots of new and inventive strategies.

Sometimes the perspectives that seem to be the most distant from your problem can give you exactly the inspiration you're looking for. If your problem is to 'increase sales' and you're viewing it from the perspective of a teenager, this might give rise to ideas such as adding more playful and entertaining features to your product that customers would be willing to pay more for. Or maybe you could introduce fashionable membership offers so people can feel part of the 'gang', thus encouraging repeat business. See how it works?

Understanding checklist: dos and don'ts

One of the simplest and most effective ways to keep your thinking on track during your creative sessions is to use checklists. For this reason, I've put

Figure 6.4 Understanding checklist

UNDERSTANDING CHECKLIST: DOs & DON'Ts

DO

- Identify the real problem – beware of treating just the symptoms
- Find out who can help
- Form opinions
- Gather facts
- Set boundaries
- Agree objectives
- Ascertain if a decision is necessary
- Use previous experience – consider best and worst results using a former solution to a similar problem
- Restate the challenge in multiple ways
- Look for dissension and disagreement
- Start out with what is right, then explore what is acceptable
- Find a measurement that fits the challenge
- Understand if this is a generic problem that fits a current model
- Demand evidence for each claim that is made

DON'T

- Start with the conclusion
- Improvise
- Assume anything
- Gather facts before gaining several opinions
- Look for consensus
- Worry about reactions of others
- Like one option over another at this stage
- React quickly (unless it's a life or death situation) – react strategically
- Concern yourself with compromises
- Proceed unless there is disagreement
- Use a traditional measurement (otherwise it is just an adjustment)

together a series of ready-to-use checklists to help you stay on brief and manage your thinking alongside the Solution Finder canvases. I like to stick these on the wall by my desk for easy reference, so I can repeatedly ground myself at different stages of the process. The Understanding checklist supports your thinking for any problem-defining activity, reminding you of all the things you do and don't need to consider when staying alert for your challenge. Download and check it each time you start any form of innovation project: **www.thinking.space**

Key takeaways

The first step in the creative process is to identify and define the problem. Problem analysis can assist you in understanding the overall nature and underlying causes of the issue, goal or opportunity you face before you set out to find solutions.

- **Define and Understand Canvas.** Set the scene for your problem-solving activity by laying out your problem statement, desired outcomes, opinions and boundaries/limitations. Reframe your challenge to look at things afresh and put a positive spin on the issue. Find out what you know (facts), what you think you know (assumptions) and what you ultimately need to know (research).

- **5W1H Canvas.** Gather data to inform your decision making. Ask Who? What? Where? Why? When? and How? to interrogate the problem and improve your understanding of it.

- **Changing Perspectives Canvas.** See the challenge through the eyes of others. Approach it from alternative angles. This helps to break your usual pattern of thinking and brings a whole new meaning to the problem.

- **Understanding Checklist.** Master your thinking as you go about defining your challenge by consulting this checklist.

References

Cotton, D (2016) *The Smart Solution Book: 68 tools for brainstorming, problem solving and decision making*, Pearson, Harlow

Lehrer, J (2012) *Imagine: How creativity works*, Houghton Mifflin Harcourt, Boston, MA

Ohno, T (2006) [accessed 13 March 2018] Ask 'Why' Five Times About Every Matter, *Toyota Traditions*, March [Online] http://www.toyota-global.com/company/toyota_traditions/quality/mar_apr_2006.html

Robertson, D (2013) [accessed 16 March 2018] Building Success: How Thinking 'Inside the Brick' Saved Lego, *Wired*, 9 October [Online] http://www.wired.co.uk/article/building-success

Salter, J (2012) [accessed 13 March 2018] Airbnb: The story Behind the $1.3bn Room-Letting Website, *The Telegraph*, 7 September [Online] https://www.telegraph.co.uk/technology/news/9525267/Airbnb-The-story-behind-the-1.3bn-room-letting-website.html

Souter, N (2007) *Breakthrough Thinking: Using creativity to solve problems*, ILEX Press, Lewes, East Sussex

Statista (2018) [accessed 16 March 2018] Airbnb – Statistics & Facts [Online] https://www.statista.com/topics/2273/airbnb/

07

The Solution Finder Step 2: Ideation

Brain-friendly brainstorming

The role of a creative leader is not to have all the ideas; it's to create a
culture where everyone can have ideas and feel that they're valued.

— KEN ROBINSON, author and international adviser
on education and creativity

Generative thinking

As we know, creativity doesn't just happen. While we sometimes get those
'Eureka' moments and flashes of inspiration, successful ideas are more likely
to occur as part of a systematic process. You've done the groundwork by
identifying your challenge in Step 1, so you know what you need to deal
with. Now it's time for the fun part, coming up with lots of ideas for your
defined challenge. Step 2 is all about encouraging the generative thinking
that produces new ideas. This means stretching reality, unleashing wild
ideas, connecting existing concepts in new ways, and building on other people's ideas. In this chapter, we'll look at how to run your brainstorming sessions to maximize your chances of success. This goes hand in hand with the
next chapter, which talks you through the range of creative techniques that
will make up your Ideation toolkit, for use in both solo and group brainstorming sessions.

Brainstorming – does it work?

Alex Osborn invented brainstorming in 1953 as a kind of creative
conference for groups of people to turn out lots of ideas and find fresh

approaches to problems. Ever since then, brainstorming has become a default ritual in most businesses. Looking for something new? Then run a brainstorm. Got a nagging problem? Gather the troops to brainstorm ways to nip it in the bud. It's by far the most widely used technique for creative thinking, and is part-and-parcel of any civilized problem-solving and decision-making process.

Brainstorming has come under fire lately from those who perceive it to be a waste of time. This is no surprise if you've spent hours stuck in a room with your colleagues, wrestling with flipcharts and plastering sticky notes everywhere, only to leave the session feeling deflated by your mediocre output, rather than bursting with enthusiasm for all the awesome ideas that were pitched.

Let's look at the dynamics that take place when a group of people get together to brainstorm for solutions to a business challenge. Imagine that Linda has thrown out an idea to solve the problem. What goes through the minds of her teammates? Almost instantly, the other members of the group analyse and judge the idea (silently or openly), and the response in their minds will predictably be one of the following:

- **I agree** with the idea and will do everything I can to back it up.
- **I disagree** with the idea so I'm going to do everything I can to make sure it doesn't happen.
- **Maybe,** I'll keep listening and give the idea some thought.
- **I wasn't listening.** What did she say?

From the outset, most members of the group have hooked into a reactive or selective mode of thinking – in their minds, they've already decided and set off down a certain path. This isn't brainstorming! These folks have shifted themselves out of the right mindset to generate or be open to new ideas.

Group brainstorming vs individual brainstorming

Since brainstorming took off in the 1950s, creativity has increasingly become a group process, especially in big organizations. As the saying goes, 'Two heads are better than one', so what better way to generate ideas than to get lots of different people together? Everyone is jumping on the group bandwagon – collaboration is in and solitude is out. That's all well and good, but here's something interesting. Academic research strongly suggests that individuals working alone come up with more and better-quality ideas than people working together in a group. Researchers Diehl and Stroebe (1987) reviewed much of the evidence from tests conducted after 1958, as well as adding their own experiments. They found that, with a time limit of only 15 minutes for idea production, the average number of ideas for individuals was a staggering 84, with those of high quality numbering 13. In stark contrast, brainstorming groups produced an average of only 32 ideas, with only three being high quality. So, compared with groups, individuals produced four times as many high-quality ideas.

What's behind this productivity loss in groups? Well, the pressure of being in a group situation can put some people off. You've probably noticed yourself that groups tend to be dominated by a few strong-minded individuals, while others stay quiet and uninvolved. Some might feel embarrassed to share their crazier, oddball ideas (known as *evaluation apprehension*). A few may feel their ideas aren't good enough so they ride on top of other people's ideas (*social loafing*), and many simply struggle to get their ideas out while waiting for their colleagues to finish speaking (aka *production blocking*).

Groupthink

Have you ever led a brainstorming session where team members were reluctant to express their own opinions or share ideas? Or have you ever held your tongue in a meeting because you didn't want to look like you were obstructing the group's efforts? If so, you've experienced the phenomenon of *groupthink*.

Groupthink crops up when team members are more concerned about securing the approval of others than expressing their true ideas and opinions, especially when these opinions might go against the consensus. This is more apparent in tight-knit groups of people who work together regularly; what can eventually happen is that the desire for group harmony and cohesion drives out common sense altogether!

The term groupthink was coined by Yale psychologist Irving Janis in 1972 after he discovered that lack of conflict or opposing viewpoints led to faulty group decisions. His research showed that, in many situations, people's desire to support group unity held them back from delving into different options and from gathering enough information to make an informed decision. Groupthink was a major factor when British Airways and UK retailer Marks & Spencer were rolling out their globalization strategies in the 1990s. In both cases, the companies underestimated the chance of failure because of the illusion of invulnerability (a key symptom of groupthink). They thought they were immune to normal business problems. Because of this over-confidence in their decision-making powers, they made lots of silly errors in judgement and their management communications got seriously blocked. Not long after, both companies suffered a massive fall in reputation and stock market valuation (Eaton, 2001).

You don't get harmony when everybody sings the same note.
— DOUG FLOYD, in Washington paper *The Spokesman-Review*

ACTIVITY

Are you an independent thinker?

Take a look at the four lines below.

Figure 7.1 Solomon Asch conformity experiment (1951)

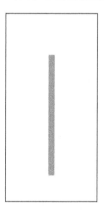 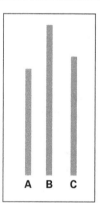

A   B   C

Your task is to pick which of the lines on the right most closely matches the line on the left. This probably isn't a huge challenge for you. One of the lines is obviously too short, one is far too long and the other one looks just about right.

Now imagine that you're doing this exercise while seated in a room with seven other participants, and the majority choose the longest line. What would you do? Would you stick to your initial response or shift your opinion to match the popular view?

During the 1950s, psychologist Solomon Asch (1951) put on a series of experiments using this line test to demonstrate the power of conformity in groups. He found that in set conditions of groups of around eight participants, people conformed to the incorrect group answer approximately a third of the time. However, when asked to individually write down the correct match, participants were a lot more accurate, choosing the correct answer 98 per cent of the time (McLeod, 2008).

Why were the test subjects so eager to deny the evidence in front of their own eyes? When interviewed afterwards, many of the participants admitted that, while they knew the rest of the group was wrong, they didn't want to risk facing ridicule or being the 'odd one out'. Others actually believed that the rest of the group must have been correct in their answers: 'They must know something I don't'. This exercise demonstrates that going along with the crowd won't necessarily lead you to the right solutions – something to bear in mind when in the throes of a collaborative brainstorming session.

The 'modern' view of brainstorming

Although preliminary academic research might not be in favour of group brainstorming, modern-day analysis presents a different, more positive view. Robert Sutton, an influential professor and co-founder of Stanford University's d.school, argues that most academic studies on brainstorming are not reflective of the real world (Sutton and Hargadon, 1996). Experiments impose hypothetical situations on participants where they are required to generate ideas that are of no real value to them, for instance: 'What would you do with an extra thumb?' or 'How many uses are there for a brick?'. Also, the way the studies are designed makes it impossible for people to build on each other's ideas or make connections with ideas that already exist.

Most importantly, Sutton identified that the so-called productivity loss shown in groups is due to the time spent listening to others speak, which is, of course, a practical element of group work. People can speak more ideas into a microphone when they are working alone than in face-to-face groups, because they don't have to wait their turn to talk. The research rules out listening to others as productive behaviour and slams meetings for being an inefficient way to get things done compared to working alone. However, let's be real. Face-to-face meetings come with the benefits of interaction, and time spent listening is not wasted as it exposes people to considerably more ideas per unit of time than in solo brainstorming. Sutton (2012) contends that 'talking and listening are both key elements of the social process underlying creativity'. Indeed, collaboration is central to the culture of some of the most admired creative companies, such as the movie masterminds Pixar.

This brings us to the notion of whether we should even be questioning whether individual or group brainstorming is better for creative work in the first place. Effective creativity depends on a mix of the two: allowing imaginative ideas to surface individually, and also be acknowledged collectively. This means that you need to consider the practical context in which you are brainstorming, and the level of skill and structure you bring to your sessions. As you'll see next, the technique can be made more useful with a good brainstorming strategy that includes both individual and group work.

Where do you get your best ideas?

When asked this question, people's answers will vary:
... in the shower;
... driving;
... cycling;
... lying awake in the morning or night.

Ideas come to us when we are relaxed and on our own. Usually they happen when we least expect them. So, why is it that most organizations choose to brainstorm in a group? Surely it's pointless?

Innovation cannot be left to chance. Alone time is important to allow your mind to wander and create freely; however, it's a mistake to rest on your laurels and assume your ideas will only come when they're ready. Creativity has to happen inside the office as well as outside it, otherwise your business will never grow. Brainstorming with others gives you a dedicated space to open up and gain new perspectives, and to share and build on other people's ideas collaboratively. CEO and founder of Heleo, Rufus Griscom, observes: 'Ideas are like people – they don't like to be isolated or treated jealously. They like to mingle, interact with other ideas' (Seppala, 2016).

A survey by creative consultancy Idea Champions asked people: 'Where and when do you get your best ideas?' (Moore and Ditkoff, 2008). The top five catalysts for best ideas were ranked as follows:

1 When you're inspired

2 Brainstorming with others

3 When you're immersed in a project

4 When you're happy

5 When you're collaborating with a partner

As declared in the report: 'We think our poll clearly shows that people rely on both social and solitary contexts for idea creation, and that inspiration can happen either way. How well an organization supports both approaches will impact how innovative it is.'

How to be better at brainstorming

Brainstorming is a technique that people can perform superbly or terribly, with all manner of results in between. It would be wrong to think that brainstorming doesn't work and give up on it completely just because you've had a few fruitless meetings; it's true that a lot of brainstorming sessions become meaningless time-traps, but that's not because brainstorming as a process doesn't work. It's because most sessions are haphazardly run and everyone's thinking goes out of focus. The good news is that, with a bit of training and pre-planning, anyone can learn to get better at brainstorming. Research by Dr Roger Firestien (1990) at the State University of New York College at Buffalo found that groups that were trained in the guidelines of creative problem solving and brainstorming generated significantly more ideas than untrained groups. Even better, this resulted in almost three times as many high-quality ideas (618 excellent ideas to 281 excellent ideas). Additionally, trained groups criticized ideas significantly less, verbally supported ideas more, and they laughed and smiled more too.

Rules for brilliant brainstorming

Rules aren't something that we like to associate with creativity. We can't help but see them as the antithesis of free, expansive thinking; and many rules are. But those for brainstorming are different – we've got to stick by them if we want to play the game and win. In his seminal book, *Applied Imagination*, Alex Osborn (1953) outlined four guidelines which have come to be known as the 'classic rules' for brainstorming. Doubtless you will have come across them thousands of times before, but can you honestly say that your sessions always adhere to them?

1. Go for quantity

Innovation is a numbers game. By extracting as many ideas as possible, you seriously raise your chances of hitting on the one breakthrough idea that surpasses all previously known limits. Keep each idea brief – just capture its essence, don't describe it in detail. Maintain momentum and stay motivated by setting a quota for your ideation, such as a minimum of 50 ideas if you're working alone or 150–200 for a group session. Any more than that is just gravy. For short bursts, try setting a timer – 'Right, I want 10 ideas from each member of the team in the next 5 minutes'.

2. Welcome wild and unusual ideas

Freewheeling is the name of the game. Inspire your teammates to embrace their wilder, madcap notions and shoot for insane and exaggerated ideas. Let them have fun with it. To be creative you need to have an 'everything is possible' mindset. As the aphorism goes: 'If at first the idea is not absurd, then there is no hope for it.' Even if an idea seems completely ridiculous or far-fetched on first sight, you can always tone it down into a more practical alternative later on. After all, isn't it better to seek ways to dazzle customers rather than just satisfy them?

Open minds are like portals to other dimensions,
where impossibility is possible....

> – DEAN CHAMBERLAIN, Quincy band lyrics

3. Postpone judgement

This may seem like an obvious one, but it's a common and tempting pitfall – there should be no criticism or judgement of ideas until you've generated a sufficient quantity to work with. Any analysis, whether positive or negative, will stunt the whole process, kill off the seeds of potential solutions and prevent people taking risks with their ideas. It's like trying to drive with one foot on the accelerator and one foot on the brake – you won't get very far.

If you keep stopping to discuss reasons why an idea is good or bad, or to shoot down outlandish ideas, you'll end up stuck with the same old familiar ones again and again. What's more, the energy and atmosphere in the room will take a nosedive as people will be afraid to speak up for fear of having their ideas rejected. You'll have plenty of opportunity to evaluate ideas later on – either at the end of the session or in another meeting where the purpose is to converge to a decision. For now, take the brakes off your critical mind and give imagination the green light.

4. Combine and build on ideas

It's very rare to find instant, fully formed solutions. This principle is about taking the seed of an idea and improving, modifying or building on it to make it even better. Encourage participants to snowball on other people's ideas to create more rounded solutions, or to springboard off their ideas to create newer ones. If you need more practical ideas, use this process to transform the more unusual ideas so that they have a better basis in reality. On the other hand, if you want to be super-radical then try combining two ideas that aren't closely related and see what happens. Take the recent innovative product Trunki: this British company married the idea of a ride-on toy with a suitcase to invent ride-on wheeled hand-luggage for children. This satisfied two customers at the same time, offering functionality and utility for parents during travel, *and* a play item for children.

Tip

When you compile many alternatives, the first third tend to be obvious, the second third are the wacky and ridiculous ideas, but the final third contains the best, most creative ideas – ones that are novel and useful. Unoriginal or unrealistic ideas are easy to come across; to find the practical and original ideas, you have to *keep* looking.

CASE STUDY   There are no bad ideas

What do you do with all the 'bad' ideas that are thrown into the brainstorming mix? Use them as stepping stones to good ideas. No idea is bad in itself, as it can always be linked to something else. The very inadequacy of an iffy idea can inspire you to journey forth and explore, transform and discover, until eventually it turns out great.

When Spencer Silver, a 3M Company employee, accidently developed an incredibly weak glue that stuck to objects but could be lifted off easily, it was initially deemed a flop. The product was shelved. Years later, Arthur Fry, a product development engineer at 3M, discovered that the adhesive was handy for sticking his page markers in his hymn book to stop them falling out, so he didn't lose his place while singing in the church choir. Fry found that the markers could be effortlessly removed without damaging the page. In that moment, the multi-million-dollar phenomenon known as the Post-it Note was born. The super-weak glue was a stepping stone to an unimaginably super-successful idea.

The 'correct' brainstorming strategy

The secret to effective, non-idea-blocking brainstorming is to capture the personal contributions of individuals while also making the most of the camaraderie and synergy of a group brainstorm. In this section, I give you a procedure for making your brainstorming work. The approach I'm going to describe is one I like to use for combining solitary and group brainstorming to draw out a bigger and better pool of ideas from my team.

Pre-session preparation

Location

Find a comfortable, quiet room and book it out for the time you need (at least an hour for a quick-hitting micro-session, but preferably two hours for broader, unrestricted thinking). Ideally, you want to brainstorm away from your usual environment or place of work, but this isn't always possible in practice. Try to create an informal atmosphere to encourage playfulness and equal discussion. Set up your room with a round meeting table if you can (think King Arthur) or seat people in open circles rather than in stiff rows. Perhaps even throw in some creative props such as interesting magazines or coloured felt-tips. Snacks and drinks won't go unappreciated either; all that brain activity burns a lot of fuel.

Pick your team

It's a well-known theory that people are a company's greatest asset, but they need to be the right people for the job. When choosing your team, try to assemble a healthy assortment of people with varying tasks and responsibilities; introverts and extroverts; experts in the subject matter and non-experts. Why is this important? People from miscellaneous disciplines and backgrounds will bring a variety of perspectives and viewpoints into the fold, so the chance for 'different' ideas to filter through is a lot greater. As Jerry Hirshberg (1998) points out in his book, *The Creative Priority*, it's the differences in the way people think that often stimulate new and interesting ideas. Try to stick to between five and ten people to keep things manageable. Too big a team and it's hard for everyone to get air time; too small and you don't have enough diversity to ignite novel debate. At Amazon, founder and CEO Jeff Bezos is said to have a rule that limits group size to the number of people that can be easily fed by two pizzas (Quinn, 2016). This generally works out to about five to eight people in any meeting. Bear in mind that you will also need a facilitator or chairperson to lead and support the session.

Tools

Gather the materials you need for recording ideas, such as a flipchart or whiteboard, markers, timer, sticky notes and several blank sheets of paper. Using tech tools or apps to collate ideas makes them easier to share later, so it may be worthwhile opting to record ideas electronically.

Have a set of ideation techniques and games ready to help spark your team's creativity and lead you to different insights. The next chapter offers an array of tools for you to pick and choose from, and these can be easily applied in a group setting.

Brainstorming is not a game

There's a misconception that brainstorming is all about playing games and building frivolous things with LEGO or playdough. Even the concept of 'gamestorming' has taken off as a fun alternative. Games, toys and ice-breaker activities can, of course, be useful to warm up and give people an opportunity to incubate their thoughts. However, games in themselves are only ancillary to the formal process of brainstorming. Brainstorming is not a game-led activity, it's a structured process to ensure that everyone is in the correct frame of mind to dig deep creatively and deliver a wealth of insights and ideas. As counter-intuitive as it may sound, structure doesn't stop it being a fun affair and good ideas continue to surface as people are guided into a state of flow, not just sporadic moments of ingenuity. For brainstorming that works, the process should always be mindful rather than mindless.

Focus

Brief the people taking part on what they can expect during the session and the rules they'll need to adhere to; you can do this in advance via e-mail. Make sure they understand what the session is aiming to achieve. It's a good idea to write down the problem statement in a nice big font and post it somewhere prominent in the meeting room, to act as a visual reminder and keep everyone on mission during the session.

Session structure

Before brainstorming

Once everyone is gathered together, make the necessary introductions and lay down the ground rules for an optimal ideation session (the four rules we looked at earlier). Set the scene by defining the problem you want solved clearly and concisely (refer to the brief you shared in advance). Provide any history, background or factual information that will ensure the group has a deep enough understanding; you want everyone on the same page before you get going. Your challenge could be naming your next line of products, reducing inefficiencies on the production line, improving internal communi-cation processes or redesigning a department – pretty much anything. This process will be relatively straightforward if you've followed the guidelines for Step 1 of the Solution Finder to accurately define the challenge. Be sure to clarify any aspects that seem confusing. Appoint a facilitator to lead the session and make sure the ideas keep coming – there should be no lengthy discussions during ideation. This person will need sharp group awareness in order to encourage equal contribution. They can also act as the scribe, taking charge of collecting and writing down people's ideas. Next, use the following three-stage process to run your session, making sure you factor in some breaks. Figure 7.2 shows you what good brainstorming should look like.

TIP

Brainstorming tip

Take breaks. Intense ideation is tiring so you need the odd break to keep the creative spark alight. Having a break also enables the incubation process, where the unconscious mind is given time to dwell on the problem and more ideas can emerge.

Figure 7.2   The 'correct' brainstorming strategy

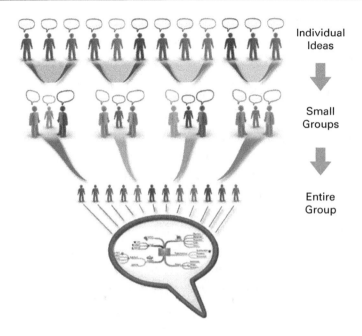

Step 1. Individual idea generation

First, ask all the members of your team to brainstorm solo in preparation for the group stage, either freestyling, or by using any of the tools in Chapter 8. In today's hectic world, we often overlook the quiet part of the creative process, preferring to jump straight into manic and (often) infertile team sessions instead. This stage creates room for thinking and a level playing field for everyone involved.

Encourage individuals to clean out all corners of their mind and jot down as many potential solutions as they can before any group discussions take place. If you wait until everyone is huddled together in a group to begin brainstorming, you'll find that the meeting becomes governed by groupthink and the harmful effects of social loafing, evaluation apprehension and production blocking. When individuals work alone, they aren't under any social pressures and are free to explore their thoughts without fear of criticism, so even the quietest members of the group are able to chip in ideas. Smart ideas don't always come from the people with dynamic and outgoing personalities; Susan Cain (2012), author of best-selling psychology book *Quiet*, says that it's usually introverts working alone who come up with the most powerful ideas. Rather than being outshone by charismatic characters or relying on stimuli provided by other members of the group, people are spurred by their own originality. And crucially, they aren't held back from thinking by having to wait for others to express their ideas.

Step 2. Small group brainstorming

The next round is to divide everyone into small groups of around three to five people, to exchange ideas and create a single document that pools together the ideas from each person. In a small group, individuals are more comfortable and willing to contribute, as it presents a safe space for them to share thoughts and ideas; the dynamics are more controlled and the strongest communicator can't dominate. Plus, people aren't automatically led into reactive thinking as they've already stated their position and sketched out their ideas in the first stage. There is much greater objectivity and focus to the whole process. Group members can work together to cross-pollinate, review their output and select the ideas they want to take forward to the next stage.

This is also a good filtering exercise since people in the group will often come up with a high percentage of very similar ideas. Collating and merging ideas reduces the quantity and gets rid of duplicates. This in turn makes the process manageable. Common ideas tend to be obvious, and therefore less innovative. Small groups should try to build on the outliers, that is, the unique ideas that members of the group have generated.

Don't wait to incubate!

One of the most powerful and often under-valued features of brainstorming is incubation – taking a break from the problem to get on with something unrelated. I cannot stress how important it is to give people time to incubate ideas that arise during brainstorming. Their minds will continue thinking about the challenge and the initial ideas and thoughts that they, or the group, have come up with. Most people think of brainstorming as a single session, but this doesn't allow participants any incubation time. Even the most creative individuals need time to let ideas marinate and turn over in their minds before the best concepts come to light.

Researchers at the University of Sydney found evidence that incubation can boost creative performance (Ellwood *et al*, 2009). For the experiment, 90 participants were split into three groups and given four minutes to list as many different uses for a piece of paper as possible. The first group worked on the task continuously for the entire four minutes, without a break. The second group was interrupted after two minutes to work on another creativity-related task (generating synonyms for words on a given list), after which they were then given another two minutes to complete the original task. The third group was also interrupted after two minutes but given an unrelated task (a Myers–Briggs Type Indicator test). Following this, participants were asked to return to the original task for the remaining two minutes. Despite working on the task for the same amount of time, the third group (which was given time for incubation) was the most successful at generating ideas post-break, with an average of 9.8. The second group averaged 7.6 ideas, while the first group with no break came up with an average of only 6.9 ideas. The results suggest that scheduling time for initial ideas to incubate, even just a short period for a break or fresh context, can significantly increase creative output.

Companies tend to plan day-long strategy or brainstorming days because it is supposedly an efficient use of time, but it's not. Brainstorming is *not* a one-off event; it is a process and needs to be respected as such. For instance, a company may want to allocate a full day to strategize a problem. Rather than conducting it in one eight-hour stretch, they could spread it across eight days and do one hour every day, perhaps in the morning when people are fresh.

One of the simplest ways to benefit from the incubation effect is to brainstorm in small bites. Incorporate lots of breaks into your workflow and change what you are doing after each break. Four 30-minute sessions are better than 120 minutes of solid ideation. During each break, your unconscious mind will keep working away in the background, resulting in more powerful ideas and improvements. In our experience, and that of several companies we've worked with, the difference between holding one big session and lots of small sessions is vast and should not be overlooked.

Step 3. Entire group discussion

The final stage is to draw everyone together in a large group to gather all their thoughts, discuss the masses of ideas generated and create a conclusive record of ideas. This is best carried out by the facilitator taking one idea serially from each person/group, putting all the ideas on a common document, either on a whiteboard, flipchart or on screen, and then giving equal time to talk about each idea (Delbecq, Van de Ven and Gustafson, 1986). A helpful option is to record ideas in the form of a diagram or Mind Map (instead of a list), which is effective for structuring ideas and clustering them into themes using colours and codes (Buzan and Griffiths, 2010).

Working around the room, the facilitator extracts all the ideas from the group one by one – the good, the bad and the average. The purpose of doing this is to start off on an equal playing field. If similar ideas are expressed, these can be grouped together. All contributions are valuable, so be sure to thank everyone and show appreciation for their input, whether the idea was an original or a duplicate.

Once all ideas have been shared, the facilitator guides the group into a discussion to clarify, develop and build on each idea, preventing people from interrupting each other and refocusing the group when the conversation gets diverted. Make it clear that this is a group effort by consistently using the term 'we'. Now this is important – all ideas should be supported and taken on board by the other members, even the ideas that seem weak, absurd or irrelevant. Remember, bad ideas can very easily be stepping stones to good ideas.

Working collectively, everyone (including the quietest members) should be encouraged to rephrase, combine and refine ideas or springboard off existing ideas to create new ones. If connections between ideas aren't clear, then make some! Produce variation by introducing some of the tools provided in Chapter 8 – reverse the challenge to explore it from its opposite angle, ask 'What if?' or abstract the problem using metaphors and analogies. Don't evaluate or judge ideas. The purpose of this phase is to consolidate ideas and make constructive suggestions for improvement without passing a final vote on the best ones. Save all that judging for later, preferably in a separate meeting. The final document or idea board then becomes the external reflection, the 'hard copy' record of the brainstorming session. Post it up on the wall to provide inspiration and input for the next phase of problem solving.

Figure 7.3 Mind Map example

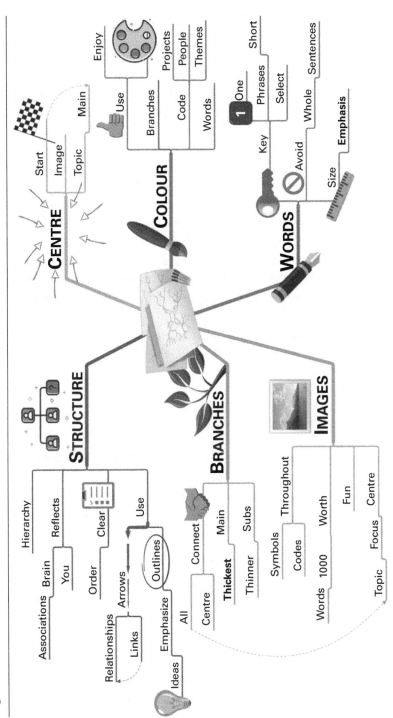

Mind Mapping fundamentals

Creativity loves connections! Instead of recording all your ideas in a big list, I recommend you try using Mind Maps to capture, develop and arrange what comes out of your brainstorming session at the large-group stage. A Mind Map is a visual diagram where ideas are laid out on branches that are connected to a central topic. Mind Mapping is in line with our natural way of thinking, which works by making associations between concepts. Most of us have used Mind Maps at one time or another, and I can't stress enough how useful they are for categorizing and expanding on ideas. Unlike conventional lists, Mind Maps work by branching from the centre outwards and they encourage your thoughts to behave in the same way without limitation or restriction. The visual nature of the map also allows you to 'see' connections between your thoughts or ideas that you might not have spotted before, and you might be able to create an even better idea from two originally separate suggestions.

An example Mind Map is shown in Figure 7.3.

Key takeaways

Brainstorming is an excellent tool for divergent thinking, but it can be severely undermined by group pressures such as social loafing, production blocking and groupthink/conformity. With a bit of foresight and planning, you can run sessions that allow time for independent thinking as well as group discussion and collaboration, so everyone gets their say.

- Devise a **brainstorming strategy** that combines solo working for better idea generation with group conditions to enhance and build on existing ideas. This is useful for collecting ideas from people who are reluctant to voice them in a group setting and prevents the louder or more senior characters from dominating the session. Try this: 1) individual idea generation; 2) small group brainstorming; 3) entire group discussion.

- Remember to fully enforce the **brainstorming rules** during this stage: 1) strive for quantity so you can go past the obvious ideas; 2) seek the wild and unusual – remove the box so you have all the space you need to discover something crazy and remarkable; 3) suspend judgement – close down the analytical brain to prevent you striking out ideas too soon, thus allowing more ideas to come forth and flourish; 4) combine and build to improve ideas in different ways – bad ideas can be stepping stones to good ideas.

References

Asch, SE (1951) Effects of group pressure upon the modification and distortion of judgment, in *Groups, Leadership and Men*, ed H Guetzkow, Carnegie Press, Pittsburgh, PA

Buzan, T and Griffiths, C (2010) *Mind Maps for Business: Revolutionise your business thinking and practice*, BBC Active, Harlow

Cain, S (2012) *Quiet: The power of introverts in a world that can't stop talking*, Crown Publishing, New York

Delbecq, AL, Van de Ven, AH and Gustafson, DH (1986) *Group Techniques for Program Planning: A guide to nominal group and Delphi processes*, Green Briar Press, Middleton, WI

Diehl, M and Stroebe, W (1987) Productivity loss in brainstorming groups: toward the solution of a riddle, *Journal of Personality and Social Psychology*, 53 (3), pp 497–509

Eaton, J (2001) Management communication: the threat of groupthink, *Corporate Communications: An International Journal*, 6 (4), pp 183–92

Ellwood, S *et al* (2009) [accessed 25 October 2018] The incubation effect: hatching a solution? *Creativity Research Journal*, 21 (1), pp 6–14 [Online] https://pdfs.semanticscholar.org/88dd/9f655716745abbb357198785064c731f4c5a.pdf

Firestien, RL (1990) Effects of creative problem solving training on communication behaviors in small groups, *Small Group Research*, 21 (4), pp 507–21

Hirshberg, J (1998) *The Creative Priority: Driving innovative business in the new world*, Harper Collins, New York

McLeod, S (2008) [accessed 30 April 2018] Asch Experiment, *Simply Psychology* [Online] https://www.simplypsychology.org/asch-conformity.html

Moore, T and Ditkoff, M (2008) [accessed 30 April 2018] Where and When Do People Get Their Best Ideas?, *Idea Champions* [Online] http://www.ideachampions.com/downloads/Best-Ideas-Poll.pdf

Osborn, AF (1953) *Applied Imagination: Principles and procedures of creative problem solving*, Charles Scribner's Sons, New York

Quinn, J (2016) [accessed 30 April 2018] Amazon's Two-Pizza Rule Isn't as Zany as It Sounds, *The Telegraph*, 12 October [Online] http://www.telegraph.co.uk/business/2016/10/12/amazons-two-pizza-rule-isnt-as-zany-as-it-sounds/

Seppala, E (2016) [accessed 30 April 2018] How Senior Executives Find Time to Be Creative, *Harvard Business Review*, 14 September [Online] https://hbr.org/2016/09/how-senior-executives-find-time-to-be-creative

Sutton, R (2012) [accessed 23 March 2018] Why the New Yorker's Claim that Brainstorming 'Doesn't Work' is an Overstatement and Possibly Wrong [Blog], *Work Matters*, 26 January [Online] http://bobsutton.typepad.com/page/5/

Sutton, R and Hargadon, A (1996) Brainstorming groups in context: effectiveness in a product design firm, *Administrative Science Quarterly*, **41** (4), pp 685–718

08
The Solution Finder Step 2: Ideation toolkit

You can't use up creativity, the more you use, the more you have.

– MAYA ANGELOU, poet, singer and civil rights activist

Creativity on demand

As adults, most of us do not consider ourselves natural creative thinkers and struggle to perceive ourselves as innovative. When we need to generate ideas, facing a blank page can be utterly daunting. In a study of over 1,100 UK workers by Microsoft Surface (2017), 49 per cent believed that learning new creativity skills would help them be more effective in their role, but 75 per cent said they had not been equipped with the relevant training and tools to nurture these skills within the past two years. Providing your team with a special set of creativity tools can be a tremendous support in stimulating ideas and overcoming the fear of getting started. We need different techniques to warm us up and trick our brain out of its usual patterns, so we can be imaginative, divergent and lateral in our thinking. This practical chapter presents a brief roundup of tools that offer a more structured and coordinated approach to creativity, especially when working in a group setting. The canvas templates are designed to feed your creative hunger and can yield results for a diverse range of business problems. Feel free to use them as much as needed and to add your own separate tools to the mix. In choosing how you go about ideation, consider the size of your group; whether there are more introverts or extroverts; the type of thinking errors you are prone to; and the physical climate you'll be working in. This way you'll have more chances to appeal to people's creative preferences, and consequently a better hope of delivering results.

Your aim in Step 2 of the Solution Finder is to draw up the broadest selection of possible ideas. Start by selecting the tool that is most appropriate to the type of issue you are working on and use it to inject fun and energy into your ideation sessions. You have to allow time and space to use new thinking tools, so that your team has the leg room to explore possibilities and insights, to play around with connections and to stretch reality beyond what is expected. *Remember*: fight the temptation to stop at your first good idea and avoid criticizing or rejecting ideas at this stage. Give your people an enjoyable experience and they'll keep those ideas coming.

The Ideation toolkit

INPUT

Clearly defined challenge

PROCESS

Generate as many ideas as possible

TOOLS

Reverse Brainstorm Canvas

Metaphoric Thinking Canvas

Combinational Creativity Canvas

OUTPUT

All ideas

Use the canvases in this chapter to break out of ingrained thinking processes and push yourself right to the edge of what's possible. If you've hit a slump in your innovation project (and this is inevitable at one time or another), introducing a tool is a great way to add a burst of energy and mental focus to get things moving again. To capture all the ideas that flow out of the session, download the ideation canvases here: **www.thinking.space**

Reverse Brainstorming Canvas

No matter what business you're in, it's a good thing to turn things upside down once in a while and challenge the way you operate. The standard corporate routine of approaching your problem from the front means you only come up with market-driven, pedestrian answers. With reverse brainstorming, however, the premise is 'do the opposite'. You take your original problem statement and use its reversal as a trigger for new ideas. Instead of thinking about 'what to do', you think of 'what not to do'. So, if you're struggling to find ways to get more customers, find ways to lose them instead. If you want to reduce the number of faulty goods you produce, find ways to create more faulty goods. If you want to maximize attendance at a training programme, find ways to make sure nobody attends. While this might sound a bit bizarre, recognizing the actions you want to avoid actually gives you better scope to find lots more surprising and market-driving alternatives for getting the results you want, from the obvious to the downright radical.

In a group, this strategy offers a playful approach leading to lively (and sometimes feisty!) exchanges over the possibilities given by the reversals. Many business assumptions we take for granted can be turned on their head, so nothing should be off limits. It's a great technique when you're stuck in a boring, conservative mode as it throws everyone off balance to start thinking afresh. Or when selective thinking has taken root, preventing the group moving past certain ideas or beliefs. Here's how it works.

Step 1. State the reverse of your problem or challenge

Start with the problem statement you identified in your problem-defining session. We'll use the example of 'How do we provide better customer service?'. Change the wording of the problem to the exact reverse or opposite. Rather than asking, 'How do I solve or prevent this problem?', try asking, 'How could I cause the problem?' And instead of asking, 'How do I achieve these results?', ask 'How could I achieve the opposite effect?' (Mind Tools, 2010). We can easily flip our problem of 'How do we provide better customer service?' to 'How do we provide awful customer service?' This switches our immediate focus from how to solve the problem to how to cause it.

Step 2. Brainstorm ideas to solve the reversed problem

When you brainstorm directly on your problem, it's easy to end up following a predictable path with the ideas you come up with. For better customer service, some typical ideas that crop up during traditional brainstorming

Figure 8.1 Reverse Brainstorming Canvas

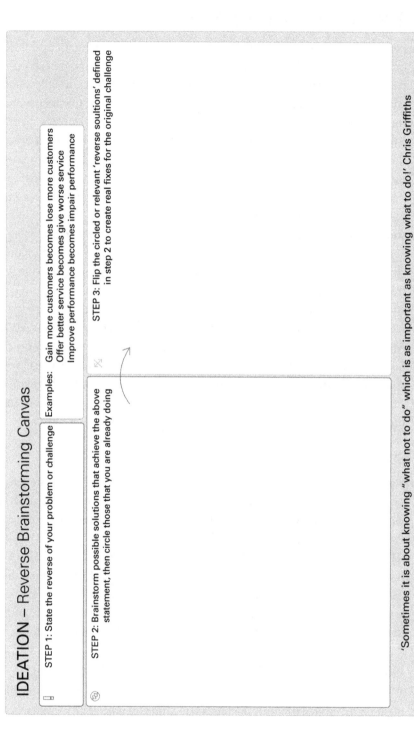

IDEATION – Reverse Brainstorming Canvas

STEP 1: State the reverse of your problem or challenge

Examples: Gain more customers becomes lose more customers
Offer better service becomes give worse service
Improve performance becomes impair performance

STEP 2: Brainstorm possible solutions that achieve the above statement, then circle those that you are already doing

STEP 3: Flip the circled or relevant 'reverse soultions' defined in step 2 to create real fixes for the original challenge

'Sometimes it is about knowing "what not to do" which is as important as knowing what to do!' Chris Griffiths

might be to answer calls within three rings or respond to e-mails within 24 hours. These are decent enough ideas, but not exactly pattern-breaking. Once you reverse the problem, however, your outlook on the situation transforms as you shift from improving the service to wrecking the entire customer experience. Get the group to call out ideas to create the problem. Whenever I perform this exercise with a company or clients, I find that their priorities change dramatically as they hit upon previously undetected elements in providing top-notch customer service and support:

- Open late and close early.
- Give customers the wrong advice.
- Have workers with very little product knowledge taking calls.
- Delete customer e-mails.
- Don't answer telephones.
- Put people on hold and forget about them.
- Use workers with poor language skills.
- Judge worker performance by number of calls answered.
- Use rude customer service operatives.
- Write e-mails with bad grammar.
- Don't share information about issues and solutions across the team.
- Don't provide a warranty.
- Always be understaffed.

Circle those that you are already doing and you might well get a shock!

Step 3. Flip your reversed solutions

Finally, flip your solutions around to find positive ways of solving your original problem or challenge. See if any of these reversed solutions provide a good fit to your problem, or whether they can be adjusted to work. As you look over your answers, you'll find that there are tons more ways to solve the original problem than you initially thought. Maybe you could provide extra training for customer service operatives to improve their product knowledge and polite handling of customers. You could share information across departments so customer complaints can be resolved quicker. You could begin working in shifts to open earlier and close later. You could test language skills during recruitment and judge performance based on quality of response rather than number of calls answered.

In any business situation, this exercise is a real eye-opener for showing you exactly what you're doing wrong and what you need to do for positive change. Be rebellious and rock the boat. Think about the constraints or rules you operate within, such as budget, systems, resources, timing, and use this technique to overturn them; for example: How could we remove this process? How could we do this for zero cost? Even if the ideas you think of aren't useful right away, with a bit of rethinking you could create something workable. Use the reversed ideas to stimulate thinking rather than taking them literally at face value. And if you don't get much out of it, at least you'll understand why the rule was there in the first place!

CASE STUDY   Do the opposite – Granada Television

In 1954, the British government auctioned the broadcasting rights for commercial TV stations for the first time. These would be regional operations that could offer advertising on TV. Many companies were eager to bid for a franchise and used demographic analysis to identify the wealthiest regions that would, naturally, generate the most advertising revenue. The result was that they focused on London and the South East of England. At the time, Sidney Bernstein was the managing director of a small chain of cinemas in southern England – Granada Cinemas. He also wanted to compete in the auction, but instead of bidding on the richest region, he decided to bid for the 'wettest' region of the UK, which turned out to be the North West. Bernstein's bid was successful and he established Granada Television, based in Manchester and serving the North of England. His theory was that potential viewers were more likely to stay indoors and watch TV if it was pouring with rain outside, whereas if it was sunny, they might be more inclined to sit in their gardens or venture out for a walk (Sloane, 2016). When everyone was looking in one direction (Which is the wealthiest region?), Bernstein triumphed by facing another (Which is the wettest region?). Granada went on to become one of the most successful independent production companies, known for its quality entertainment and high-profile programmes, such as *Coronation Street*, *University Challenge* and *World in Action*.

Metaphoric Thinking Canvas

Thinking metaphorically is a potent way to escape the constraints of conventional thinking and embrace ambiguity. A metaphor can change our way

Figure 8.2 Metaphoric Thinking Canvas

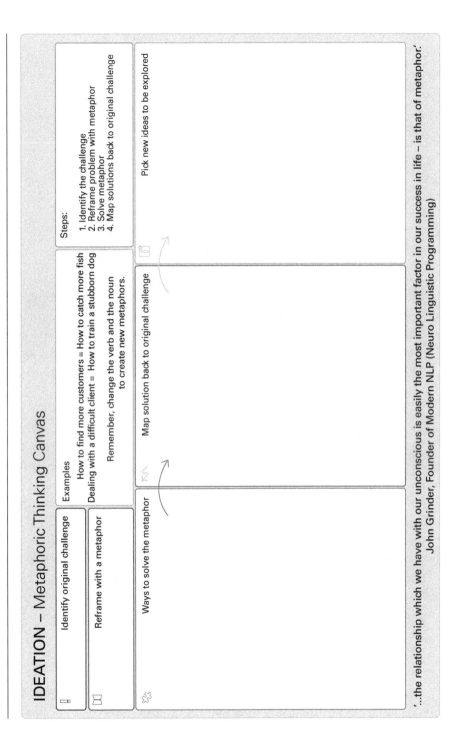

IDEATION – Metaphoric Thinking Canvas

Identify original challenge

Reframe with a metaphor

Examples

How to find more customers = How to catch more fish
Dealing with a difficult client = How to train a stubborn dog

Remember, change the verb and the noun to create new metaphors.

Steps:

1. Identify the challenge
2. Reframe problem with metaphor
3. Solve metaphor
4. Map solutions back to original challenge

Ways to solve the metaphor

Map solution back to original challenge

Pick new ideas to be explored

'...the relationship which we have with our unconscious is easily the most important factor in our success in life – is that of metaphor.'
John Grinder, Founder of Modern NLP (Neuro Linguistic Programming)

of looking at the world by forcing us to understand one thing in terms of another. These familiar expressions are all metaphors:

- Life is a rollercoaster.
- Financial watchdog.
- It's a jungle out there.
- Time is money.
- Operational bottleneck.
- The ball is in our court now.
- All the world's a stage.
- A leap of thought.
- She marches to the beat of a different drummer.

One of the reasons metaphors work so well for creative thinking is that they're symbolic and tell a story that invites others to be more abstract and open-minded in their thinking. By applying a metaphor to your problem, you place it in a new context, which can unclog your brain and spark all sorts of jazzy and totally different ideas. Business adviser and author Kevin Duncan (2014) calls it the 'analogy springboard', and the possible sources of inspiration from it are effectively endless.

A good metaphor triggers the mind to look for similarities between concepts that might at first seem totally unrelated. For instance, the pea pod inspired a new way of opening cigarette packages and is now a method used in the packing industry all over the world. The benzene molecule, discovered by Friedrick Kekule, the renowned German chemist, was first described as a 'snake biting its own tail'. And sticky Velcro was inspired by a comparison with plant burrs. Remember, life and business aren't always logical. When you reframe your problem as a metaphor, you release old characteristics and assumptions from it to allow new and original insights to bubble to the surface. From these you can draw relevant connections and ideas back to your task. What follows is a simple process for using metaphors for idea generation. Notice how the energy in the room changes once you introduce this technique.

Step 1. Identify the challenge

Define your challenge in the form of a statement. For the purpose of illustration, we'll use the problem 'I want more customers'.

Step 2. Reframe the problem with a metaphor

Now rephrase the original problem into a similar or unrelated problem by means of a metaphor. An easy way to do this is by replacing the verb (which represents the process) and noun (the content of the challenge). Start by breaking down the verb and noun as follows (Figure 8.3):

Figure 8.3   Isolate verb and noun

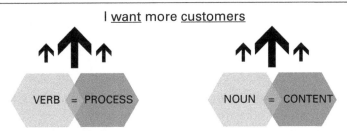

Think of how you could change the verb and noun to create a new statement. There are no limitations, so go wild with your imagination. For instance, you could substitute 'want' for 'how' and 'customers' could be changed to 'fish' to produce the new challenge of 'How to catch a fish'. Now you've got an alternative way of looking at the issue (Figure 8.4):

Figure 8.4   Change verb and noun

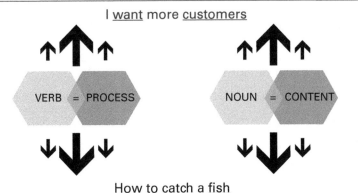

To give you more examples, the challenge 'Dealing with a difficult person' could become 'Training a stubborn dog', while 'Reducing the bureaucracy at work' could be analogous to 'Weeding the garden'.

Ask yourself: What does the problem make you think of? Is there anything that it could be compared to? It's better if there's some sort of vague similarity between the old verb and new one (since verbs represent process), otherwise you could battle to relate the concept back to your problem. As human beings we're essentially curious and stimulated by obscure tasks. But if a task is too fuzzy, we're likely to ignore it rather than get to grips with the difficulties it presents. It becomes a block rather than a stimulus for creative thinking. Then again, we've also got to be wary of working with metaphors that are too close to the problem at hand, as we won't be making the familiar strange enough to gain any useful insights or ideas (Proctor, 1989).

An idea is a feat of association, and the height of it is a good metaphor.
                          – attributed to ROBERT FROST, American poet

If you're fretting trying to come up with a metaphor, ask yourself if your challenge might be similar to a distant parallel activity. This could come from nature or any other realm that's different from the environment of your problem. It's important to pick the right metaphor for your problem, otherwise you could go down the wrong track. Some of the best metaphors are those where there's some action taking place such as:

- riding a bike
- planning a holiday
- cooking a gourmet meal
- going on a diet
- parenting a child
- negotiating a contract
- growing plants and flowers
- running for political office
- going fishing
- building a house
- rock climbing
- playing a sport, eg football.

Step 3. Solve the metaphor

Next, focus your attention on solving the problem presented by the metaphor. Completely blank out all thoughts of the original problem from your mind. Take the metaphorical subject of 'How to catch a fish' and generate ideas and associations to solve it as if it were the real issue. See how far you can extend the comparison. What solutions work in that particular scenario? Some possible solutions for this example could be:

- Use correct bait.
- Ask a fisherman.
- Buy a boat.
- Get a good rod.
- Use a net.
- Go spear-fishing.
- Use explosives.
- Read a book on it.
- Use a lure.
- Learn the habits of fish.
- Watch fishing shows on TV.
- Buy a fish from the pet shop.
- Get a fishing game.

Step 4. Map it back to the original challenge

In this final step, map each key idea that you generated to solve the metaphor *back* to the original problem. How might you relate the same actions or responses? For example, some of the ideas from Step 3 could be converted like this:

- Use correct bait – use appropriate advertising, make products more appealing.
- Ask a fisherman – ask or employ a sales expert/consultant, find a mentor.
- Use a net – make sure the message appeals to as wide an audience as possible, find affiliates, spread web links.
- Go spear-fishing – target individual customers, focus on repeat sales.
- Use explosives – conduct a huge PR campaign.
- Read a book on it – study new sales techniques.

Select the ideas with the most potential and explore them on your canvas (Figure 8.5). Taking a metaphorical view often reveals some awesome ideas that you probably wouldn't have picked up while looking at your problem face-on. It adds distance to the problem, which helps to remove the emotions

Figure 8.5 Mind Map: How to catch a fish

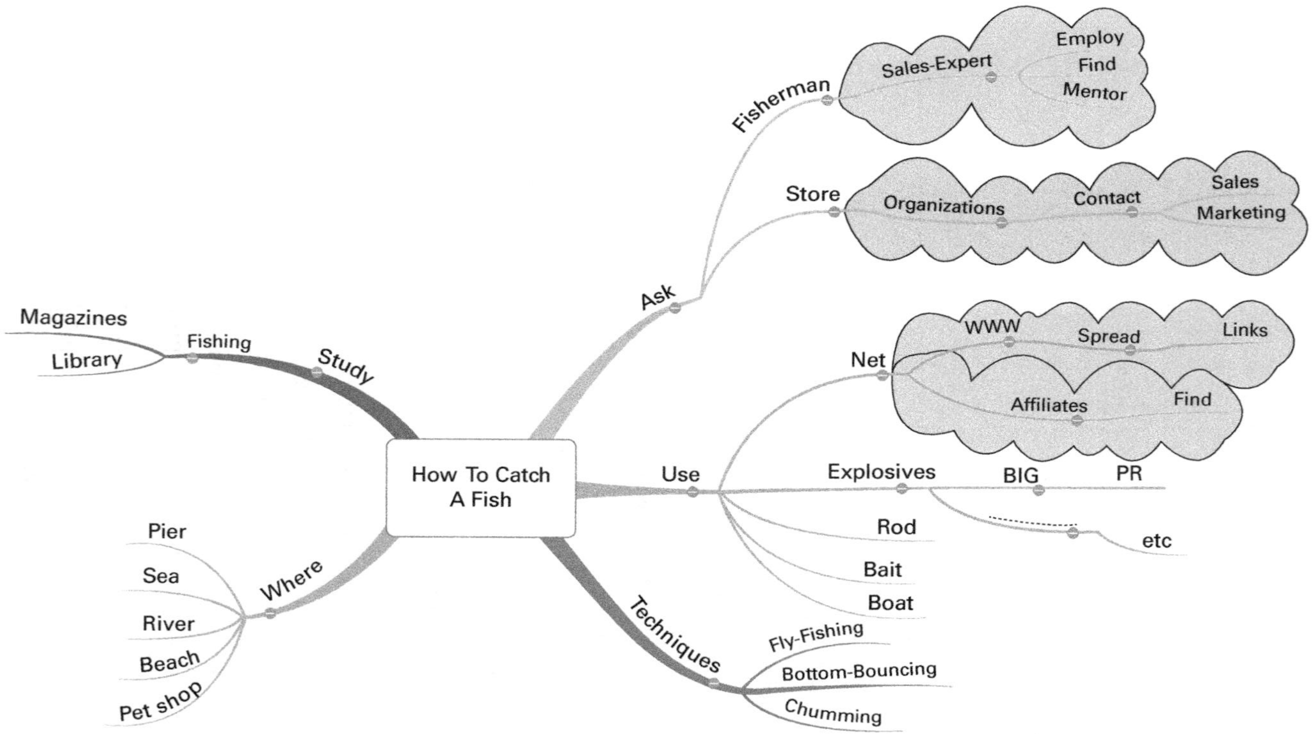

How To Catch A Fish

Study
- Fishing
  - Magazines
  - Library

Where
- Pier
- Sea
- River
- Beach
- Pet shop

Ask
- Fisherman
  - Sales-Expert
    - Employ
    - Find
    - Mentor
- Store
  - Organizations
    - Contact
    - Sales
    - Marketing

Use
- Net
  - WWW
    - Spread
    - Links
  - Affiliates
    - Find
  - BIG
    - PR
  - etc
- Explosives
- Rod
- Bait
- Boat

Techniques
- Fly-Fishing
- Bottom-Bouncing
- Chumming

and restrictions surrounding it. Consequently, the discussion around it is less fraught and the decision becomes easier to carry out. Try using a metaphor for your next challenge. I'm sure you'll agree that it's a valuable prompt for moving you beyond predictable ideas to make extraordinary discoveries.

Tip

Using a Mind Map to 'back-map' your metaphoric solutions to the original problem helps you make use of the natural drive of the human brain to look for and create connections between two different ideas.

Combinational Creativity Canvas

As we already know, creativity can happen in many ways. The ability to make connections is accountable for vast quantities of novel ideas across every field, and this technique takes advantage of this kind of 'combinational creativity'. Yes, that's a thing.

Ideation is all about freewheeling and generating as many ideas as you can – routine ideas, crazy ideas, useful ideas and so on. The more ideas you have, the more ammunition there is to tackle the situation. Resist the temptation to stop brainstorming once you've delivered a few practical, doable solutions. Your first set of ideas are critical for getting the flow going, but they're unlikely to be ground-breaking. Your thinking needs to go beyond these. This approach allows for three stages of ideation to take you from the mundane, sensible ideas through the madcap, non-sensible ideas, ultimately culminating in the most winning and workable solutions (a combo of sensible and non-sensible ideas). It takes real strength to keep looking when you feel ready to quit, so it's worth setting an agenda that you can stick to. High-energy ideation needs at least 30–120 minutes to get the best results, so the running order shown in Table 8.1 might be useful if you can only spare an hour for a session. Feel free to adjust the timings to fit your particular group needs.

Stage 1. Sensible ideas

You've probably noticed when brainstorming that obvious, sensible ideas tend to come out first. These are likely to be ideas that quickly resonate with others in the group, but they won't be unique (Harris, 2009). They might

Figure 8.6 Combinational Creativity Canvas

IDEATION – Combinational Creativity Canvas

| Stage 1: Sensible Ideas | Stage 3: Combine Sensible with Non-sensible | Stage 2: Non-sensible Ideas |

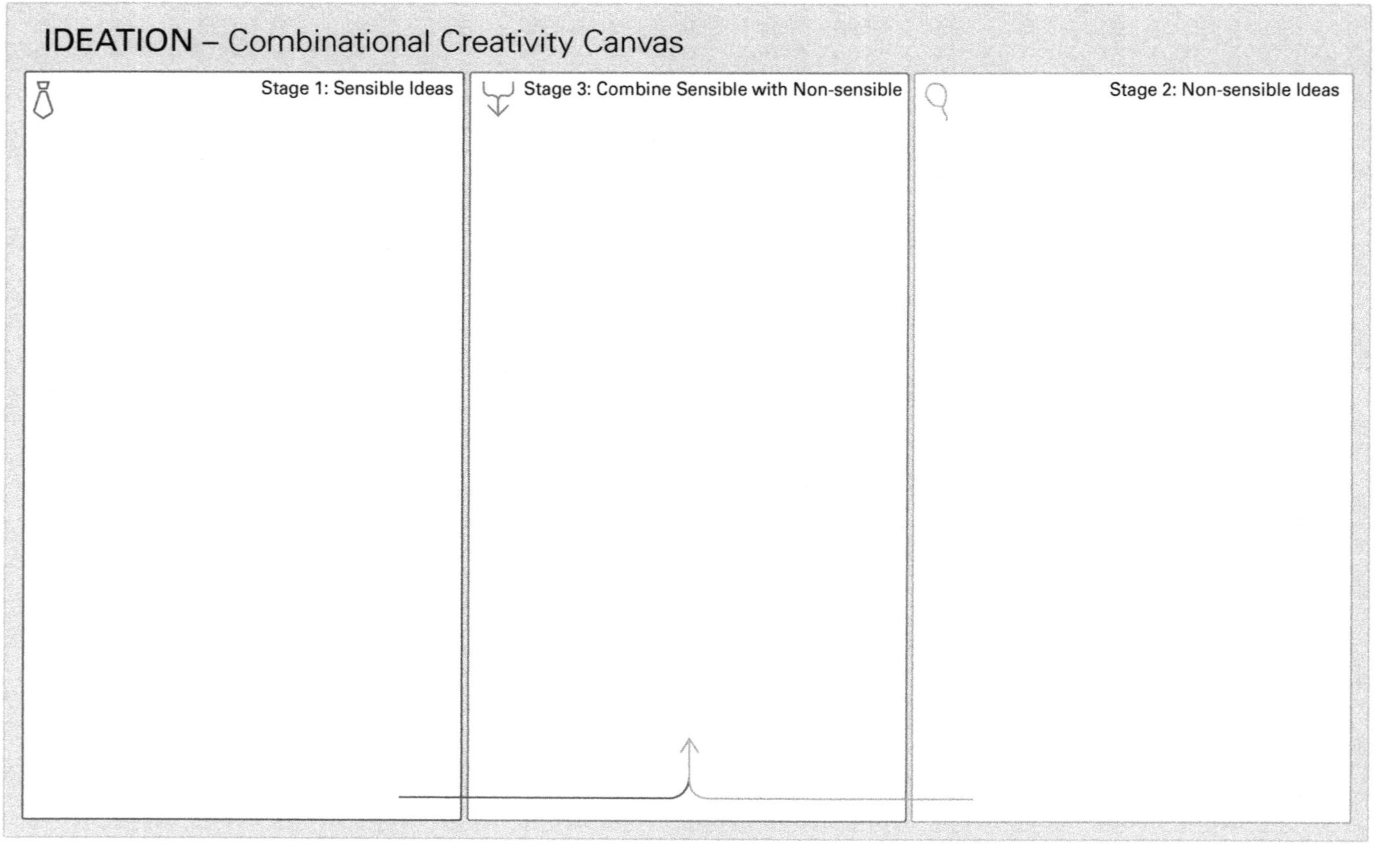

Table 8.1   Ideation session agenda

Ideation session agenda (60 minutes)	
10 mins	Introductions. Establish ground rules. Set out the challenge.
30 mins	Solo and group ideation with generative thinking tools. Sensible and non-sensible ideas.
5 mins	*Break*
10 mins	Discuss and combine sensible and non-sensible ideas.
5 mins	Wrap up the session. Next steps.

only represent an incremental improvement rather than a market-driving innovation. If an idea is too 'safe' then it won't have the imaginative power to change the way things are done for the better. Look at these initial insights as the starting point; you might return to explore and build on them later but don't be tempted to pull the plug just yet. Just repeat 'Yes, what else?' to signal that you want people to persevere and maintain a continuous stream of ideas. And don't forget to treat all ideas equally. If you show any preferences for certain categories of ideas, your team will start trying to second-guess what you're really after (Rawling, 2016).

Stage 2. Non-sensible ideas

If you really fling yourself into the ideation process, you'll hit a point when the ideas start looking a bit outrageous. Notice that as you gain more confidence, your ideas get more radical and ambitious. This is probably because you're making suggestions for more disruptive and transformative change rather than incremental improvement.

Don't kill the excitement by dismissing these outlandish ideas out of hand. The more extreme the idea, the less viable it will seem at first, but it can still hold the seed of possibility. You might prefer practical ideas that you can realistically find profit in straight away, but your customers or target audience might be craving the 'wow' factor. This comes down to your mindset. Logical decision-makers can't stand ambiguity; they like things to make sense and will force-fit them into patterns to help them solve problems. Being fearful of ambiguity tricks people into reactive thinking where they skip the wild, generative phase completely and bolt into important decisions. Creative people, on the other hand, can throw themselves happily into a swirl of chaos and confusion. Indeed, this is what helps them make the conceptual leap that takes them miles beyond the obvious, logical approach. It was by ignoring the supposedly 'logical way' of making cars that Henry Ford came up with that paradigm-changing innovation – the assembly line. Previously, the method of making cars involved teams of men moving from one car to another. Ford turned this upside down by putting the car frames on belts and moving them past the workers.

Chaos often breeds life, when order breeds habit.

      – HENRY ADAMS, American journalist and historian

Ask 'What if?'

If you're getting bogged down by conventional thinking and constantly playing it safe with your ideas while brainstorming, try asking 'What if…?' questions to trigger some riskier options. It's an ideal way to boost your visionary skills and speculate about possibilities that could occur. The 'what if' questions can be anything you like and can focus on any condition, idea or situation, no matter how wacky or far-fetched. The whole point is that it gives you the freedom to think along different lines and to focus on what you *can* do, not what you cannot do. A great way to use this technique is to place yourself in the future: 'Two years from now, if we were celebrating our success, what would have happened?' Write the story!

    Suspend any disbelief and throw yourself completely into the imagined scenarios – act as if they're real and already happening. What hole in the industry might you have filled? How might you have made your product better/bigger/faster/smaller/more fun? What rules or assumptions might you have challenged? What blind spots will you have overcome? You'll be surprised at how easily this creative guesswork can turn insane ideas into genuine opportunities that can be further explored.

Stage 3. Combine sensible with non-sensible ideas

It's a myth to think that new ideas are all 'light bulb' moments, popping into your head spontaneously. Most creative achievements depend on making connections between existing pieces of inspiration, attributes, knowledge, materials and practices, and recombining them to make new formations. This concept underlies many of the innovations and breakthroughs we find in the fields of technology, art and science. Johannes Gutenberg combined the pressure of a wine press with a coin-imprinting mechanism to create the printing press in 1440, transforming the spread of information throughout the Western world. The revolutionary Smart car is the result of an unlikely marriage between premium carmaker Mercedes-Benz and Swatch, the fashion watch brand (Sloane, 2010). Mercedes' precision-engineering knowledge was partnered with the trendy design and microtechnology skills of Swatch to build a small, stylish car suitable for city driving. Cleverly, the name Smart stands for 'Swatch Mercedes Art'. From the start, easyJet modelled its strategy on the US domestic service Southwest Airlines and took inspiration from how buses were run to introduce 'no-frills' affordable air travel in Europe (Sull, 1999). Nothing is entirely original; everything is an extension on what came before.

Chance favors the connected mind.

– STEVEN JOHNSON, innovation and popular science author

To combine ideas, you need a lot of ideas to start with. So, take the ideas you've generated so far and do a mashup. Randomly pair them with each other or with ideas already 'out there' to create something new. Even a dumb or absurd idea may have value when linked with more practical elements. Don't be scared to throw two contradictory or disconnected ideas together either. It may feel weird, but this technique can stretch people's minds further as they experiment with their colleagues' ideas. Give positive reinforcement to encourage combinations; for instance, openly acknowledge someone's idea and then expand on it with your own input. Let's look at an example. If you're generating ideas to increase levels of motivation in your team, you might have sane and nutty suggestions such as those listed in Table 8.2.

Now match some of these ideas together to gain fresh insights into solving the problem. If you were to pair the unorthodox suggestion to 'work naked in the office' with 'pleasant work environment', what does this evoke? Being naked suggests a feeling of freedom, so perhaps you could allow people to dress down in the office to create a more relaxed atmosphere. Not a birthday suit, but not a business suit either! Or perhaps you could hold a pyjama party for the next brainstorming session, where people can come to work in their pyjamas and slippers.

Employing multiple ideation tools makes for more fruitful creative sessions because introducing a new tool can build on the progress made by

Table 8.2 Ideas for motivating people

SENSIBLE IDEAS	NON-SENSIBLE IDEAS
Focus on individual strengths	Form a cult
Ask people what they want	Work naked in the office
Recognize accomplishments	Give Friday off
Build team spirit	Action only the most absurd or fun ideas
Flexible working	Promote the whole team
Create attainable 'stretch' goals	Unlimited holiday allowances
Pleasant work environment	Arm-wrestling competitions
Opportunities for learning/training	Ignore missed deadlines
More decision-making input	Matchmake workers
Encourage creativity	Train people in non-job-relevant skills
Create a 'praise calendar'	Reward failure generously (more than success)
Demonstrate trust	Host an in-office 'happy hour' every day
Diverse rewards	Encourage dangerous office pranks
Insist on work–life balance	Ban all meetings
Measure output not input	Free cooked meals to take home after work
Learn what de-motivates	Allow half the week for pursuing hobbies
Celebrate successes	Encourage people to give up if a task is too hard
More colour in the workplace	Delegate jobs to the 'wrong' people
Say 'thank you'	Allow unlimited procrastination
Be transparent	Give bonuses for punctuality
Shared vision/purpose – focus on the 'Why'	Allow in-office protests and open conflict
Opportunities for advancement	Schedule 'gossip time'
Use performance coaching	Hold elections for new leadership positions
Offer meaningful incentives/perks	Unlimited mobile phone use
Be positive	Give monthly raises
Communicate and consult regularly	Create an in-house social network

(continued)

Table 8.2   *(Continued)*

SENSIBLE IDEAS	NON-SENSIBLE IDEAS
Bring in speakers, mentors and teachers	Rehire individuals for different jobs
Increase salaries	Encourage drinking on the job
Give frequent feedback	Allow delegation of all unwanted tasks
Encourage friendly competition	Get rid of all furniture
Grant autonomy	Set up an office nightclub
Set clear expectations	Build a cinema room
Support new ideas	
Work-sponsored outings	
Set challenging tasks for growth	

previous tools. Instead of starting from scratch, gather all the ideas you've generated and continue mixing and matching from that point using a second, third or fourth tool. By combining the obvious and non-obvious, you can produce ideas that are new, functional and unexpected, forming the basis for true innovation.

Once brainstorming/ideation is over, it's time to come together as a team to review and analyse the ideas, converging on a solution. This is ideally done in a separate meeting or after a break to allow time for the ideas to percolate and incubate in your mind. The evaluation stage is critical in moving your ideas from vision to reality (see Chapter 9).

Ideation checklist: dos and don'ts

The purpose of the ideation checklist shown in Figure 8.7 is to provide constructive guidance for prepping and running your ideation sessions, whether formal or informal. There are right and wrong ways to brainstorm. Make your meetings work by reinforcing positive behaviours (Dos) and reining in creativity killers (Don'ts). Download the Ideation checklist from **www. thinking.space**

Figure 8.7   Ideation: dos and don'ts

IDEATION CHECKLIST: DOs & DON'Ts

DO

- ✓ Establish the correct environment
- ✓ Keep an open mind
- ✓ Suspend judgement
- ✓ Brainstorm individually first, then in groups
- ✓ Involve others
- ✓ Focus on quantity
- ✓ Give yourself time to utilize thought experiments (focused daydreaming)
- ✓ Expand and build on ideas
- ✓ Link seemingly random ideas – connect the unconnected
- ✓ Capture all ideas
- ✓ Take breaks
- ✓ Listen to others
- ✓ Have multiple small ideation sessions rather than one long meeting
- ✓ Borrow another person's point of reference
- ✓ Look outside for inspiration – mirror others and improve
- ✓ Sleep on it – allow incubation time
- ✓ Ignore discouragement from doubters
- ✓ MAKE IT SERIOUSLY FUN

DON'T

- ✹ Be self-conscious
- ✹ Rush idea generation
- ✹ Create and evaluate at the same time
- ✹ Be negative at this stage
- ✹ Bully others with your ideas
- ✹ Try and be sensible
- ✹ Wander off topic
- ✹ Multitask when trying to generate ideas
- ✹ Dismiss insane ideas as being impossible
- ✹ Fall foul of 'listening to the experts' syndrome
- ✹ Lack confidence
- ✹ Brainstorm without structure

Key takeaways

Creativity needs a playful mind. For collective idea generation that works, you should aim to foster a positive and good-humoured environment where people can share their ideas without judgement. Use special ideation tools to trigger your thinking so you can diverge freely and build your tolerance for ambiguity.

- **Reverse Brainstorming Canvas.** Instead of looking for ways to provide better customer service, look for ways to make it worse. You'll rejig your mind and see things you don't usually notice. Use this tool to eliminate the silly, unnecessary rules and conventions that hold your team back from doing their best.

- **Metaphoric Thinking Canvas.** The metaphor is a powerful force for generating new ideas. Compare to create! Follow these steps: 1) identify the challenge; 2) reframe with a metaphor; 3) solve the metaphor; 4) map solutions back to the original challenge.

- **3 Stage Ideation Canvas.** Fuse the mundane with the mad to spark innovation. Stage 1: Generate sensible ideas; Stage 2: Think up non-sensible ideas. Ask 'What if?' questions to encourage your imagination to break free from current constraints; Stage 3:) Combine sensible ideas with non-sensible ideas to form creations that are both functional and novel.

- **Ideation Checklist.** Get the most out of your brainstorming sessions by following these simple dos and don'ts with your team.

References

Duncan, K (2014) *The Ideas Book: 50 ways to generate ideas visually*, LID Publishing, London

Harris, P (2009) *The Truth About Creativity*, Pearson, Harlow

Microsoft Surface (2017) [accessed 11 May 2018] British Companies at Risk of 'Creativity Crisis', Microsoft Surface Research Reveals, *Microsoft News Centre UK*, 27 July [Online] https://news.microsoft.com/en-gb/2017/07/27/british-companies-risk-creativity-crisis-microsoft-surface-research-reveals/

Mind Tools (2010) [accessed 13 May 2018] Reverse Brainstorming: A Different Approach to Brainstorming [Online] https://www.mindtools.com/pages/article/newCT_96.htm

Proctor, RA (1989) The use of metaphors to aid the process of creative problem solving, *Personnel Review*, **18** (4), pp 33–42

Rawling, S (2016) *Be Creative – Now!*, Pearson, Harlow

Sloane, P (2010) *How to be a Brilliant Thinker: Exercise your mind and find creative solutions*, Kogan Page, London

Sloane, P (2016) *Think Like An Innovator: 76 inspiring lessons from the world's greatest thinkers and innovators*, Pearson, Harlow

Sull, D (1999) Case study: easyJet's $500 million gamble, *European Management Journal*, **17** (1), pp 20–38

09
The Solution Finder Step 3: Analysis

Innovation is saying 'no' to 1,000 ideas.

– STEVE JOBS, co-founder of Apple

Evaluate ideas

You've had fun playing around with the challenge and, hopefully, you've stockpiled a bunch of ideas. Now it's time to evaluate. Good analysis is what helps you get a handle on the mass of information that flows out of brainstorming, allowing you to make the transition from idea to solution. This means sorting and screening to ditch the weaker ideas and selecting the best ones to take forward. According to Stevens and Burley (1997), it can take up to 3,000 raw ideas to produce just one commercially successful solution. Of these, around 300 are submitted to a more formal idea-screening process. Analysis plays an indispensable part in creative prosperity.

Analysis is the convergent stage of the solution-finding process and calls for a different mindset to the divergent, ideation stage. Things can get complex. The range of interpretations around a problem can be vast and there are multiple ways of looking at ideas. You can end up in 'analysis paralysis' trying to make sense of everything. This chapter presents you with a small set of easy-to-understand analysis tools to measure your ideas using a balanced approach, giving you the confidence to say 'no' to the weaker ideas and offering a platform for nurturing those with the highest merit. Which ideas do you want to take forward?

Remember: there might be more than one solution for the problem. If you specify that you need to exit the evaluation stage with one perfect idea, you are in 'either/or' thinking. This is too restrictive. You need to have a 'both/and' outlook while working through this process to improve your chances of spearheading the most innovative concepts with real potential. Just because you're narrowing down options and converging on solutions, it doesn't necessarily follow that you should also close down your mind.

The big picture

Here's an activity for you to get your analytical teeth into.

ACTIVITY

Who's the richest?

Your task is to decide which business personality is the wealthiest out of three possible alternatives. Here are some facts to help you choose:

Profile A

- o   Lives in the same house that he bought in the 1950s
- o   Drives a Cadillac XTS
- o   Dines on fast food and drinks five cokes a day
- o   Doesn't carry a cell phone or have a computer at his desk
- o   Plays bridge as a hobby

Profile B

- o   Drives a Volkswagen hatchback with manual transmission
- o   Goes to work every day in a T-shirt, jeans and hoodie
- o   Got married in his backyard
- o   Lives in a five-bedroom home
- o   Founded his own charitable foundation

Profile C

- o   Possesses a string of luxury properties
- o   Has an extensive art collection
- o   Maintains a fleet of luxury yachts and a private jet

- o Owns multiple supercars (worth $50m)
- o Holds lavish parties where celebrities perform.

Which of these would be your choice?

Judging purely on facts, the logical profile might be C, as this person appears to lead the most extravagant lifestyle.

Here are the businesspeople:

- Profile A is Warren Buffet, chairman and CEO of Berkshire Hathaway – net worth of **$84 billion**. #3 on *Forbes* 2018 'The World's Billionaires' list.

- Profile B is Mark Zuckerberg, founder and CEO of Facebook – net worth of **$71 billion**. #5 on *Forbes* 2018 'The World's Billionaires' list.

- Profile C is Roman Abramovich, investor and owner of Chelsea Football Club. Net worth of **$10.8 billion**. #140 on *Forbes* 2018 'The World's Billionaires' list.

The uber-wealthy don't always live the high life. We cannot automatically take things at face value when thinking analytically.

With the evaluation stage, there is always the danger that data are 'king', but – as in the above exercise – factual data alone will never give you the whole picture. Of course, in a commercial enterprise the need for logical thinking is self-evident if you're going to be objective in evaluating the feasibility of ideas. Data give you something on which to ground your judgements and help you weigh up the risks against the expected gains. However, placing too much faith in logic can lead you to the wrong conclusions; in launching the ill-fated New Coke venture, Coca-Cola had all the facts and stats they could have wanted, but it still didn't stop them making a huge mistake in how they interpreted them… cue disastrous results. Rather than overspending time examining the data, it's best to focus on getting a 'big picture' view of your challenge. Look at the forest, don't get lost in the trees.

Chess is considered to be one of the most analytical sports around. During experiments, fMRI scanning of amateur chess players showed that the analytical left side of the brain is more likely to fire up when they are working out a chess problem. But when scientists performed the same tests on chess grandmasters, who are expert players, they found that they used *both* sides of the brain equally to make decisions during games (Schultz, 2011). They engaged the visually focused right side to recognize patterns from previous games and the analytical left side to evaluate the next best logical move, rendering them more advanced thinkers. As with chess, being highly logical can make you a good innovator, but if you want to be a superstar innovator, you need to have 'whole brain' thinking. This involves recruiting both sides of the brain to process the problem intuitively and rationally at the same time.

'Logic is the beginning of wisdom... not the end.'
— SPOCK, STAR TREK VI: The Undiscovered Country

Where is the love?

One of the saddest things about being locked into logical thinking is that we end up ignoring one of the mind's most prized resources – **emotion**. It's a myth to imagine that without emotions, we would develop reasoning super-powers precise enough to rival Spock from *Star Trek*. In our society, we're taught to regard emotion as a weakness that will lead our judgements astray. Yet the idea that emotion has no place in decision making is a misjudgement in itself, as the work of neuroscientist Antonio Damasio (1994) demon-strates. He studied patients who, because of an accident or disorder, lost the ability to experience normal emotions and feelings, such as irritation, pain, passion and so on. You would think that this would make them perfectly rational creatures, able to use their full intellect to execute the best decisions possible; instead, they became immobilized in their decision making, help-less to ascribe value to anything or reach simple conclusions. Even the most basic decisions, such as choosing between a red or blue pen to fill out a form, were an excruciating process, because they were cut off from the subtle emotional signals that help people select between given options. Damasio reports: 'When emotion is entirely left out of the reasoning picture, as hap-pens in certain neurological conditions, reason turns out to be even more flawed than when emotion plays bad tricks on our decisions.'

It's true that emotions can be irrational and will occasionally throw us off track. Every so often they make us feel that we're right even when we're not. However, the role of emotions in providing essential support to the reasoning process cannot be overstated. As the mind faces a number of choices, it is the emotions that give the thumbs up or down by fleetingly signalling how the consequences of a specific choice would make us feel (Gibb, 2007). Emotion does not come at the expense of logic, but rather feeds into it. Using the methods in this chapter, you can learn to bridge the heart and head so that your ability to feel is equally as strong as your faculty of valuing and judging. How do you feel about the idea? How do others feel about it?

Emotions have taught mankind to reason.
— LUC DE CLAPIERS, Marquis de Vauvenargues, French moralist

CASE STUDY   Emotional advertising

The most successful brands have long known that the best ad campaigns appeal to the heart, not the head. People rely on emotions rather than content to make purchasing decisions; therefore, ads that induce an emotional response are more influential than those with a rational message. Through comprehensive meta-analysis of the UK Institute of Practitioners in Advertising (IPA) database, Les Binet and Peter Field (2013) found that emotional advertising is twice as efficient as rational-based advertising and delivers twice the profit over the long term. Their research draws on 996 advertising effectiveness case studies from 700 brands, and spans over 30 years of IPA Effectiveness data. The trend towards Big Data encourages tightly targeted and rationally persuasive campaigns as opposed to emotional, creative campaigns. The former will produce short-term effects, but the latter will build brand fame, leading to bigger long-term paybacks (Roland, 2013). Ads by John Lewis, Hovis, Nikon and British Gas are highlighted as examples of memorable campaigns that tap into feel-good emotional factors.

The Analysis toolkit

INPUT

All ideas

PROCESS

Mine for diamonds

Sort, screen and select the best ideas

TOOLS

Heart/Head Pros/Cons Canvas

Force Field Evaluation Canvas

OUTPUT

1 or more best/most creative idea(s)

My formula for whole-brain analysis involves a concise three-stage process which steers you into making the right choices for your particular challenge – **Sort, Screen, Select.** This simplifies the evaluation activity by breaking it down into small steps and ensures it remains both rational and intuitive. You can use it to assess ideas on your own or in a workshop/meeting with others. Download the Analysis canvases from **www.thinking.space**

1. Sort

Before jumping into detailed analysis of your ideas, you need to look at editing them down to a manageable quantity – a shortlist of between three and six is ideal. This first pass-through is crucial to stop you drowning in a sea of possibilities. Your focus should always be on the original creative brief, that is, the opportunity or problem you set out to address. If you've got a huge volume of ideas to work through, say 50 to 100, it helps to first categorize them into clusters or groups based on meaningful themes (that's if you haven't already done this at the end of your brainstorming session). For instance, you could distinguish groups of ideas according to the type of innovation they promote: product innovation, technical/technological innovation, organizational innovation, managerial innovation or methodological innovation (Rebernik and Bradač, 2008). Or, if you're developing a new product or service, you could create clusters that relate to 'practicality', 'differentiation', 'safety', 'fun' or other design-related elements. Another quick and dirty option is to categorize your ideas in terms of time and cost requirements, such as 'simple', 'hard' and 'difficult'. Simple ideas are those that can be put into action with minimal expenditure of time and money. Hard ideas need a bit more investment, while difficult ideas demand the most expenditure (Moore, 1962).

There are no hard and fast rules, so choose the categories that work best for your challenge; just make sure you keep it simple. Once your ideas are in clusters, it becomes easier to pick out which ones you can kill off. It could be that they don't fall into any obvious grouping for helping to solve the problem. Perhaps even whole clusters can be thrown out if they don't fit in with your ultimate goal.

Use the principle of **positive judgement** to keep an open mind while you're doing this so that your attention is drawn to the more exciting and intriguing options. Judgements starting with *'no, because...'* or *'yes, but...'* should be avoided like the plague during the sorting process. These negative openings put a dampener on things and close the door to further evaluation on an oddball idea that might have real potential. If you begin a judgement with 'yes, if...', this invites further speculation. It keeps you focused on the positive and novel aspects and gives the idea a chance to breathe. You never know, it could eventually shape up into a wonderfully practical solution.

By the end of this stage, heaps of your original ideas will have been discounted, while the few most promising and attractive ones remain to be explored further. These ideas form your input into the screening process. If you don't have a huge volume of ideas or need to move fast, you can skip the sorting stage and jump straight into the evaluation deep-end.

2. Screen

How do you decide which ideas are better than others? It's my personal belief that 'ticking off' ideas against a long list of pre-set criteria is a pretty lame way to evaluate. For one, it doesn't make good use of the rich and complex workings of all our cortical skills, and, because the procedure is so fixed, hardly any positive judgement is engaged. We need to employ a whole brain approach if we're to effectively exploit our resources and connect with both the quantitative and qualitative sides of our thinking. To assist with this, pull out your Heart/Head Pros/Cons Canvas.

Heart/Head Pros/Cons Canvas

After the sorting process, you should be left with a small pool of ideas you'd like to investigate a bit more (no more than eight). In an ideal world, at least some of them will be paradigm-breaking ideas – ones that you wouldn't normally have thought of, ones that may even be a little crazy. The procedure that I like to use for screening ideas is one that encourages balanced left- and right-brain analysis, and helps you stay generative while making a decision. Evaluate each of your ideas in turn using the following measurement factors:

a **Heart vs Head Rating.** Take one of your ideas and begin your evaluation by looking at it from the perspectives of both your heart (emotions) and head (logic). Individuals in a group can do this separately and then compare scores.

Figure 9.1 Heart/Head Pros/Cons Canvas

ANALYSIS – Heart/Head Pros/Cons Canvas

Potential Solution 1	♡ = Score (1–10)	⚒ = Score (1–10)	Total =

⊕ Pros	⊖ Cons

Potential Solution 3	♡ = Score (1–10)	⚒ = Score (1–10)	Total =

⊕ Pros	⊖ Cons

Potential Solution 2	♡ = Score (1–10)	⚒ = Score (1–10)	Total =

⊕ Pros	⊖ Cons

Potential Solution 4	♡ = Score (1–10)	⚒ = Score (1–10)	Total =

⊕ Pros	⊖ Cons

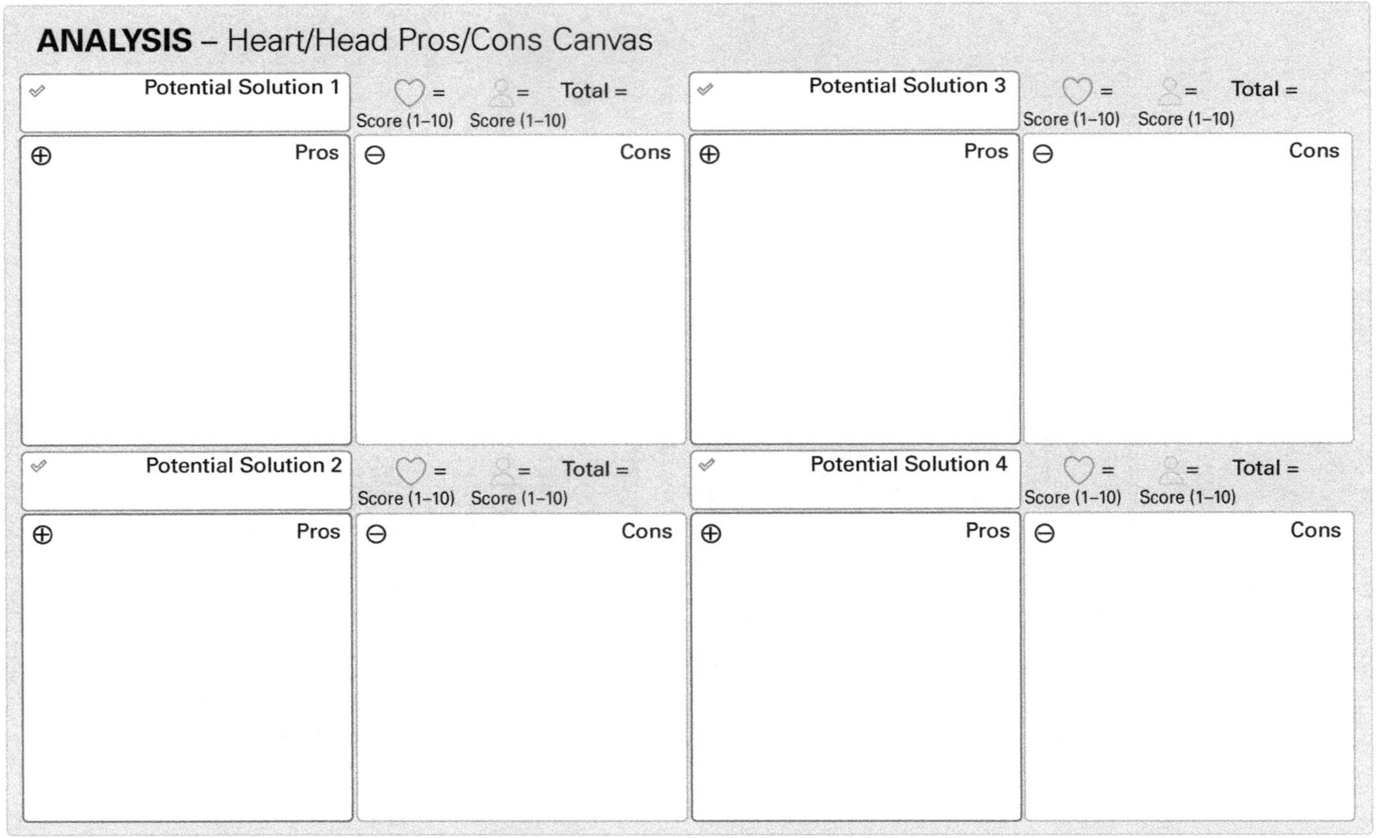

o   *Heart:* Consider how you 'feel' about the idea – think with your heart. What's your gut feeling on it? Does it excite you? Assign a rating to the idea that best signals how positive you are about it emotionally. Use a 10-point scale where 10 indicates that you feel 'very positive' and 1 'very negative'.

o   *Head:* You then follow the same process using intellectual reasoning – think with your head. Does the idea make sense to you logically? Is it robust? Can you rationalize and justify it? Score it on this basis from 1 to 10.

The results of this activity are usually fascinating. You could find that for some ideas your heart says yes but your head says no, and for others both your heart and head see eye to eye. Now total up your heart and head scores to get a balanced score that incorporates both rational and intuitive thinking. Rating scales such as this are quantitative forms of analysis and offer a clear-cut and definite way to work out your best ideas. A strongly positive score says it's an attractive option, whereas a strongly negative score suggests it's a bit of a humdinger. A wide spread of scores across the team indicates a lack of consensus. Further exploration can provide more insight to help you move forward.

While figures and scores are helpful for evaluating alternatives, we also need to use more qualitative, generative thinking to broaden and deepen our analysis. To do this, study the idea from following angles.

b Pros and Cons. Break your idea down into its positive and negative aspects – it's pros ('greens') and cons ('reds'). Get everyone involved and use generative thinking to take into account important financial, marketing and organizational implications, for example costs, timescales, novelty, brand fit, impact, competition, reliability, quality, attractiveness, morale, associated risks, legal issues, scale, income potential, ease of implementation, safety, company practices, feasibility and so on. Again, you want a 'big picture' view of the idea, so make sure you observe it in the context of your current market, environment and product mix, not in isolation. Some quick calculations may be necessary to estimate any numerical inputs or outputs. In certain cases, the canvas could throw up more questions and you might need to get hold of additional data and research to feed the analysis.

o   *Pros (the 'greens'):* What are the positive aspects about this solution? Its strengths? What do you like about it? Why might it succeed? What might others like about it? What are the possible future gains? Work your way round the room and ask everyone to say something positive about the idea being discussed. Carry out a detailed examination of all the positive attributes and their interrelationships. Briefly consider whether you can build on these attributes to make the idea bigger and better. By the time you're done, you'll have a terrific list of selling points that you could use to pitch the idea for implementation.

o   *Cons (the 'reds')*: What are the negative aspects of the solution? Its weaknesses? What do you dislike about it? Why might it fail? Why will others reject it? What are its limitations in the 'real world'? Be its worst critic. Explore all the flaws and downsides of the idea in depth. Keep an open mind and think about how you could erase a red point or even transform it into a plus. After all, you don't want enthusiasm for the idea to dip at this early stage. Change your perspective if you need to. For instance, if one of your negatives is that the solution would cost too much, switch your thinking to: 'How could I afford to pay for this?' If you're able to come up with answers to the question, the barrier is no longer a negative, is it?

Follow this activity for all your shortlisted ideas and you'll end up with a complete and robust description of each one. This exercise can completely change the dynamics of decision making; an idea can score high on the head/heart scale, but still have lots of weaknesses. Or it could have a low score but come with numerous pros. Without you even realizing it, the process compels you into an inclusive left- and right-brain analysis.

Some people might criticize this approach for being too rough, simplistic or 'soft' – that is, not 'analytical enough'. But lots of more complex analytical systems fall apart precisely because they're too analytical. As we've seen, being logical is great for decision making but it can be catastrophic when we overdo it. Having to apply intricate measurements and weights to different attributes can jumble our choices and leave us confused, resulting in the dreaded analysis paralysis. This system rides past these limitations by bringing generative thinking into the mix and factoring in the richness of emotion. It helps to build consensus by engaging the group in an interesting discussion as opposed to just ticking off ideas against a long list of exhaustive criteria.

3. Select

Now it's time for the final stage – choosing the solution. If you've followed the steps by the book so far, it's likely that one or two options will stand out more than others. You will know what you like about them and why. Working in a group, a simple voting system should be enough for selecting the ideas worth pursuing. You could post the ideas up on the wall and ask people to vote with coloured sticky dots (allocate a fixed number to each person), or just ask for a show of hands. For more sensitive or controversial issues, you might want to hold a secret ballot. Each person writes their preferred option on a slip of paper and posts it in a box. This overcomes the problem that people may be unduly influenced by their colleagues' choices.

Refer back to the defined challenge to make sure that the solution(s) you choose will meet your original objectives. A knockout idea usually contains these essential FAD characteristics, balancing both risk and opportunity:

- **Feasibility**: We can actually do it.

- **Acceptability**: We get a satisfactory return.

- **Desirability**: People want it.

While it would be nice to have one all-out winner that clearly hits the target, there may be one or two second-best ideas that you also want to suggest for implementation. It could be that a certain idea has merit but needs some reworking to fully make the grade, or you might need to rank your ideas to figure out which ones to prioritize. Before you make a firm decision, put your main ideas to the test with the Force Field Evaluation Canvas.

Force Field Evaluation Canvas

Force field analysis has been around for decades and was originally developed by Kurt Lewin (1951) as a change management model. Broadly speaking, it works on the basis that in any decision, there are going to be two forces at play – driving forces, which support the execution of an idea, and resisting forces, which are barriers that may hinder the change. Its value during this stage is that it helps teams consider a high-potential solution in terms of how feasible it is to put into practice. The canvas contains columns where you can identify the forces for and against the solution and assign scores to each one, giving you a whole-picture view: an idea is deemed viable if its driving forces outweigh its restraining forces. The benefit of doing this as a team before an idea is carried out is that people who are likely to be affected by the solution can have their say early on. This initial involvement can improve the chances of success once the initiative is under way. Let's work through an example together.

Figure 9.2 Force Field Evaluation Canvas

ANALYSIS – Force Field Evaluation Canvas

Total =

Total =

STEP 1	STEP 2 Driving Forces	Score STEP 3	STEP 4 Options to increase score	Score STEP 5	Score STEP 3+5

STEP 2 Resisting Forces	Score STEP 3	STEP 4 Options to decrease score	Score STEP 5	Score STEP 3+5

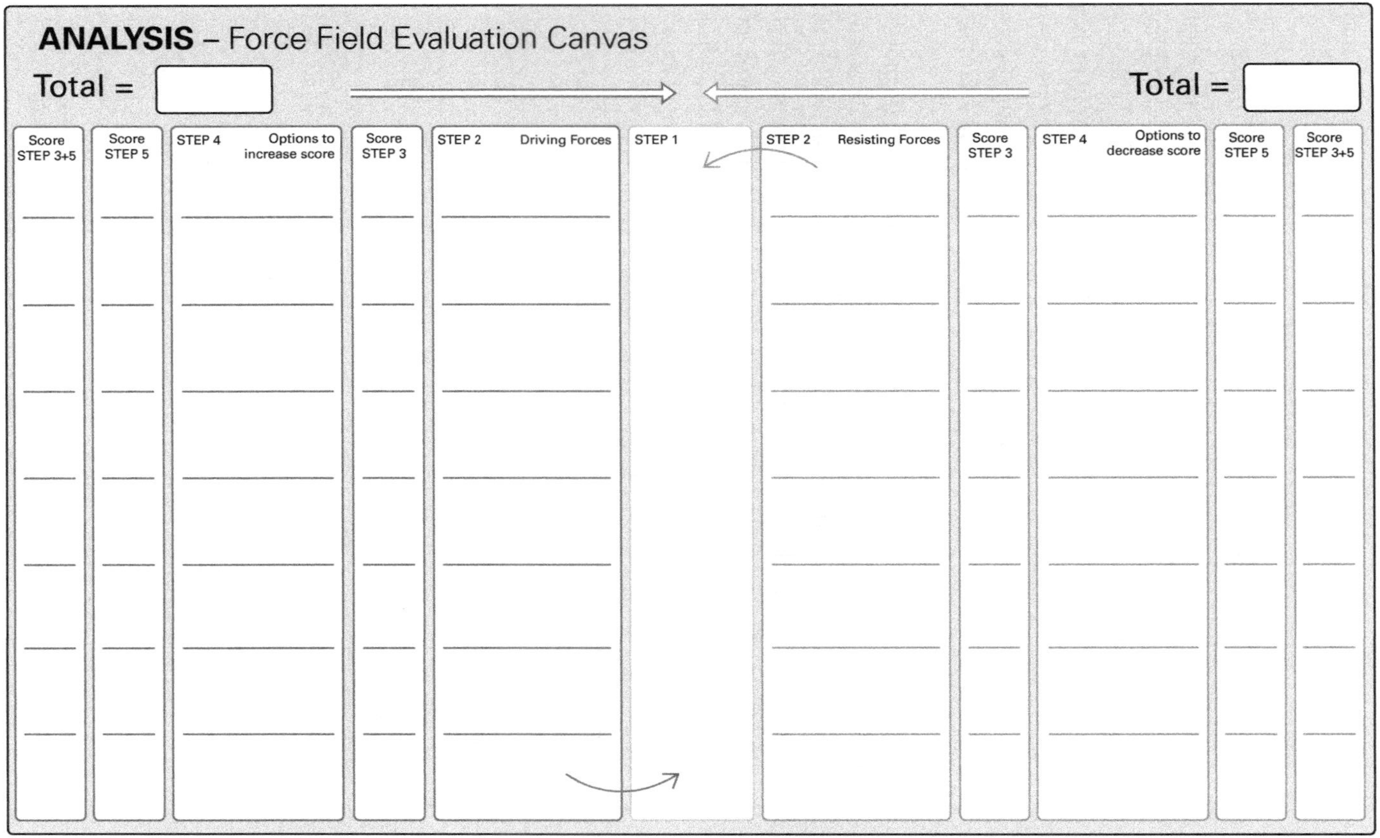

Step 1. Current or desired state

Write a brief description of your current situation or goal in the middle column. For example, you might be proposing an office relocation.

Step 2. Examine the driving forces and resisting forces

Consider all the things that will help the idea work and list them in the Driving Forces column. These can be existing or anticipated helping forces, as well as internal or external forces. For instance, will it make you more competitive? Can it be implemented quickly? Is it profitable or more efficient? Does it mesh well with the overall business model/vision/strategy? Who or what can assist to make the idea a success? Driving forces can include things like new technology, changes in the market, legislation, competition or strategic initiatives from the leadership.

Next, contemplate all the things that would make implementation of the solution difficult. What could go wrong with the solution after it is implemented? Could it create more problems in the long run? Does it only partially solve the problem? Who or what can deter the progress of the idea? Factors such as organizational inertia, worker hostility or fear of failure count as restraining forces. Sometimes the solutions with the greatest potential can also carry the greatest risk. List these inhibiting factors in the Resisting Forces column (Figure 9.2). Examples of driving and resisting forces for an office relocation can be found in Figure 9.3.

Figure 9.3   Driving forces vs Resisting forces: office relocation

Driving forces	Resisting forces
New office lease incentives	Unsettling for team
Move closer to client base	Moving expenses
Reduce operation costs	Planning required
Tap into new market	Disruption of 'business as usual'
Fresh start for the business	Currently in a good location
Improve image	Adapting a new space
More space needed	Recruitment difficulties
	New environment and regulations

Step 3. Assign ratings

Evaluate the driving and resisting forces by allocating a score to each one according to its strength on a 1–5 scale (1 = weak, 5 = strong). Add up the scores for all the driving and resisting forces. To move ahead with confidence, you would need a high driver score. If your totals are 21 (driving) vs 32 (resisting), then you might be inclined to decide against an office relocation at this time. However, there will be some flexibility around the forces. If you really want to proceed with a project and make it successful, this analysis can help you work out how to push it through by strengthening the supporting forces and reducing the opposing forces.

Step 4. Review options to increase/decrease scores

Examine each of the driving forces in turn and discuss options to strengthen the score; in other words, ways to make the solution easier to implement. For example, you could put systems in place to minimize the disruption to the business and use incentives to make the move more attractive to the team. Then focus on decreasing the score of the resisting forces by exploring how to reduce or remove them completely. Tackling the latter might well make the idea even stronger, swinging the balance to a heavier positive weighting. Notice that this activity expands your evaluation and fuses your final decision with both generative and analytical reasoning.

Step 5. Total up your new scores

Check your new totals. Can you go ahead?

Court challenge

Would the idea stand up in court? As we've seen, innovation is both logical and emotional. It's normal to become attached to our own ideas and make decisions based on our optimistic feelings for a project. But the more positive we are about an idea, the less likely we are to see all its flaws. A powerful approach for overcoming this kind of selective thinking is to deliberately seek out and consider evidence against your favoured idea in an idea 'court case'. Encourage your colleagues to put across opposing facts and play devil's advocate. Allow any lingering doubts to come out. Keep poking holes in the idea and you might soon spot a pattern. This is a great technique for challenging and stress-testing ideas, showing you which aspects are underdeveloped. Highlight any issues that might require further action before you fully commit.

There is no decision that we can make that doesn't come with some sort of balance or sacrifice.

— SIMON SINEK, leadership guru and author of *Start With Why*

No solution is ever going to be 100 per cent perfect; there will be compromises involved. But if you've followed the process in this chapter, you'll be fully aware of the positive/negative balance. Once the winning solution(s) is chosen, it's hugely important to thank everyone involved in the process for their contribution. It takes courage for people to speak up about their ideas and they may have spent considerable time and energy on them. Always offer clear feedback on why certain ideas are not being progressed and be respectful about how people may feel about their rejected ideas (Gower, 2015).

Analysis checklist: dos and don'ts

In creative problem solving, there is a need for a more holistic approach to idea evaluation. A good decision is based on analysis of many different points of view. If you rely on just one type (such as 'factual' data), you'll fail to see the whole picture. Use the Analysis checklist to support your thinking as you dig about your ideas in different ways. It will help you stay systematic and avoid the bias traps that can trip you up if you do not consciously think about the things you should and should not do during evaluation. Download the checklist from **www.thinking.space**

Figure 9.4   Analysis: dos and don'ts

ANALYSIS CHECKLIST: DOs & DON'Ts

DO

- Agree on the evaluation criteria to ascertain what is really important
- Decide on the best potential solutions to evaluate
- Remain generative in your thinking – use whole brain thinking
- Remember: facts only tell part of the story
- Include emotional feelings
- Note: the 'map is not the territory'
- Welcome constructive criticism
- Assess potential risk and reward for each viable alternative
- Get others involved in the evaluation stage
- Get fresh perspectives to consider what others would make of the solutions
- Capture the pros and cons of any potential solution
- Gauge support for an idea – use voting to see how others feel about the alternatives
- Directly compare options
- Use tried and tested analytical processes
- Evaluate for feasibility, acceptability and desirability
- Assess how sustainable the idea is in the long run
- Schedule time for second guessing a selection

DON'T

- Overthink the solution
- Rely just on numbers
- Focus on just one or two alternatives – have at least four
- Base your hypothesis on confirming evidence alone
- Avoid individuals that you know will ask the difficult questions
- Wing it
- Get stuck in the comfort zone of doing more research
- Consider it a one-time process
- Be afraid to rethink and generate additional ideas
- Allow psychological biases to predetermine your selection
- Proceed if the preferred solution doesn't feel right
- Ignore simple alternatives that can be tried immediately at little cost
- Settle for the status quo
- Be afraid to reverse a decision
- Analyse too soon
- Use 'either/or' thinking. Consider using 'both/and'

Key takeaways

Step 3 of the Solution Finder is when you shift from ideas to solutions (via analysis). Sort and screen your captured output against measured criteria and select solutions for best 'fit'. The objective is to engage your *whole brain* in the analytical process – your emotions and generative faculties (right brain) as well as reason and logic (left brain), like chess grandmasters.

- **Heart/Head Pros/Cons Canvas.** Screen an idea by examining it from the perspective of both your heart (what is my gut feeling on it?) and head (is it logical and practical?). Is your idea complete? Assess it by its pros ('greens') and cons ('reds') to get a big picture view of the data.

- **Force Field Evaluation Canvas.** Analyse the forces for and against an idea: step 1) define your current or desired state; step 2) examine the driving forces and resisting forces; step 3) allocate ratings to help you evaluate; step 4) review options to increase the scores of the driving forces and to decrease those of the resisting forces; step 5) check your new totals. Have you got a sure-fire solution?

- **Analysis Checklist.** Stick to these evaluation rules to outsmart your biases and assess the whole picture before you make a big decision.

References

Binet, L and Field, P (2013) [accessed 29 May 2018] The Long and the Short of It: Balancing Short and Long-Term Marketing Strategies, *IPA* [Online] http://www.ipa.co.uk/page/the-long-and-the-short-of-it-publication#.Ww18Y_ZFxPY

Damasio, AR (1994) *Descartes' Error: Emotion, reason and the human brain*, Avon Books, New York

Gibb, BJ (2007) *The Rough Guide to the Brain*, Rough Guides, London

Gower, L (2015) *The Innovation Workout: The 10 tried-and-tested steps that will build your creativity and innovation skills*, Pearson, Harlow

Lewin, K (1951) *Field Theory in Social Science: Selected theoretical papers*, Harper & Row, New York

Moore, LB (1962) Creative action – the evaluation, development and use of ideas, in *A Sourcebook for Creative Thinking*, ed SJ Parnes and HF Harding, Scribner's, New York

Rebernik, M and Bradač, B (2008) [accessed 22 May 2018] Module 4: Idea Evaluation, *Creative Trainer* [Online] http://www.innosupport.net/index.php?id=6038&L=%273&tx_mmforum_pi1[action]=list_post&tx_mmforum_pi1[tid]=4096

Roland, L (2013) [accessed 29 May 2018] The Long and Short of It: Measuring Campaign Effectiveness Over Time, *WARC*, 12 June [Online] https://www.warc.com/newsandopinion/opinion/the_long_and_short_of_it_measuring_campaign_effectiveness_over_time/1727

Schultz, N (2011) [accessed 21 May 2018] Chess Grandmasters Use Twice the Brain, *New Scientist*, 11 January [Online] https://www.newscientist.com/article/dn19940-chess-grandmasters-use-twice-the-brain/

Stevens, GA and Burley, J (1997) 3,000 raw ideas = 1 commercial success! *Research Technology Management*, 40 (3), pp 16–27

10

The Solution Finder Step 4: Direction

There are no old roads to new directions.

– attributed to the Boston Consulting Group

Turn ideas into action

An idea isn't an innovation until you make it happen. In many businesses, creative problem-solving endeavours come to a halt once the solution has been decided. Owing to procrastination, lack of courage or neglect, even the most transformative solutions are left on the shelf gathering dust, destined never to see the light of day. Don't fall into this trap. Nothing kills team motivation and creativity faster than new proposals that come to nothing. Creativity is just as much about moving on your ideas as it is about generating those ideas in the first place; we are talking about **applied creativity**, after all.

The implementation stage is crucial for turning ideas into positive change – whether in a process, a product, a department, a method, a culture, a way of thinking or a way of working. This phase is the culmination of all your earlier thinking. You've got your most promising idea ready – the first three steps of the Solution Finder saw to that. Now it's time to strengthen the practical version of your idea, give it concrete shape and structure, and drive it forward through goal setting and action planning. Your idea needs a clear path of deployment to put it in the best position to survive out there in the wild.

It's at this point that you can use **positive selective thinking** to fully commit to what you are doing. You can have belief in your idea and your capability to succeed because you've undertaken all the necessary mental groundwork to get here via the previous three steps of the Solution Finder. Your belief is what will bolster your actions through early dialogues, designs, prototypes, tests, pilots and beyond launch, supporting you and your team all the way in your innovative adventure.

Genius is 1% inspiration, 99% perspiration.

– THOMAS EDISON, American inventor

99% perspiration, continual innovation

Without a doubt, you will need motivation, discipline and perseverance to make your idea a reality. You've reached the final hurdle, but the hard grind is far from over. Just as you've got to keep going during ideation to find the best ideas, so you have to keep going during implementation to make sure your solution will be a lasting one. When you take your idea forward, you shouldn't stop being creative – keep making it stronger all the way through. Keep learning. You will need high adaptability after the serious work of implementation begins, and there should be a continuous and dynamic process of development as you figure out what works, what doesn't, and what to do next. The guys at Rovio went through thousands of iterations of the mobile game *Angry Birds* before they hit upon the addictive formula that went on to seize the world's attention (Cheshire, 2011). The first concept was just the starting point. And since the game's release in 2009, the innovations have kept coming – we've seen more levels, new versions, spin-offs, cuddly toy merchandise, a cartoon series, books, an animated feature film and many other novelties. It has been the #1 paid app on iTunes in 68 countries, as well as the best-selling paid app of all time. Make no mistake, there will be copious amounts of hard work involved. Persistence is the fuel needed to build upon your best ideas and navigate the highs and lows that accompany implementation. Welcome to the unglamorous side of the creative process! Indeed, because innovation is so heavy going, it's important to be on the lookout for victories and celebrate them along the way.

CASE STUDY   Success doesn't come easy

When you look at the success stories of some of the world's most esteemed creators, it's clear that none of them had it easy. Their history is often speckled with setbacks. Walt Disney's first animation company went bankrupt and he was turned down 302 times before he got the financing for Disney World. It took James Dyson 15 years to bring his game-changing concept of a dual cyclone bagless vacuum cleaner to life, persevering through 5,127 prototypes before he hit the jackpot (Malone-Kircher, 2016). He then launched the Dyson company to produce his design when no other manufacturer would take it on. Elon Musk, the multibillionaire behind SpaceX and Tesla, has taken a good few knocks during his career and been ridiculed for his high ambitions. He was famously ousted from PayPal (a company he co-founded) while on his honeymoon, his first three rocket launches all failed and his two companies almost went bankrupt in 2008. Instead of lying low, he continues to show unmatched spirit and resilience in championing his innovations for a world of clean energy, revolutionized transport and space colonization. And how could I not mention inventor Thomas Edison, who tried over 9,000 designs before successfully developing a working electric light bulb? Why have these people become household names, looked up to by millions? Because they kept going and didn't take 'No' for an answer.

Belief matters

In Chapter 2 we looked at all the negative side effects that come with selective thinking, so you might very well wonder why I'm encouraging you to be selective in your thinking at this stage. As we've seen, selective thinking is dangerous for ideation because it causes you to charge ahead with the first decent idea, closing your mind to other opportunities and pathways. During the active Direction stage, however, you can fully commit to your idea because you've carefully journeyed through the steps of the Solution Finder, giving yourself the best probability of making it work successfully. Up to this point, you've applied the optimal thinking formula, so you can have trust and confidence that you've chosen the correct way forward.

In a research report prepared for Nesta innovation foundation, Patterson *et al* (2009) found 'self-belief/confidence' to be essential characteristics that contribute to innovative working. This is connected to the work of pioneering psychologist, Albert Bandura (1977), who developed the theory of self-efficacy – a person's belief in their ability to succeed in a particular task or situation. Your level of self-efficacy enhances your power to make your ideas happen. When you truly believe in your solution, you possess the motivation, conviction and determination to build on it and see it through to the very end.

I have learned a deep respect for one of Goethe's couplets: Whatever you can do, or dream you can, begin it. Boldness has genius, power, and magic in it.

– WILLIAM H MURRAY, The Scottish Himalaya Expedition

Self-efficacy for entrepreneurs

A strong sense of self-efficacy, a belief in one's ability to do a task well, can be gained from more productive decision making and is especially valuable for entrepreneurs. Psychology researchers at the University of Giessen, Germany, found that self-efficacy has a significant correlation to business creation and success (Rauch and Frese, 2007). In fact, this correlation is as high as the one between the weight and height of adults in the United States, one of the highest medical correlations ever found (Bharadwaj Badal, 2015). High self-efficacy encourages behaviour patterns that lead to enterprise success. Namely, it:

- motivates people to take the initiative;

- helps them persevere in the face of problems and better cope with challenges;

- gives them confidence in their ability to perform various (often unanticipated) tasks;

- provides a hopeful outlook for the future.

The Direction toolkit

INPUT

One or more best/most creative idea(s)

PROCESS

Develop the final solution

Plan and start implementation

TOOLS

Building Solutions Canvas

SMART Goals Canvas

Action Plan Canvas

OUTPUT

Implementation underway

In the final step of the Solution Finder, use the Direction canvases to build up your solution, set smart goals and implement an action plan to take your innovative idea to market. Download these from **www.thinking. space**

Building Solutions Canvas

Your initial idea won't be mature, but it will be fertile and full of potential. In its budding state, your idea needs the right treatment to help it grow and develop into a robust and workable solution. For example: the concept for electric cars isn't as new as people think. Electric vehicles first materialized in the 19th century, but soon lost out to the affordability and simplicity of internal combustion engines. It wasn't until recent development efforts that electric innovations were complete enough to offer a direct replacement for conventional petrol-powered cars, allowing the idea to pick up speed in the 21st century.

Before getting stuck into any goal setting or planning, you need to craft and refine your solution ready for launch. Remember, even after your plan is under way, you should continue developing your idea to make it the best it can be. Constantly ask, 'How can I make it better?'

Build on the work you began during Analysis to translate your interesting idea into something more actionable. Use force field evaluation, the court challenge (see Chapter 9) and tools such as SWOT (Strengths, Weaknesses, Opportunities and Threats) analysis to prod and poke your idea, and to strengthen it from multiple angles. Rethink your idea against your challenge and objectives to find ways of powering it up to make it even more feasible, acceptable and desirable.

This is a necessary exercise to give you all the back-up required to win support and gain maximum acceptance for your idea. You will need this buy-in to galvanize and lead others involved in the implementation. To be successful, every new solution must become part of an existing web of people, technologies and capabilities. For instance, look at all the people (customers, workers, stakeholders) who will have to use your idea or change to accommodate your idea (McKeown, 2014). Anticipate any reluctance they will have to your proposed solution and consider other factors that might help or hinder implementation (places, things, office politics, rules, skills, timings or actions). This is how you construct a heavy-duty solution that can weather the change process.

Figure 10.1 Building Solutions Canvas

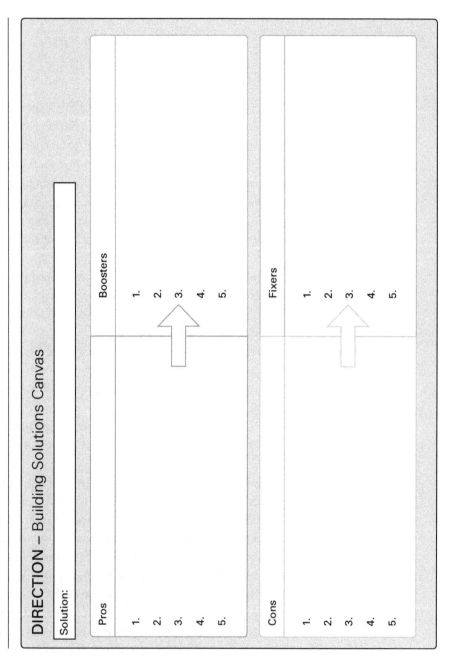

Don't oversell the idea by positioning it as the ultimate end-solution or definitive way forward. Instead, offer it up as a preliminary idea and involve others in building it up so it becomes their idea too. This will give people their own reason to jump on board and show active commitment. Share the glory. Set your ego aside and don't fret about losing some of the credit for being the one to come up with idea. People will come to recognize you as a team player and as someone who's proactive at finding new directions and goals for the business.

Refer back to the pros and cons audit you performed in Step 3 of the Solution Finder. Now come up with practical ways to 'boost' the positives and 'fix' the negatives.

Boosters

Starting with the pros (the 'greens'), note down all the ways in which each one might be strengthened, emphasized or improved. Is there something you can add to the solution to make it bigger and better? Can you scale it up? Make it more solid? More cost-effective? Longer-lasting? Is there anything else the idea might allow you to accomplish? Say you've come up with a top marketing idea for increasing attendance at your company's seminars and workshops; perhaps you could take it to the next level and brand your approach to make it even more attractive to your target market.

Fixers

Next, examine all the ways in which you can overcome your idea's shortcomings and eradicate its flaws. How might you counter other people's concerns about it and dispel any potential risks? Don't simply patch over the cracks; go further and convert any possible objections into positives. For instance, if your idea involves introducing a new management approach into your organization, think of how stakeholders might challenge the proposed change initiatives. Then prepare for this by considering ways to make it better for the company, its workforce, partners and customers.

An idea by itself is not the sum total of the creative process; it is only the beginning.

— PROFESSOR JOHN ARNOLD, Stanford University

Testing, testing

Part of the process of building up your solution is to try it out and see how it works. By modelling, prototyping or 'live' testing an idea, you might identify practical shortcomings or flaws you hadn't thought of. You can then redevelop and 'de-risk' the idea before committing yourself fully. Here are some quick ways to test it out:

- **Prototype.** A sample or working model of your idea. Your idea works in theory, but it's not until you start physically building it that you can understand how it will work in practice. Being able to see and touch the idea brings it to life and helps others understand it better than if you were to just give a formal presentation on it. Don't worry about giving your prototype a polished look – a bit of cardboard, sticky tape and some marker pens should do a decent enough job, or sketch out a few skeleton screens on paper for websites or apps.

- **Usability testing.** Create a test environment or simulated experiment and invite potential consumers to try out your product or service. Observe them closely to see how people interact with your idea. Are there features that no one really needs? Are there moments in the process that the user finds stressful or confusing ('pain points')? The goal in capturing this sort of feedback is to identify what people like about your idea, as well as any problems that can be fixed before launch.

- **Pilot.** Trial the new system, product or procedure for a short time in real-life conditions to see what happens. Think of it as the dress rehearsal before the big show. Innocent Drinks started out after testing their original smoothies at a music festival in 1998. The founders planted a sign in front of their stall asking customers if they should give up their day jobs to make smoothies (O'Neill, 2009). Customers responded by throwing their empties in a bin marked 'Yes' or 'No'. By the end of the weekend, the 'Yes' bin was full while the 'No' bin contained just three bottles. The founders resigned from their jobs the very next day.

The results of prototyping and testing help you to refine and validate your idea before it's rolled out at scale. Is your innovation really ready? Test it and find out.

SMART Goals Canvas

Your goal for your innovation project might seem obvious to you, but it may not be so clear to others. You need to state your goal in crisp, concise terms that you can measure so that you, and everyone else involved, can tell when success has been achieved. This is even more vital if your goal is something intangible, such as increasing worker motivation or creating a culture shift in the business. Research shows that people who have clear written goals are more successful in achieving them. In a study of 149 participants, Dr Gail Matthews (2015) at the Dominican University in California discovered that those who wrote down their goals, set action commitments and shared their goals and progress with friends had a much higher success rate (76%) than participants who only thought about their goals (43%). Furthermore, a survey of 4,960 individuals by training and consultancy company Leadership IQ found that people who can vividly describe or picture their goals are anywhere from 1.2 to 1.4 times more likely to successfully accomplish their goals (Murphy, 2010). Committing your goals to writing forces you to clarify your intentions and makes them more real to you. And by breaking them down into milestones, you're motivated to follow through on them. If you're working with others, setting goals helps the group focus on the right priorities and empowers them to make better decisions. Having crystal-clear objectives also enables you to see and celebrate your wins as you make your ideas materialize.

There are lots of methods out there for goal setting and you should use whatever clicks with you. The SMART technique works well for creating neatly defined goals for meeting any kind of challenge; on your SMART Goals Canvas, you're encouraged to (surprise, surprise) set yourself SMART goals to describe what a successful innovation outcome would look like. These are targets that are specific, measurable, attainable, relevant and timely: vague objectives are not helpful. The completed canvas gives you a visual concept of success to work from. Not only will it channel your attention, but it will also serve as an internal document to channel the focus of others who'll be involved in making the initiative happen.

Take stock. Before you start smartening up your goals, take a moment to inspect your current situation and the problem you're trying to solve. Consider your intentions. These form the core purpose of your goals and are usually at the root of your motivation for wanting to crack this particular challenge. For instance, birth-control activist Margaret Sanger's goal to develop the oral contraceptive pill was born of the intention to give women the right to control their bodies.

Figure 10.2 SMART Goals Canvas

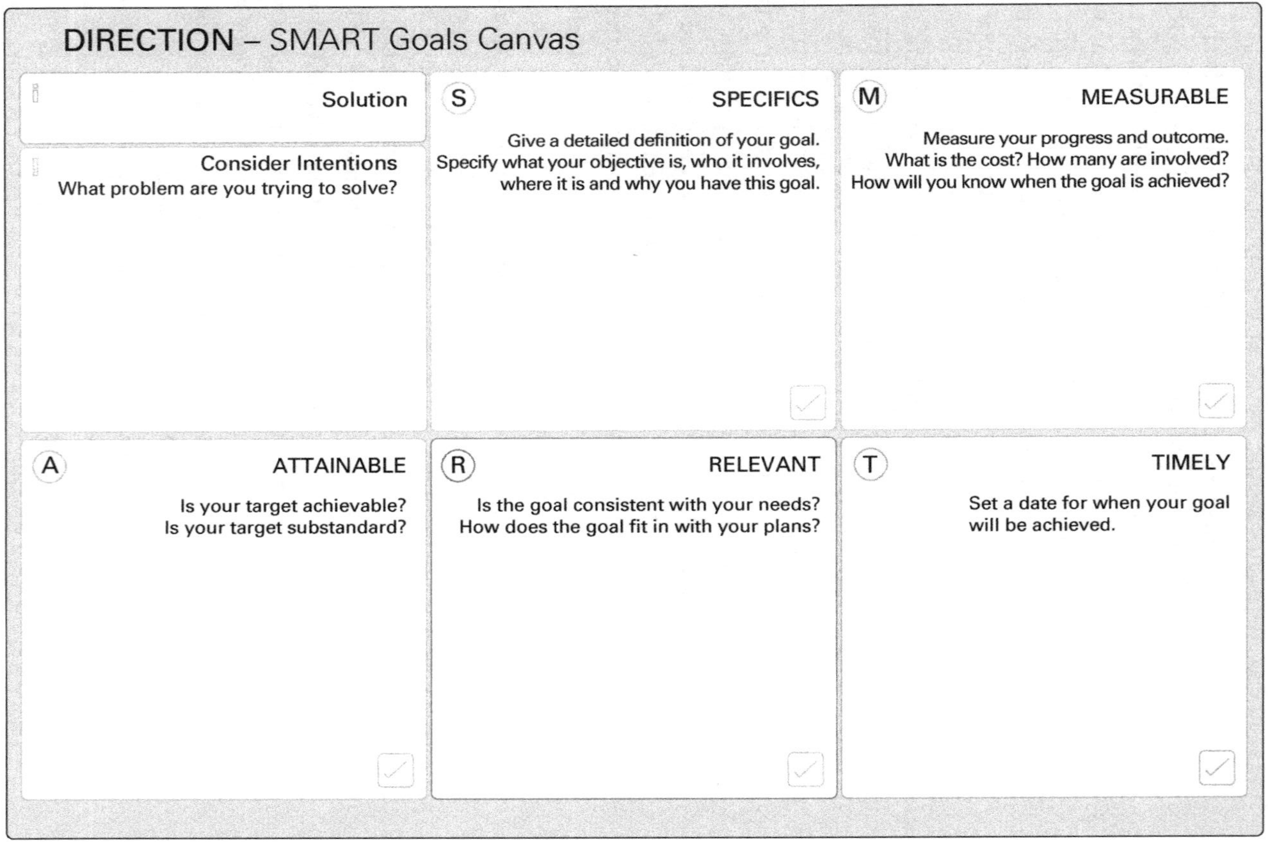

DIRECTION – SMART Goals Canvas

Solution	(S) SPECIFICS	(M) MEASURABLE
Consider Intentions What problem are you trying to solve?	Give a detailed definition of your goal. Specify what your objective is, who it involves, where it is and why you have this goal.	Measure your progress and outcome. What is the cost? How many are involved? How will you know when the goal is achieved?

(A) ATTAINABLE	(R) RELEVANT	(T) TIMELY
Is your target achievable? Is your target substandard?	Is the goal consistent with your needs? How does the goal fit in with your plans?	Set a date for when your goal will be achieved.

SPECIFIC. Give a detailed definition of your target outcome/goal. Lay down what your objective is, who it involves, where it is and why you have this goal. For example, 'To fully train all analysts in using our new business intelligence software, so we can obtain more comprehensive data for strategic and tactical decision making across all work units'.

MEASURABLE. Add precise targets, metrics or best practice standards so you can measure your degree of success. What is the cost? How many are involved? How will you know when the goal is achieved? If your goal is to improve customer satisfaction, what percentage improvement are you aiming for? If you're launching a new product, what level of sales are you targeting? According to a McKinsey study, more than 70% of corporate leaders cite innovation as one of their top three business priorities, yet only 22% set innovation performance measures (Barsh, Capozzi and Davidson, 2008). An innovation goal can be a tricky thing to evaluate, but it's important to establish metrics that will help you gauge the success of your efforts, whether based on financials, popularity or practicality.

ATTAINABLE. Is your target achievable? Is it substandard? Set your goal too high and it might be out of reach, set it too low and you won't create any noticeable change. Your goals should represent substantial growth or progress, but make sure they are within your sphere of control and don't eat into your other key responsibilities.

RELEVANT. Is the goal consistent with your needs? How does the goal fit in with your plans/the bigger picture? Don't set certain goals just because you think you should, otherwise you won't be as passionate or committed to achieving them. Whether you're hoping to create a new trend, make more money or have more fun, make sure your goal is part of the overriding culture and operation of your business. There should be a clear line of sight between your objectives and those of the department or organization.

TIMELY. Set a date for when your goal will be achieved. Personal development author and life coach Anthony Robbins defines a goal as a 'dream with a deadline'. Deadlines add a sense of urgency to a goal, bringing quicker achievement, and are the final anchor in making your goal real and tangible. For example, 'Find two new component suppliers by the end of June', 'Reduce monthly expenses by 10% within three months', 'Double traffic to the website within six months' or 'Implement a new CRM system by the end of Q3 2019'. Without a time limit or start date for the objective, it's easier to procrastinate and allow everyday tasks to get in the way of what you really want. You can also set cut-off dates for key achievements along the route to a major goal, such as deadlines for the planning, development and implementation of a new IT system, and then further time frames for testing the system and training the team to use and understand it.

The whole idea of this kind of goal setting is to lead innovation by ushering in something new (new customers, new projects, new markets, new products, new approaches and so on). But goal setting alone isn't enough to guarantee successful execution of your initiative or solution: you must get there step-by-step. Too often we get so fixated on the eventual outcome that we forget to plan all the steps that are needed along the way. This puts us at the mercy of external forces and leaves us wide open for the critical aspect of ourselves to take hold: 'I'm never going to get this done on time' or 'This target is impossible'.

Action Plan Canvas

With your SMART goals set, you know exactly where you're going – but how will you get there? Proactive planning helps to break down your 'Big Idea' into discrete, manageable steps and overcomes the tendency for reactive thinking by making sure that everyone's responses and day-to-day actions are in line with your ultimate goals.

To kick off your innovation project, draw up a battle plan using the Action Plan Canvas. Your plan doesn't have to be super-intricate and exhaustive, just organized. If you involve other people in your planning, you give them a chance to buy in to the project and claim some ownership over it.

Step 1. Identify tasks

Map out all the tasks you need to complete to achieve your target. It's helpful to start at the beginning and work through your tasks step-by-step. What's the very first action you'll need to take? Once that's done, what comes next? Focus on the jobs that are critical to the objective and will move you forward the most. Using Post-it Notes, group your tasks into the canvas columns of Now, Next and Soon by order of priority so you can clearly see the sequence in which you need to finish each task. Specify task-relevant details such as 'target date' and 'owner' on each Post-it for greater accountability. Some tasks will be dependent on others and some will be standalone actions – keep any dependencies in mind when working out your timeframes.

Figure 10.3 Action Plan Canvas

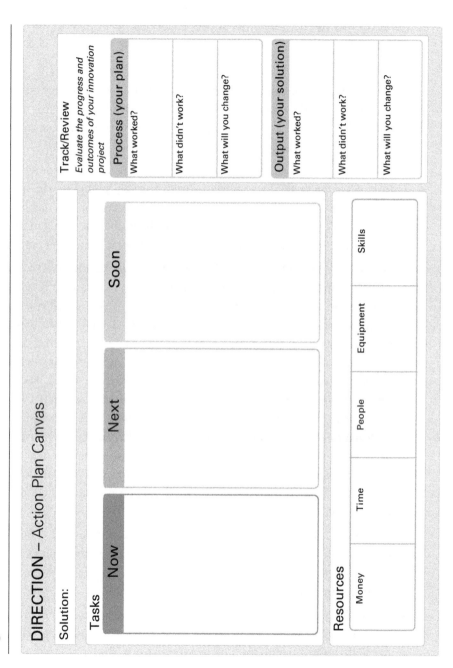

DIRECTION – Action Plan Canvas

Solution:

Tasks

Now	Next	Soon

Resources

Money	Time	People	Equipment	Skills

Track/Review
Evaluate the progress and outcomes of your innovation project

Process (your plan)
What worked?

What didn't work?

What will you change?

Output (your solution)
What worked?

What didn't work?

What will you change?

Step 2. Allocate resources

Now that you can see all your tasks clearly, study them in more detail. What resources will you need in terms of people, money, facilities, time and expertise to do what needs to be done? Use the following pointers to check that you cover everything:

- **Money.** What financial resources will you need to complete all your action steps? Is the money available now? If not, how can you get hold of the funds you need? Your response to this might hint at extra action steps for your plan.

- **Time.** Add timescales for each of your action steps. Is there enough time to reach your goal? The canvas helps you easily pinpoint which tasks might have to be shuffled around to accommodate others that would need to be done beforehand. If you don't have enough time for certain tasks, work out how you might be able to borrow it from other activities.

- **People.** Is there sufficient human resource to make the plan happen? Whose support and contribution can you rely on? Can they handle the increased workload, or will you need to recruit? Make sure all your tasks are allocated to the right people. A task that's left unassigned can very easily be left undone. It's a good idea to delegate or outsource the activities that you're no good at – get an assistant to help with admin or use skilled freelancers for detailed technical, analytical or creative work. Focus on the areas where your strengths and natural abilities mean that you add the most value, for example strategic decision making or communicating with major clients. People can help you in different ways – some may offer their time, knowledge, money or influence, others their moral support. Once you've defined who these people are, ask yourself how you might engage them even more. Does this suggest additional action steps for your plan?

- **Equipment.** Do you have the essential equipment, systems and facilities to carry out the plan? If you've already got the material resources you need, include them in your project plan. If not, write down how you'll go about getting them.

- **Skills.** Do you and your associates have the knowledge and training needed to accomplish each action step? How much training will you need? If you're going to need more expertise or knowledge, map out how you'll get it.

You now have a platform for action. For smaller projects, you probably won't need to think about all of these factors. For instance, if you're working on a small internal project to create a departmental database, you might only have to consider 'People', 'Skills' and 'Equipment'. For larger, more complex projects, you could find it helpful to use formal project management techniques and tools such as Gantt charts or task and project management software to manage all your activities.

Step 3. Communicate the plan

If you want people to back your brilliant solution, then you'll have to sell it to them. How can you build enthusiasm and acceptance? Who might object or need to be persuaded? New plans aren't always accepted automatically; in fact, much of the time they're resisted. This resistance could be down to any number of sources, such as fear of the unknown, lack of information, threats to status, fear of failure and lack of perceived benefits; so be prepared for a negative reaction, and don't let it prevent you from acting on your idea. Think about how you can deflect any potential negativity instead.

As part of his theory of change management, Kurt Lewin (1958) maintains that people must be introduced to change before change is introduced. Good communication is vital for outlining the merits of your case and getting people on your side. Tell it like a story. Give it a catchy headline and describe the journey that your idea will take, complete with potential obstacles, choices and lucky encounters. Refer back to the list of pros you identified in Step 3 of the Solution Finder (Analysis) and put together compelling facts and figures to back them up. Avoid clichés and jargon – use everyday language to state your message clearly in a way that people can best hear it, understand it and act on it. Keep it simple by focusing on the core problem and how you intend to address it creatively. But most important of all, be passionate and purposeful. To sell an idea, you need to demonstrate your belief in it.

Step 4. Implement the plan

Finally, after all the thinking and planning comes action. This is the point where you inject energy and enthusiasm into launching the idea for real. Don't wait too long. If you insist on holding out for perfect conditions with every provision in readiness, you may never get started. If you're deploying a large-scale solution or change, I would suggest looking into change management skills and techniques to make the transition as smooth as possible.

No matter how great your idea is, it will never be perfect, and you can only guess at how it will turn out once it's flung into the real world. Despite the best of intentions, new businesses, decisions and projects can go pear-shaped or miss the mark. Always have a good Plan B in place, just in case things don't go as expected with Plan A. Be on the lookout for potential pitfalls or constraints that could impact the plan. Make sure you have an efficient report-back system in place which will monitor progress and quickly draw attention to any hurdles that crop up on your way (see next step). For instance, have new competitors entered the market? Is the current management structure hindering growth? Are important skills lacking? Stay open to emerging information, watch what happens and be prepared to change direction if you're not on the right path.

The point of all this planning is not to look for guaranteed certainty. It's hard to get it right 100 per cent of the time... almost right will do. Having a plan doesn't future proof your business. It doesn't mean you will never make mistakes or be reactive again. But it does help to reduce how often and severe your mistakes or reactions are.

Everybody has a plan until they get punched in the mouth.

– MIKE TYSON, Former Professional Boxer

CASE STUDY   Powerful people can slip up

According to a study led by Jennifer Whitson at the McCombs School of Business, powerful people are inclined to be more action-orientated and goal-focused than those who lack power (Whitson *et al*, 2013). While this tendency to take decisive action can be a driver of success, it can also bring problems in that people in leadership positions might struggle to see obstacles in the way of their goals. Whitson set up experiments in which participants were randomly assigned to either a powerful or powerless position. In one exercise, both groups were asked to imagine themselves either planning a trip to the Amazon rainforest or as an entrepreneur starting a flower-selling business. They were then presented with a number of statements to consider in their planning; half were advantageous ('you have prior experience visiting jungles') and half were goal-constraining ('you are afraid of some of the native animals'). On being asked to recall these statements later on, the researchers found that the high-power participants recalled significantly fewer constraining statements than the powerless subjects. The latter group remembered equal numbers of advantages and constraints. This led Whitson to conclude that people in positions of power may well have a harder time seeing obstacles or challenges (Collins, 2015).

If you are a manager or CEO, then, understand that your ability to identify unforeseen obstacles may be reduced. You might not have the mental tools to know what needs to be done to strengthen and implement the solution. Your workers, on the other hand, may have a more balanced view and can help you stay grounded. They can give you the prod you need to spot problems lurking in the mist. The best answer is to allow for routine collaboration with others who can point out risks and clear the way for decisions to be carried forward to the finish.

Step 5. Review and celebrate progress

How do you know for sure if the decision you made is the right one? Innovation thrives on feedback. A pivotal aspect of the implementation stage is the gathering of data to help you evaluate success, learning or failure. Checking these data as you go along helps you manage and modify your activities more or less in real time, to keep you moving in the right direction. If you've botched something up, you'll have time to remedy it while it's merely a nuisance, before it can evolve into a major problem. Work out transparent ways of measuring how well you're doing in pulling off your goals. As part of your review, you need to judge the effectiveness of your process (the plan) as well as your output (the solution). An idea that's a 'sure thing' could flunk because you target the wrong customer base, the technology is too costly, or project management is too erratic:

- **Process.** Was the plan carried out according to schedule? If the plan wasn't followed as expected then consider: Was the plan realistic? Were there enough resources to accomplish the plan? Was there an absence of systems or processes to support the change? Were there any aspects that were overlooked? Did any major errors occur? Were people resistant to it? Where did you waste time? If you think you'll be going for a similar goal again, work out what steps were successful and keep these elements as part of your revised implementation. Then modify all the things that you could have done better: for instance, allow more time for certain tasks, or get hold of extra funds so you don't fall short.

- **Output.** How you track the effectiveness of your decision depends on the type of solution you've put into action. Some solutions are based on numerical factors and involve comparing changes in quantities – for instance, the frequency of faulty products, or complaints/errors before and after the solution is implemented. In these cases, you can take a quantitative approach by collecting statistics and other mathematical information to check your results. Other solutions involve changes in people's attitudes, opinions, satisfaction or morale and these will benefit from a more qualitative approach. For example, we can solicit feedback from the people affected by the solution through a mixture of methods such as surveys or focus groups. Their responses will give us a sense of how successful they believe the solution is.

As the results start rolling in, it's important to take a step back and be objective on why your innovation strategy is or isn't working. What happened? What went well and what didn't? What will you do differently next time?

Take time to reflect on your achievements and celebrate them. Perfectionists often struggle to move forward because they're never happy with what they have accomplished. Learn to recognize the formula that brought success so you can repeat it again and again. Celebrating team wins is an ideal way to nurture a vibrant, 'family-like' and creative atmosphere; it gives people a chance to bond over shared activities and incites them to generate more ideas and make them happen. Simple things like an off-site team lunch or picnic will do the trick. Celebrate the progress made, not just the end results. In any innovation journey, there will naturally be project milestones along the way. These are good times to recognize how far you've come and celebrate the small triumphs.

Missed your goals? Don't get disheartened; even the most successful innovators blow it from time to time. Remember failure is a stepping stone, not a stumbling block. It was the disappointing performance of the ROKR E1, a collaboration between Motorola and Apple to integrate the iTunes music player into a mobile phone, that spurred Apple's decision to forge ahead with a smartphone of their own. It's our mistakes and let-downs that often teach us the most. The critical thing is to maintain a positive attitude. Creativity thrives in a climate of optimism, adventure and commitment, so stay focused on opportunities that fit your vision. Pin down what went wrong, find creative ways to adapt and rework your target to get you back in the game.

We do not learn from experience. We learn from reflecting on experience.

– JOHN DEWEY, in *How We Think* (1993)

CASE STUDY Reflect and learn

Research shows that taking time to reflect on our work leads to better performance. In a Harvard Business School field study, employees of outsourcing company Wipro were split into three groups: reflection, sharing and control (Di Stefano *et al*, 2014). In the reflection group, participants were given a paper journal and asked to spend the last 15 minutes of their workday reflecting on the day's activities and writing about the key lessons they had learnt. The sharing group did the same reflecting exercise for 10 minutes but also spent an extra five minutes explaining their notes to a colleague. Those in the control condition continued working until the end of the day. The result after 10 consecutive days was that the journaling workers had 22.8 per cent higher performance than those who did not reflect.

Regular self-assessment and learning is key to a 'be better' culture. It gives people an opportunity to pause and mentally sift through the day's experiences – by capturing the lessons learnt during the day, workers are able to carry them forward to improve their future productivity. So, it's important to monitor and reflect on the progress of your solution every so often. Don't just look at what's off track; let people celebrate the small wins as and when they occur. This provides a cumulative effect that builds confidence in people's ability to conquer a goal, making it more likely that the solution will be executed successfully.

Step 6. Repeat

Is reviewing the last stage of innovation or the first? Implementation isn't a strictly linear process; it's a continuous cycle of development. Launching your new idea in the marketplace or within your business is just the start. Allow your plan to keep evolving via an ongoing feedback loop. The Japanese philosophy of **Kaizen,** or continuous improvement, encourages you to make small changes to your work bit by bit. In time, these little changes accumulate to make a massive difference. Many companies get complacent and smug following a big victory, but one outstanding innovation isn't enough to deliver perpetual success; the momentum that led to innovation must be sustained so you are driven to test and implement more original solutions. As a creative leader, you should constantly be on the lookout for opportunities to do things better and fine-tune your business in response to changing conditions. Keep track of your internal and external environment with useful tools such as SWOT and PESTLE (Political, Economic, Social, Technological, Legal and Environmental) analyses. Ask questions such as:

- Why are we doing it this way?
- What's missing?
- What are we putting up with?
- Are we adapting to the changing needs of our customers or the market-place?
- What opportunities have we overlooked?
- In what ways are we running at risk?

Amazon is a prime example of an organization that uses its creative re-sources to continually develop the business. 'It's always day one' according to founder and CEO Jeff Bezos, and that's the mindset that promotes inno-vation at scale, making it part of the company's DNA. Rather than settling down in its comfort zone, the online retailer continues to expand and ex-periment on many fronts. Some of its most striking successes include Alexa (the company's AI-based digital assistant), 1-click purchase, Kindle, Amazon Marketplace (allowing third-party suppliers to sell via its platform), Prime (its membership programme), music streaming, TV/film content, and auto-mation of fulfilment through robots. I could go on.

The Amazon ethos is about innovating early and often without losing sight of core goals. Bezos said at Amazon's 2011 shareholder meeting: 'We are stubborn on vision. We are flexible on details.' The advice here is: have a plan, but stay nimble and agile so you can be ready to embrace new trends. Be committed but fluid. After all, how many plans have you seen through until the end no matter what? Again, don't look for perfection. Amazon hasn't always got it right first time. Its third-party seller business took three tries before it stuck.

Direction checklist: dos and don'ts

It's not easy to keep your thinking on the straight and narrow while in the throes of action. Are you behind your decision 100 per cent? Do you have the resources and competencies to manage ideas? Does your strategy reflect long-term goals balanced with an element of flexibility? Refer to the Direction checklist to help you reap the full benefits of your plan and become a true champion of innovation. Download it from **www.thinking.space**

Figure 10.4   Direction: dos and don'ts

DIRECTION CHECKLIST: DOs & DON'Ts

DO

- Believe in yourself and your team
- Take action
- Use the Decision Radar tool
- Consider if you have allocated resources to implement
- Set clear achievable goals with time frames
- Create an implementation plan
- Consider what might go wrong – have contingency plans
- Communicate the decision with stakeholders
- Reflect regularly on the decision and how it is progressing
- Monitor, document and share outcomes
- Remember you are unlikely to be 100% right – 'almost right' will do
- Use visual tools to manage your project
- Have regular progress meetings
- Connect the dots along the way
- Celebrate when a successful outcome is achieved
- Get behind your decision 100% – give it a chance
- Be passionate and purposeful
- EXECUTE YOUR PLAN

DON'T

- Miss the big picture – see the wood AND the trees
- Assume everyone understands the goal/objective – explain and clarify
- Let fear of making a bad judgement call hold you back
- Constantly look backwards
- 'Third' guess your decision
- Change your mind unless there is no choice
- Expect it to be easy – anything important rarely is
- Expect immediate results
- Be afraid to try and make the decision better
- Ignore any lessons that can be learnt from successes and failures

Key takeaways

Pursuing innovation means taking action. In this last step of the Solution Finder, you build a strong, communicable case for your idea and formulate a working plan for implementation. With belief and confidence in your solution, there'll be no stopping you! Stay fluid, track progress, keep innovating and celebrate success.

- **SMART Goals Canvas.** Use the SMART formula to clearly set out your goals so you have a visual concept of success to work from.

- **Building Solutions Canvas.** Search for ways to make your idea more robust, popular, attractive, beneficial, practical and/or effective. How can you build on the positive 'greens' and counteract the negative 'reds'?

- **Action Plan Canvas.** Outline a broad strategy of action steps and cite how obstacles will be overcome. Allocate your resources (money, time, people, equipment, skills), communicate to important stakeholders, and get going! Develop a feedback loop for reviewing performance and adapt for continuous innovation.

- **Direction Checklist.** Keep an eye on these helpful dos and don'ts as you action your idea and move closer to your innovative goals.

References

Bandura, A (1977) Self-efficacy: toward a unifying theory of behavioral change, *Psychological Review*, 84 (2), pp 191–215

Barsh, J, Capozzi, MM and Davidson, J (2008) [accessed 12 June 2018] Leadership and Innovation, *McKinsey Quarterly* [Online] https://www.mckinsey.com/business-functions/strategy-and-corporate-finance/our-insights/leadership-and-innovation

Bharadwaj Badal, S (2015) [accessed 5 June 2018] The Psychology of Entrepreneurs Drives Business Outcomes, *Gallup* [Online] http://news.gallup.com/businessjournal/185156/psychology-entrepreneurs-drives-business-outcomes.aspx

Cheshire, T (2011) [accessed 8 June 2018] In Depth: How Rovio Made Angry Birds a Winner (and What's Next), *Wired*, 7 March [Online] http://www.wired.co.uk/article/how-rovio-made-angry-birds-a-winner

Collins, M (2015) [accessed 15 June 2018] In One Ear and Out the Other: What Powerful People Do Differently, *Texas Enterprise*, 6 February [Online] http://www.texasenterprise.utexas.edu/2015/02/06/research-brief/one-ear-and-out-other-what-powerful-people-do-differently

Dewey, J (1933) *How We Think: A restatement of the relation of reflective thinking to the educative process*, D.C. Heath and Company, Boston, MA

Di Stefano, G *et al* (2014) [accessed 18 June 2018] Learning by Thinking: How Reflection Aids Performance, *Harvard Business School Working Paper No. 14-093* [Online] http://www.sc.edu/uscconnect/doc/Learning%20by%20Thinking,%20How%20Reflection%20Aids%20Performance.pdf

Lewin, K (1958) Group decisions and social change, in *Readings in Social Psychology*, ed GE Swanson, TM Newcomb and EL Hartley, Holt, Rinehart and Winston, New York

Malone-Kircher (2016) [accessed 5 June 2018] James Dyson on 5,126 Vacuums That Didn't Work – and the One That Finally Did, *New York Magazine*, 22 November [Online] http://nymag.com/vindicated/2016/11/james-dyson-on-5-126-vacuums-that-didnt-work-and-1-that-did.html

Matthews, G (2015) [accessed 12 June 2018] Goals Research Summary, *Dominican University of California* [Online] https://www.dominican.edu/academics/lae/undergraduate-programs/psych/faculty/assets-gail-matthews/researchsummary2.pdf

McKeown, M (2014) *The Innovation Book: How to manage ideas and execution for outstanding results*, FT Publishing, Harlow

Murphy, M (2010) [accessed 12 June 2018] The Gender Gap and Goal-Setting: A Research Study, *Leadership IQ* [Online] https://www.leadershipiq.com/blogs/leadershipiq/the-gender-gap-and-goal-setting-a-research-study

O'Neill, R (2009) [accessed 13 June 2018] Quitting Day Jobs to Make Smoothies, *Financial Times*, 10 April [Online] https://www.ft.com/content/a6b255be-25e7-11de-be57-00144feabdc0

Patterson, F *et al* (2009) [accessed 8 June 2018] Everyday Innovation: How to Enhance Innovative Working in Employees and Organisations, *Nesta* [Online] https://media.nesta.org.uk/documents/everyday_innovation.pdf

Rauch, A and Frese, M (2007) Let's put the person back into entrepreneurship research: A meta-analysis on the relationship between business owners' personality traits, business creation and success, *European Journal of Work and Organizational Psychology*, **16** (4), pp 353–85

Whitson, JA *et al* (2013) The blind leading: Power reduces awareness of constraints, *Journal of Experimental Social Psychology*, **49** (3), pp 579–82

Part Three
The End of the Beginning

11
Commit to 'thinking differently'

There are only two options regarding commitment. You're either in or out. There's no such thing as a life in between.

— ATTRIBUTED TO PAT RILEY, professional basketball executive/former coach and player

Putting it all together

Hey, congratulations! You're almost there; we're at the final section of the book. In Chapter 1, we explored what was currently going on in your thinking using the Decision Radar and uncovered all the potential areas of change. After that, we delved into the common biases and errors of the mind, looking at faulty programming and how it can mess up our thinking. We then went on a solution-finding journey where we defined our challenge, got out of our comfort zone and probed our ideas before acting on our best decision/s (see Figure 11.1).

Even if you didn't systematically work through the book and just dipped into the chapters that seemed most relevant to you, you'll have absorbed new knowledge and insights designed to make you a better, more creative decision maker. It's almost time we tested your thinking again with the Decision Radar to assess your 'new and improved' skills. But first, you need to understand a bit about reasoning.

What is reasoning?

Innovation needs good, strategic decision making – ideas must be generated, discussed, developed and ultimately put into action to make their mark on the world. The Solution Finder brings together the key skills of Understanding, Ideation, Analysis and Direction in the correct order, so we can make sure our thinking is relevant to the task we're working on. Underlying and

Figure 11.1 The Solution Finder Matrix

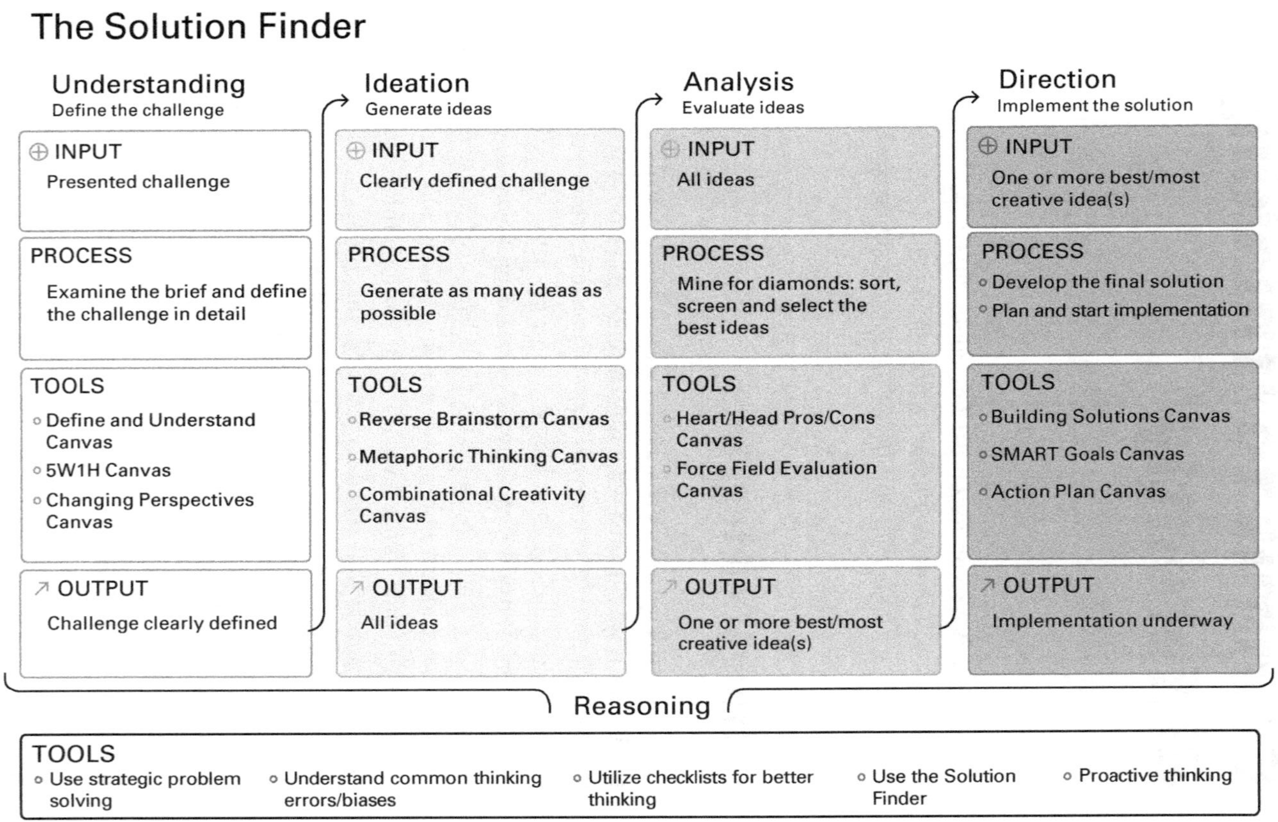

The Solution Finder

Understanding Define the challenge	**Ideation** Generate ideas	**Analysis** Evaluate ideas	**Direction** Implement the solution
⊕ INPUT Presented challenge	⊕ INPUT Clearly defined challenge	⊕ INPUT All ideas	⊕ INPUT One or more best/most creative idea(s)
PROCESS Examine the brief and define the challenge in detail	PROCESS Generate as many ideas as possible	PROCESS Mine for diamonds: sort, screen and select the best ideas	PROCESS Develop the final solution Plan and start implementation
TOOLS ○ Define and Understand Canvas ○ 5W1H Canvas ○ Changing Perspectives Canvas	TOOLS ○ Reverse Brainstorm Canvas ○ Metaphoric Thinking Canvas ○ Combinational Creativity Canvas	TOOLS ○ Heart/Head Pros/Cons Canvas ○ Force Field Evaluation Canvas	TOOLS ○ Building Solutions Canvas ○ SMART Goals Canvas ○ Action Plan Canvas
↗ OUTPUT Challenge clearly defined	↗ OUTPUT All ideas	↗ OUTPUT One or more best/most creative idea(s)	↗ OUTPUT Implementation underway

Reasoning

TOOLS
○ Use strategic problem solving
○ Understand common thinking errors/biases
○ Utilize checklists for better thinking
○ Use the Solution Finder
○ Proactive thinking

connecting these four stages, however, is Reasoning. It is through our reasoning that we turn ourselves into **proactive** thinkers with a conscious and focused approach to problem solving. Reasoning gets us thinking about *how* we think, rather than simply *what* we think (aka metacognition). Many of us are familiar with each type of thinking, but the key to creative success is using the right types at the right times. This keeps us in check to work through our challenge comprehensively, toning down our unproductive biases. The more we repeat good reasoning, the more it becomes a positive habit.

There's nothing ground-breaking about this approach. Many of the things discussed in this book might seem everyday common sense. Yet common sense is often not common; most people don't spend a great deal of time reorganizing their thoughts when they get creatively 'stuck'. Little effort is made to smash down bad thinking and the behavioural barriers that cause it. Sometimes the simplest, most 'obvious' things are the hardest to put into practice; but they become easier and more intuitive the more you do them.

Reasoning checklist: dos and don'ts

When you're proactive in how you think, you're equipped for any situation. Refer to the Reasoning checklist (Figure 11.2) to pull your thinking together as you aim to work more objectively, explore more creatively and plan more effectively. By switching on good reasoning, you put yourself and your team in a better position to create peak conditions for innovation. Over time, it will become easier to balance and orchestrate when you need to be generative, analytical and selective as you go about your daily business. Download the checklist from **www.thinking.space**

Decision Radar V2

Now that you're bursting to the brim with new knowledge and real-life experience of using the strategies in this book, visit **https://decisionradar. opengenius.com/** to complete the Decision Radar again, implementing the lessons you've learnt. It's recommended that you take the full test again for a more accurate profile, but if you're strapped for time, you can opt for the quick 10-minute test to get a general evaluation.

Review your new results. What do you notice? Which areas have developed into strengths and which still require attention? Green is good, so the aim is to work towards getting everything into the green area (the outer rings).

Figure 11.2 Reasoning: dos and don'ts

REASONING CHECKLIST: DOs & DON'Ts

DO

- Stay objective – keep an open mind
- Study metacognition – create a strategy behind your thinking
- Look for disconfirming evidence
- Share your ideas with others
- Be aware of the impact of self-image – ask who you are trying to impress
- Pay attention to what information you use
- Understand how you frame the problem changes the solution
- Be confident, but not overly so
- Listen to gut instinct early on in the decision-making process
- Use negative and positive thinking techniques
- Break the rules when appropriate
- Avoid the pressure caused by the 'group' or the 'masses'
- Be aware of the impact of the various types of bias
- Understand that common sense isn't common
- Embrace imperfection
- Think big, but break it down into small steps

DON'T

- Make conclusions too early
- Ignore your emotions
- Be selective in what you look for
- Make choices primarily because they are self-serving
- Fall foul of confirmation bias
- Avoid conflict or disagreement
- Fear failure
- Be trapped by false limits
- Be unduly optimistic about estimates
- Allow heuristics and assumptions to dictate the response on important decisions
- Follow hunches without testing them first
- Act now and think later
- Suffer from hyper-seriousness
- Ignore common thinking errors
- Always follow the rules
- Have a bias blind spot

This may take time. Often people overcompensate for their biases in certain areas, which in turn creates a deficiency in another. For good reasoning, you are looking for balance across the scale.

Take a moment to reflect and consider:

- What have you learnt overall? Note down the key lessons relating to your progress and any unique patterns that arise.

- What are you good at? List some ideas for how you can play to your strengths even more.

Figure 11.3 The Decision Radar

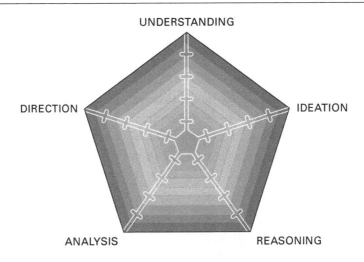

Figure 11.4 Example Decision Radar V2 profile

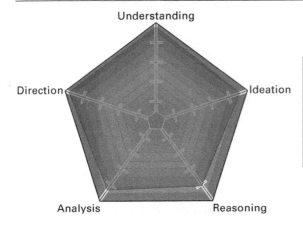

Test date:
03 July 2018 07:56

Understanding	96%
Ideation	92%
Reasoning	81%
Analysis	87%
Direction	97%

- What are your areas for development? Write down the actions you can take to improve your skills and overcome any blind spots.

- What can you take forward right now? Creative decision making is a big undertaking that requires a varied skill-set. Don't put yourself under pressure to excel at everything right away; instead, start with the areas that you're most interested in or that can make the biggest difference in your role, career or business.

In revisiting the Decision Radar, it's likely that you will show a stronger, more balanced approach in your decision-making abilities. Taking this time to reflect on your learning and improved skills will help to build greater self-awareness and confidence. It also provides a fitting opportunity to re-examine the areas that you'd like to work on some more.

Keep a record of your scores and the date you complete the radar. To get a greater return on your creative investment, you may want to complete the radar on a regular basis, say at the beginning of every quarter or following a big challenge. This allows you to observe how your decision making improves as you continue to build your understanding and experience of the creative process. For example, did working on one area help to enhance another?

The Decision Radar can be used twofold:

- **Individually.** To identify areas for improvement as a basis for a coaching conversation to set goals and actions.

- **In teams/organizations.** To gain a snapshot of group abilities. Managers and leaders can then ensure there is a balanced team created to work on problems, with collective strengths in all areas of decision making.

Commitment

The skills and strategies in this book will be of little value if you don't take time to develop them. We learn most by doing, so to truly master your thinking you need to commit to putting positive skills into action and eradicating the behaviour you don't want. By visually identifying your unique thinking patterns, the Decision Radar will help you choose strategies to manage your own everyday biases and those of your team. Sharpening up your thinking is a long-term endeavour which can be tough to maintain in the modern day, what with working longer hours to combat overflowing in-trays, data being thrown at us non-stop and the immediacy of communication technologies. We all know what it feels like to start something new all hyped up and full of zest, only to have our enthusiasm tail off once we're in the thick of things. To make a lasting impact, you'll need a tremendous amount of self-discipline. A formal or public commitment to change will help you continue to learn and grow and target your energy where it is needed most.

Commitment Traffic Lights

How can you make a commitment to be a better thinker? I devised the Commitment Traffic Lights exercise as an easy way to help you get going. For each aspect of your creative decision making, write down the following:

- What will you stop doing? (Red)
- What will you continue to do? (Amber)
- What will you start doing? (Green)

The Commitment templates for Understanding, Ideation, Analysis, Direction and Reasoning are available from **www.thinking.space**

Some people have trouble changing in a particular area because of their existing habits or preferences:

- Individuals who are strong in Ideation have no problems generating multitudes of ideas, but if they are comparatively weak in Analysis, they may never get around to evaluating those ideas or making a timely decision.

  Advice: A well-balanced, methodical process such as the Solution Finder will guide you towards a successful outcome.

- Someone who is overcautious and strongly analytical may need to set commitments to embrace mistakes as future lessons, avoid analysis paralysis and make greater use of divergent tools to gain confidence in their creativity.

  Advice: Remember, a mind, like a parachute, works best when open. Let yourself daydream to access your unconscious mind. Work on creating a safe culture for you and your team to have the time and space to come up with non-sensible ideas. Use the ideation techniques in this book to spark more ideas.

- Selective thinkers would do well to move away from confirmation bias and 'one right answer' thinking by extending the Ideation stage and involving others to challenge their thinking.

  Advice: Consider using both individual and group brainstorming to solicit different perspectives and confront any assumptions.

- Reactive thinkers can benefit by sleeping on things and using a systematic process (the Solution Finder) to delay decisions.

  Advice: Administering a well-constructed process is a key step towards proactive thinking and helps to squeeze out many of the thinking errors that might be present.

Figure 11.5   Reasoning commitment

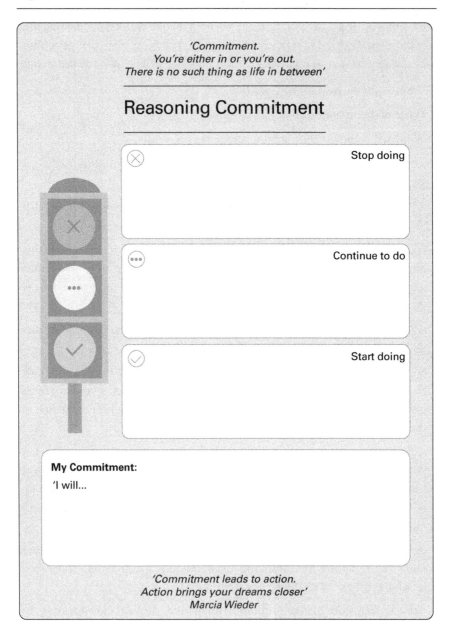

'Commitment.
You're either in or you're out.
There is no such thing as life in between'

Reasoning Commitment

Stop doing

Continue to do

Start doing

My Commitment:
'I will...

'Commitment leads to action.
Action brings your dreams closer'
Marcia Wieder

Maintain momentum on your commitment progress by checking in daily, weekly or monthly. It's worth reminding yourself frequently that every little bit you do now counts towards your creative growth.

Making time for creativity

Now, more than ever before, creativity is at a premium. But people often lament that they simply don't have time to be creative. Small business owners and managers commonly fall into this trap as their day-to-day responsibilities leave them feeling sapped. Time is the most precious resource we have and is by far the most difficult to manage. Making time to be creative is no different from making time for anything else. Without some form of time management, you can easily lose hours/days/weeks on the wrong things or end up running in circles, trying to do everything all at once. Worse, you might even delay getting started on the big projects that count, for example your next innovation. This is why forward-looking brands such as LinkedIn, 3M, Apple and Intuit give their workers free time to tinker with new ideas and work on side projects.

It's not unusual for creativity to get crowded out by pointless busywork or sudden distractions. According to research by Julian Birkinshaw and Jorden Cohen (2013) published in *Harvard Business Review*, knowledge workers spend an average of 41 per cent of their time on discretionary activities that offer little personal satisfaction and could be handled competently by others. Why? From a psychological standpoint, this occurs because the brain attempts to 'simulate' productive work by avoiding heavy projects and tackling lots of menial, low-value tasks instead. It cleverly tricks you into thinking that you're super busy, but the real work that produces measurable results remains undone.

Even if you're already creative and have piles of eyebrow-raising new ideas, without managing your time your ideas will never happen. To be successful, your creativity needs to be productive, otherwise you're just paying lip service. But how can you maximize your creativity without losing productivity? Life is never going to stop being 'crazy busy'. The biggest gains often come from the small investments you make, the minor tactics and habits that improve your efficiency across the gamut of professional disciplines and obligations, including creativity. Here are some strategies to help you walk the talk of creativity and deliver more innovative value using the time you have.

1. Find your focus

For years, businesses have put the ability to multitask on a pedestal as something to be revered in their workers. Many of us like to believe that it makes us more creative and helps us get a better handle on our responsibilities. Unfortunately, the science says 'not likely'. Teresa Amabile (2002) and her colleagues at Harvard Business School evaluated the daily work patterns of more than 9,000 individuals involved in projects that required creativity and innovation. Their key discovery? Focus and creativity are very closely connected. People are more likely to be creative if they're allowed to concentrate on just one activity for an uninterrupted length of time and when they collaborate with only one other person. By contrast, when people have disjointed days with lots of bitty tasks, e-mails, meetings and group discussions, their creative thinking pretty much goes to pot.

Think about this for a moment. When you stop to respond to an e-mail alert or tweet, or to speak to a colleague, it's not just a case of reading a message and writing back, or quickly giving your input. You also have to recover from the disruption and refocus your attention. Now I don't know about you, but I find it a real pain to get back into the swing of things once I'm interrupted, especially if I'm working on a creative task. If you need to make an important decision, bouncing around quickly from thought to thought or task to task doesn't give your mind a chance to make the best choices.

Take a look at your diary. Is it booked all day with back-to-back meetings and discussions? What about your to-do list? Is it crammed full of data demands and tasks that could probably be done by others? This is a major problem with executives and leaders and takes them away from the high-profile problems and innovative challenges where they're most needed. A good way to guard against this and other distractions, such as social networks and the like, is to schedule time specifically for creating and thinking. To be really creative, you have to be able go into the deepest darkest depths with your thinking, and this can only happen if you make time for it. I like to do a lot of my thinking when I'm driving, flying or on the train, when I know I'll have a decent amount of uninterrupted time. But you might prefer to book 'alone time' when you're still in the office. The actor and comedian John Cleese used to arrange an 'oasis' of quiet, uninterrupted time and space for generative thinking when he was writing for *Monty Python*, usually around 90 minutes, and consequently found that much of his sketch-writing was more creative than that of his comedic colleagues (Rawling, 2016).

> ## Personal R&D
>
> When scheduling 'time to think' into your weekly planner, consider it a meeting with yourself. Almost all companies have Research and Development (R&D) departments or units. If you don't like the idea of setting aside time to create or think, look at this as your own R&D time instead. Blocking out two hours on a Thursday afternoon for a bit of R&D doesn't sound too bad.

Concentrate all your thoughts upon the work at hand. The sun's rays do not burn until brought to a focus.

– ALEXANDER GRAHAM BELL, scientist and inventor of the telephone

Good days/bad days

A sensible way to go about finding your focus is to look at your good days and bad days during the week and organize your thinking within that. As reported in a survey by staffing firm Accountemps (2013), US executives believe Tuesday to be the most productive day for workers by far. Monday is seen as a 'catch-up' day following the weekend, with most scheduled meetings occurring then. Wednesday and Thursday follow jointly as the next productive days, and Friday lags behind as the weekend beckons. Does this pattern fit you? What are your good, bad and best days to think?

Best time to be creative

Do you know when your optimal creative time is during the workday? According to an article published in *TIME* magazine (2006), it comes down to whether you're a morning person or a night owl.

Morning person:

Table 11.1 The morning person's mental clock

TIME	ACTIVITY	
6 am to 8 am	Creativity	For the early riser, creativity peaks early in the wake cycle when there are fewer distractions and the inner critic is still asleep.

(continued)

Table 11.1 (*Continued*)

TIME	ACTIVITY	
8 am to 12.30 pm	Problem solving	The brain has warmed up and is primed for more analytical problem-solving activity.
12.30 pm to 2.30 pm	Low concentration	Routine tasks are best kept for early afternoon when the body's biological clock shifts, lowering concentration.
2.30 pm to 4.30 pm	Problem solving	Another productive time for analytical thinking.
4.30 pm to 8 pm	Rejuvenation	Refresh the mind with breaks, exercise and brain-building activities such as reading and puzzle solving.
Tip	It's a good idea to schedule appointments and meetings in the afternoon to keep the working memory free for higher-order thinking in the morning.	

Night owl:

Table 11.2 The night owl's mental clock

TIME	ACTIVITY	
8 am to 10 am	Low concentration	This is a bad time to focus on heavy tasks as the night owl struggles to wake up.
10 am to 12 pm	Creativity	The creative window occurs after they have shaken off the morning grogginess.
12 noon to 1 pm	Problem solving	Peak time for activities such as analysis and memorization.
1 pm to 3 pm	Low concentration	The mind enters its afternoon lull, so this is a good time for low-key tasks or engaging with colleagues.
3 pm to 6 pm	Rejuvenation	Renew and replenish energy with exercise or meditation. Stay mentally sharp by reading and doing light mental puzzles.
6 pm to 11 pm	Problem solving	Gear up to concentrate on the stuff that matters when the mind is better able to filter out distractions.

Whether you're a morning person or night owl, observe your daily patterns and note when you are at your most creative. If you find you have more insights and can think more broadly in the afternoon, then block out an hour of 'creative time' after lunch. Make sure your team knows that you're in a focused ideation session; shut down e-mail, close web browsers and set your phone calls to go to voicemail. No one can bug you then. Once you've had your private session, you can let yourself get caught up in e-mails, hang out on social networks or catch up with colleagues without feeling guilty because you won't have neglected your creative work.

2. Chunk it

In any innovation project you're likely to have a mixture of both creative and productive tasks. For a new website, tasks such as brainstorming ideas and designing the layout are creative, for example, but actions such as proofing and publishing web pages are more about being productive (DropTask, 2016). You can make the project more manageable by breaking tasks down into smaller, bite-sized chunks and then identifying whether productivity or creativity is best suited for each one.

Breaking tasks down in this way makes them much easier to tackle psychologically. When planning your day, aim to batch similar types of activities together and work on them in sequence, so you have fewer of those jarring start-up moments. Make sure you carve out time away from your usual activities for the more creative tasks, so you can brainstorm and let your imagination flow without being distracted by everything else on your plate.

When working through the Solution Finder process, chunk it into several 'mini' sessions so that people have time to take those all-important breaks to renew and incubate ideas. For instance, break up each stage over four days instead of trying to squeeze it into one day. To prevent energy plummeting, take frequent breaks and 'change the channel' after each break so that everyone's thinking can reset to work on a new technique or phase of the process. Remember to keep it short – four 30-minute sessions are better than a straight run of 120 minutes. This approach is mentally satisfying as it injects lots of quick wins into your process, fuelling your enthusiasm to take the next step, then the next, and so on.

ACTIVITY

Take a city break

Give yourself a minute and see if you can think of at least seven major cities that begin with the letter 'M'...

...This probably wasn't too difficult. There are lots of cities around the world beginning with this letter.

What cities did you think of?

Did you notice your mind starting to dry up after thinking of seven cities?

Now hold off on thinking about the problem until tomorrow morning. I promise that when you wake up you will probably be able to think of at least seven more cities beginning with the letter 'M'. This is because taking a break from the problem allows your unconscious to do its job. When you consciously work on a problem, you plant a seed in your mind. Then, when you back away this seed continues to grow, sending out roots into your brain and making more and more connections. Try it and see.

3. Daydream purposefully

Most people think of daydreaming as goofing off – something you might do during those lazy moments when you're supposed to be working. But I'm a firm believer that daydreaming is one of the most profound creativity tools you can get, and it's totally free to boot. Do your most creative, unusual ideas come when you're trying to force them during a long session in front of your computer? Or do they come when you're out walking, driving, in the shower or when you wake in the middle of the night? Well, you're not alone. This happens to all of us. It seems that inspiration bubbles up during times when we switch our minds off and aren't actually 'working'. Many of the world's greatest minds reached moments of true brilliance through the simple act of daydreaming. Here's just a few:

- Sir Isaac Newton and his discovery of gravity and the theory of orbit;
- Thomas Edison and his countless inventions (including the working light bulb);
- Albert Einstein and his theory of relativity;
- Wolfgang Mozart and his legendary musical compositions.

Einstein was very outspoken about his love of daydreaming – or what he called his **'thought experiments'**. He even credited these 'experiments' for giving him the ideas that led to his greatest works. It's said that he came up with the theory of relativity by picturing himself sitting on a beam of light and imagining the journey he was going to take through the universe. Edison had his own unique way of harnessing the power of daydreaming. He would hold ball bearings in each hand, sit down in a comfortable chair and doze off. Just as he was relaxing into sleep, his hands would loosen their grip and the ball bearings would fall to the floor, waking him up. Immediately after waking, Edison would note down any ideas that had come to him (Gilliard, nd). The great Austrian composer Mozart would daydream about music on long walks through the countryside, imagining sounds that would become the basis of his powerful compositions (Fries, 2009).

There's no reason why we can't benefit from daydreaming and thought experiments in the same way as Einstein or Mozart. Our creative thinking is often influenced by what we're used to in real life and what we see around us. The beauty of daydreaming is that it gives us permission to let go of the reality we're used to, so that the ideas we generate are likely to be more extraordinary and engaging. There have been more than a few occasions when I've struggled for hours – days even – to solve a problem without any success. That's when I know I need to stop aggressively forcing myself to find an answer, and instead find a way to relax and unwind, letting my mind drift. Sure enough, a creative solution soon blossoms, seemingly out of nowhere and when I least expect it.

How to make daydreaming 'work'

Whenever I try to convey the benefits of daydreaming to people, I often get a remark along the lines of: 'If daydreaming is so effective, why aren't I coming up with brilliant ideas all the time? I'm always staring out of the window!' And my answer is simple. As with all good creativity techniques, daydreaming has to be focused, goal-orientated and deliberate to be successful. Usually we daydream without any preparation and without a goal in mind. But daydreaming for creativity is more than just relaxing, being passive or placing the problem on the mental backburner. The key to using daydreaming as a creativity technique is to put the legwork in beforehand and hold an awareness of what you want to achieve.

The science of daydreaming

Thanks to its reputation as a time-squandering and self-indulgent activity, daydreaming at work is usually out of bounds. But the tide is changing, and support for daydreaming as a tool for creativity is growing all the time. Over years of studies, scientists have found that our brains have two separate modes – an executive network and a default network. When we're doing active creative work, high-level problem solving, getting important stuff done or learning something new, we are in 'focused' executive mode (see 'Find your focus' above). When we are relaxing, gardening, doodling or walking, our brain assumes the 'diffuse' default mode. This is when we're not really controlling the direction of our thoughts and our mind starts to mull over the past or speculate on the future. In this wandering state of mind, we begin to visualize and make our own spontaneous connections and ideas.

Building on this research, Kalina Christoff and colleagues (2009) at the University of British Colombia discovered that more areas of the brain fire up when we daydream than when we're engaged in vigorous, conscious thought. The researchers discovered that, in addition to the default network, the brain's executive network is simultaneously engaged when we daydream. Prior to this, scientists had supposed that the two networks operated on an either-or basis – when one was activated the other was thought to be dormant. There we have it – daydreaming sends the brain into overdrive! Far from being vacant, our brain is at its busiest and most creative when allowed to daydream. Next time you're fretting over a sticky problem, distract yourself, take a 'brain break' and allow the magic to happen in the background.

Step 1. Do your homework   Either alone or with your team, take your problem and look at all the information relevant to it, exploring all the possible solutions you can think of by using more active ('conscious') creativity techniques, such as reframing the problem, challenging your assumptions and reverse brainstorming. This works to brief and program the deeper parts of your mind so your unconscious has lots to think about. When you use a metaphor to solve a problem, you're effectively going into a daydream, and tools such as the canvases in this book will help put you and/or your team in a different state of mind without you even realizing it.

Step 2. Switch off Once your prep is done, get away from the pressure of the problem by doing something else for 30 to 60 minutes. Consciously turn the issue over to the active powers of the unconscious mind, then go outside or do something enjoyable and relaxing. Let your thoughts meander in solitude while all the information 'incubates'. Encourage your team to do the same – send them to a coffee shop for a change of scenery or to find somewhere peaceful where they can be free to daydream about the problem.

In doing this, you set the unconscious mind free to roam productively, play with concepts and generate new insights and ideas – ones that you might never come across while tackling your challenge directly. By giving your mind the space to go about its business, it will do the imaginative work for you.

This kind of purposeful daydreaming is a great way to push through a project when you're stuck, or when you have too many options. There are masses of ways to get into the right state of mind for daydreaming:

- Take a head-clearing walk in the park or around the block
- Listen to music
- Sit on a bench somewhere
- Visit a museum or art gallery
- Have a bath or shower
- Ride a bicycle or go for a drive
- Do some gardening
- Go to a café
- Doodle
- Go fishing
- Run errands
- Meditate
- Lie awake in the morning or night
- Clear up your desk or wash the office cups (yes, even that!)

I like to do a lot of my 'mind wandering' when I'm out travelling, whether I'm on a train, on a plane or in a car. Other people prefer to take a stroll. For example, Charles Darwin liked to take long walks around London. Inventor Thomas Edison would fish off the end of his dock for an hour almost every day, even though he wasn't very good at it. He never even used bait. When asked about it later in life, he admitted that he didn't do it to catch fish. His response was, 'Because when you fish without bait, people don't bother you and neither do the fish. It provides me my best time to think' (Kothari, 2016).

Fishing worked for Edison. It's well worth experimenting to find what works best for you. While daydreaming, allow ideas to percolate and filter through. Always – and this is really important – pay close attention to any ideas that come up and note them down in a notepad or record them using your mobile phone/dictaphone. It's no good having an awesome idea and then immediately forgetting it!

Use your senses (mindfulness)

Creative thinking requires a deliberate shift into a new zone. A good trick for creating the right mental climate for ideas to fizz through is to use **mindfulness**. This is the art of paying careful attention to the details of the present moment, without judgement. Don't be scared off by how 'new age' and unbusiness-like it sounds. Studies show that mindfulness meditation stimulates divergent thinking to open your mind to original ideas (Colzato, Ozturk and Hommel, 2012) and increases cognitive flexibility, which is critical to the creative process (Baas, Nevicka and Ten Velden, 2014). Mindfulness helps you develop your inner sensitivity and awareness so that you're open to even the slightest suggestion of an idea. If you're at home or in the office and agonizing over a problem that seems intractable, go on a short excursion to help you tune out, preferably somewhere in nature. Or set aside five minutes to sit in a quiet room. Think 'mindfulness'. Take a leaf out of Leonardo da Vinci's book and get in touch with your senses to make the experience richer and more engaging. Look around you with the eyes of an artist, hear through the ears of a musician, feel with the sense of a sculptor, smell with the nose of a perfumer and taste with the palate of a chef. This exercise heightens your awareness in just 20 seconds and brings you into focus to look at your situation with lots more clarity. Take a notebook and record the things you notice. What ideas do these things stimulate as you relate them to your challenge? What new connections come to mind? Is the problem the real problem? If not, consider whether you need to redefine it. The more you train yourself to be aware of what you are hearing, seeing, feeling and thinking, the more data you'll be transferring into your unconscious thinking system. The result? More associations and ideas.

The greatest geniuses sometimes accomplish more when they work less.
– ATTRIBUTED TO LEONARDO DA VINCI, Italian Renaissance artist,
scientist, engineer and all-round genius

Key takeaways

Commit to seeking, developing and sustaining the capacity to think differently using the knowledge and tools you've been given throughout the chapters in this book. Good reasoning skills are the only way to become aware of your own cognitive biases, and with awareness comes the ability to do something about them and make better-quality decisions. With some careful time management and a healthy respect for breaks and daydreaming, you and your team can infuse creativity into your day-to-day work.

- **Reasoning Checklist.** Bring more strategy into your problem solving and keep your objectivity in check with these comprehensive dos and don'ts.

- **Decision Radar V2.** Re-do the Decision Radar assessment to see how you've progressed in carrying out the teachings in the book. Take the opportunity to reflect on your learning and improved skills, as well as to re-examine the areas you'd like to continue working on.

- **Commitment Traffic Lights.** Avoid procrastination by making a formal commitment to positive change. For each aspect of your decision making, what will you stop doing (Red), what will you continue to do (Amber), what will you start doing (Green)?

- **Got no time for creativity?** Make it! Your brain has a natural ability to solve problems. Tap into both the executive (focused) and default (diffused) powers of your mind to tackle complex challenges:

  - Find your focus by scheduling quiet, undisturbed time for thinking in your busy work calendar.

  - Use purposeful daydreaming to slow down, switch off your conscious mind and allow new ideas to bubble up. Imitate Leonardo da Vinci and use your senses. Become mindful of what you're seeing, hearing, tasting, smelling and feeling. When you relax your mind and body, you can visualize more vividly, stir up your imagination and create better with your thoughts. Remember to note down your ideas afterwards!

References

Accountemps (2013) [accessed 10 July 2018] Workplace Productivity Peaks on Tuesday, *Robert Half*, 16 December [Online] http://rh-us.mediaroom.com/2013-12-16-Workplace-Productivity-Peaks-On-Tuesday

Amabile, TM *et al* (2002) Time Pressure and Creativity in Organizations: A Longitudinal Field Study, Harvard Business School Working Paper No. 02-073

Baas, M, Nevicka, B and Ten Velden, FS (2014) Specific mindfulness skills differentially predict creative performance, *Personality and Social Psychology Bulletin*, **40** (9), pp 1092–106

Birkinshaw, J and Cohen, J (2013) [accessed 5 July 2018] Make Time for the Work That Matters, *Harvard Business Review*, September [Online] https://hbr.org/2013/09/make-time-for-the-work-that-matters

Christoff, K *et al* (2009) Experience sampling during fMRI reveals default network and executive system contributions to mind wandering, *Proceedings of the National Academy of Sciences of the United States of America*, **106** (21), pp 8719–24

Colzato, LS, Ozturk, A and Hommel, B (2012) Meditate to create: the impact of focused-attention and open-monitoring training on convergent and divergent thinking, *Frontiers in Psychology*, **18** (3), p 116

DropTask (2016) [accessed 11 July 2018] Productivity vs. Creativity [Blog], 8 June [Online] http://blog.droptask.com/productivity-vs-creativity/

Fries, A (2009) *Daydreams at Work: Wake up your creative powers*, Capital Books, Herndon, VA

Gilliard, M (nd) [accessed 13 July 2018] Thomas Alva Edison, *Innovation-Creativity.com* [Online] https://www.innovation-creativity.com/thomas-alva-edison.html

Kothari, A (2016) *Genius Biographies*, Notion Press, Chennai

Rawling, S (2016) *Be Creative – Now!*, Pearson, Harlow

TIME (2006) [accessed 11 July 2018] Making the Most of Your Day, 16 January [Online] http://content.time.com/time/covers/20060116/pdf/Day_Night.pdf

12
Creative leadership

Leadership is the art of giving people a platform for spreading ideas that work.
— SETH GODIN, American Author and Former Dot Com Business Executive

Innovation is a core leadership skill

Big or small, young or old, all companies must find a way to inspire creativity and nurture it within their ranks. Without a healthy and consistent supply of ideas, most organizations will pass their sell-by date for usefulness. It's no joke; the pressure to stay current is always on, making innovation a top priority for leaders. The creative approach can be different for every business, but ultimately the goal is to get people working together to deliver new ideas and solve problems. People make change happen, and so your success as a first-rate leader hinges on building a culture where innovation is everybody's job, from Sam in HR to Louise in Accounting.

Innovation isn't only about new paradigm-shifting products, services or technologies, it's about any new idea that can help you do things better, whether it's cutting costs through more efficient production methods, dreaming up ways to increase brand value or deciding what jobs need to be done within each department. Kaizen (continuous improvement) is just as relevant as disruption. Creative leadership means empowering people to take on playful, daring, idea-hungry and solution-finding behaviours in their day-to-day work so the company can move fast towards a shared purpose. Having the right tools and processes, such as the Solution Finder, is super-important, but innovation won't blossom to its full potential without an overall culture or environment that supports it. Are you a team of one? Not the CEO? No matter, you can still lead creatively in your department, with your co-workers in other functional units or within your sphere of influence. In practical terms, 'flying the flag' for innovation means:

- **Championing a grand mission and vision.** The ability to set a meaningful direction for the business that excites others, rather than bland statements that are long on puffed-up platitudes and short on inspiration.

- **Pulling insights from failures as well as successes.** Creativity is given the space it deserves through risk taking and experimentation. Any failure is a learning opportunity to create better results for future choices.

- **Making play a corporate priority.** Injecting fun into workplace practices is a key way to help creativity flow. The more you play, the more it is accepted as a cultural norm.

- **Being a source of optimism.** Shifting attitudes to change from antagonism to anticipation. Maintaining a can-do spirit. A consistently positive leader sees the good in everything and overcomes moods to keep the team moving forward.

- **Ushering in support systems to enable experimentation.** Supplementing the formal organizational structure with informal systems and networks that allow information sharing and cross-fertilization of ideas across work units.

The end game

The biggest challenge in creative leadership is motivating people to want to be involved in innovation. Many people don't see themselves as creative, or they feel it's not their job to have new ideas; and to be honest, organizational systems are often designed in a way that stifles creativity rather than making it happen. One of the most powerful ways to inspire and focus people towards positive change is to connect to your higher meaning – the purposeful mission and big-picture vision you hold for the company or a specific innovation project. Your mission is what you are doing today; your vision is your ambition for the future.

Work that matters (mission)

Why do you do what you do? What is the overriding purpose of your business? This should be about more than money; your business must have a meaning that people can embrace, share and believe in. According to a survey by American Express (2017) , 62 per cent of millennials in the United States,

UK, France and Germany want to make a positive difference in the world, and 74 per cent believe that the successful businesses of the future will have a genuine sense of purpose that resonates with people. This offers valuable insight for creative leaders in how to engage their workers for the long term. Leadership needs to make a convincing case that working for the organization will provide meaning and value to each person, and that they have a cause worth pursuing over and above the extrinsic rewards they get from the job.

A well-defined mission represents the soul of the organization/team and generates power. For example, LEGO's (2012) mission is 'to inspire and develop the builders of tomorrow', while Google (nd) promises to 'organize the world's information and make it universally accessible and useful'. Your own mission acts as an anchor for workers to dedicate their creative efforts to tasks and activities that align with the goals and values of the company. As a team, explore your strengths, values and passions to get to the crux of why you exist (Mühlfeit and Costi, 2017):

- **Strengths.** What are your strengths as a team/company? Does anything stand out as your unique superpower? Think of your strengths in terms of the product offerings or services you provide, the level of talent you have and the resources at your disposal. Are you masters of engineering excellence? Can you boast a whip-smart sales team? Or, like British retail giant Tesco, is creating value for customers your thing?

- **Values.** What are your team/company values? These are the principles, philosophies and positive intentions that you stand for and that help you connect to your customers and workers at a deeper level. To get a sense of your core values, ask your team, 'What's important to us?' and pay attention to the language they use. Are you all about 'having fun' or are you more interested in speed, diversity, integrity, teamwork or entrepreneurial spirit? Also think about the image you present to the public. When people look at your business, what would you like them to see? For Ford, 'quality is job one' (Petersen, 2007), as emphasized in former ad campaigns, while Virgin (nd) has insatiable curiosity, heartfelt service and smart disruption as part of its underlying philosophy.

- **Passions.** What are you passionate about as a team/company? Consider why you are in this business in the first place. What ignited your interest in starting or working for the company? Your passion tells people why they should do business with you; it's the infectious energy that makes the brand come alive and which others can see and feel. Are you passionate about building an empire, sustainability, innovation, people or entertainment? Find out what drives your company and embrace it.

'Move' people (vision)

What does success look like? Where do you want to be in three, five or ten years' time? You cannot expect your team to be innovative if they don't know where they are headed. With a clear understanding of the past and present, a creative leader paints an inspiring and distinctive picture of the future vision that excites others to follow. There is a sense that you are all embarking on a journey or adventure together. Your chosen horizon should be grounded on more than maximizing shareholder value, profits or any other financial target. That's not going to get people leaping out of bed to seize the day. Make it memorable. Make it bold. 3M's (2018) vision is 'to advance every company, enhance every home and improve every life'. And Amazon (nd) aims 'to be the Earth's most customer-centric company, where customers can find and discover anything they might want to buy online'. Ask 'What if?' questions to bring to light what you really want innovation to do for your company. For instance, 'What if we had a million pounds to spend on our solution?' or 'What if we scrapped our current business model?'

Striving for a better future will always involve change – people are more willing to accept the challenges ahead when you empower them to use their own creativity to forge a path forward. This participation can't come about if your vision is not clear or transparent. It's up to leaders to demonstrate that there is a bigger risk in standing still and that organizations with no vision for the future are the ones destined to stagnate.

Be strategic

The mission and vision are the starting point for strategic plans and objectives. You have your internal mission that defines your work and *'why'* you exist; and then you have the external vision that represents *'where'* you are going and what you intend to do. Together, these help you to set priorities and devise strategies to reach your goals. Engage others in co-inventing the detail of the end game and a roadmap of how to get there. Once you have strategies in place, you and your team can focus your energy on delivering the vision and mission without constantly trying to figure out what comes next.

CASE STUDY   The living company

Why do so many companies die young? Arie de Geus (1999), a business executive at Royal Dutch Shell, studied companies that lived longer than most, ranging from 100 to 700 years, including names such as DuPont, Mitsui and Siemens. His team observed that prosperous, long-standing organizations tend to operate as a living community of people held together by clear values and a strong sense of identity, rather than merely focusing on the bottom line. Even in the most widely diversified companies, workers feel like parts of a whole. On top of this, companies that last are very good at 'management for change' (de Geus, 1997). There is a high level of tolerance for experimentation, which creates the space for more innovation and learning. The opposite of the 'living company' is the 'economy company', which exists only to make money. Are profits or people your purpose? If it's the former, then you might not make it to the next decade.

Freedom to fail... and learn

We all know that in the business world there are hits and misses; if you're aiming for a hit, you're bound to miss some of the time. That's just the way it goes – any innovator will tell you. Creativity thrives in a climate of adventure and experimentation; a climate fed by risk. It's not easy to embrace risk and take chances that could potentially lead to error. Not only is implementing new ideas nerve-wracking, but the process of innovation can distract people from their day-to-day work and the 'normal' activities of the business.

If you're not failing every now and again, it's a sign that you're not trying anything very innovative.

> – ATTRIBUTED TO WOODY ALLEN, American Screenwriter and Director

The big, bad unknown

At a corporate level, fear of the unknown is blatantly widespread. Big companies thrive on predictable outcomes; they need to be able to forecast the future to make optimal strategic decisions. And this is where the problem lies. CEOs can very quickly shoot down new and fresh ideas that might lead the organization to places it's never been before. There's a reluctance to play around with the business model or aspects of strategy that have worked well for them since the 90s: 'If it ain't broke, don't fix it'. Most companies are still on some illusory search for the 'holy grail' of ideas – a brand spanking new idea that also brings the reassurance of having been tried and proven in the past. That's never going to happen. New ideas are risky. They take you into uncharted territory. Oddly enough, fear of the unknown usually gets worse the *more* successful you become. The more accomplishments you've achieved, the higher your footing, and the more you stand to lose by making a mistake.

Learning from failure

Although we hate failure, it's our mistakes that often teach us the most. Some of the most venerated people and organizations are the ones that take chances, get things wrong and bounce back to try again. Pixar is flying high right now, but it acknowledges that there was a 16-year journey of experiments and mess-ups – including a major corporate shift from making computers to creating commercial animations – before the company got around to successfully releasing its first full-length movie, *Toy Story*. When Pfizer first tested a new drug to treat high blood pressure and angina, the results turned out to be far less effective than researchers predicted. In an interesting twist, however, male subjects in the clinical trials reported that it had one particular side effect. Instead of binning the drug, Pfizer flipped their strategy and the so-called 'potency pill' Viagra was born. Bill Gates' first venture with Microsoft co-founder Paul Allen was Traf-O-Data 8008 – a device that could take a look at traffic tapes and then process them into useful data. It never took off. However, Allen (2014) looked back at the experience with a positive mindset: 'Even though Traf-O-Data wasn't a roaring success, it was seminal in preparing us to make Microsoft's first product a couple of years later.'

For these innovators, failure was a stepping stone instead of a stumbling block and helped them forge their own unique path. We could all benefit by seeing it in the same way. If we're more concerned about getting it right first time, we'll bypass the playful, imaginative phase of the creative process. We won't spend time reframing the problem to find more answers, challenging assumptions, changing perspectives or testing different ideas. All of these techniques can bring up errors, but these errors might also take our thinking somewhere completely new. The best thing we can do is learn from our blunders; but to do this we have to free ourselves to make them in the first place. Do you allow yourself to make mistakes? How tolerant are you of your team making mistakes? As a leader you need to learn to see the positive side of failure:

1 Failure is a sign that you're diverging from the well-trodden route. You're pushing the boundaries; and that's a good thing.

2 Failing at one thing means that you learn what doesn't work. We all learn by trial and error, not trial and rightness! The important thing is to reflect on the lessons learnt from failure so that you don't make the same mistakes again.

3 Each failure gives you an opportunity to try a new approach.

How to manage mistakes

Errors are inevitable and necessary to make creative progress, but how can we manage them? To make it easier to stomach, try calling failure something different in your organization. For example, Four Seasons Hotels & Resorts chose to stop labelling something as a failure or a mistake, preferring to use the term 'glitch' instead (Gower, 2015). Each department holds a daily 'Glitch Report' meeting, in which team members discuss the previous day's mishaps, looking at how to correct course and achieve the best possible outcomes. A failure or mistake can sound final, as if it can't be recovered from, but a glitch is an opportunity to identify areas to improve.

Aim for a 'no blame' culture and empower your team. Obviously in some industries, such as medicine, there is less room for error, but empowerment can still be a powerful tool for finding unconventional approaches. Acceptance of failure is a key cultural element of enlightened brands such as Pixar, Amazon, Dyson and Google. The leadership at animation company Pixar prizes an environment where employees know they can fail without fear of dismissal or embarrassment. Co-founder and president Ed Catmull talks pragmatically about the subject: 'We will fail, and we need to make it safe for you to do that. If you get over the embarrassment, you become more creative because it frees you up' (Graham, 2015). Give your co-workers the time and space to grow their skills, bring more ingenuity to their work and 'be all they can be'. Encourage them to take managed risks. To get the best out of your team – especially the highly creative types – set aside rigid, uncompromising job descriptions and focus on broad guidelines that can be adapted to each person and the context they're working in. Specify goals, not methods, so people can go ahead and raise their game. By all means, set the boundaries for your empowered workers ('This is as far as you can go'), but understand that you can't control every variable and eventuality of every decision or task.

Yes, they *will* make mistakes. Maybe lots of them. But that's something that you will have to learn to cope with. Mistakes can occur for all sorts of reasons, such as poor prioritization, conflict with other projects/within teams, negligence, not collecting enough data, and so on. Many times these can be traced back to the common thinking biases (selective, reactive and assumptive thinking), such as misdirected confidence in a certain solution. Let's say the worst happens – you annoy shareholders, waste funds or damage the company's reputation. What then? A major loss can be devastating for individuals and teams alike. These times call for leaders who can see the positive side of failure, take stock of the situation and get everyone back on track and moving again. If your people are worried about getting it right first time, they'll steer clear of any exploration or testing of different ideas. Following the steps in this book will go some way in helping to minimize the possibility of failure, but please understand that there will always be uncertainty involved when leaving your comfort zone. Use these strategies to manage risk:

- **Make small bets.** Consider your personal attitude to risk. How comfortable are you with getting things wrong? You don't have to bet the whole company. Place the odd bet on a small idea every now and then and see what comes of it.

- **Reframe failure.** Call it a 'glitch' or something else less painful-sounding.

- **Risk vs reward.** For each big idea, ask yourself: What might happen if you take a chance on it? What might happen if you don't?

- **No such thing as a 'fail'.** What would you do if you knew you could not fail? Take steps towards it. If you knew you couldn't get things wrong, would that change your attitude to experimentation?

- **What could go wrong?** Use force field evaluation and the court challenge (Chapter 9) to find the blind spots and consider all the things that could go awry with a project at the start. Build mitigating strategies into your plan to prevent them happening.

- **Share learning.** Get together with your team to talk about past 'failed' projects and what you can learn from them for the future. What were the silver linings? Reflect on the risks you took and whether it was worth the experience in hindsight. This helps to make the topic of failure less awkward for the team.

- **Worst-case scenario.** What's the worst that can happen? Prepare yourself for any losses by making contingency plans. Often this helps you realize that the anticipated failure is ultimately 'not that bad' and can be managed.

- **Don't blame.** If a project fails, find out what went wrong and why, but don't reproach the people involved. Nonetheless, if the same mistakes keep recurring, make it clear that ongoing poor performance will need to be dealt with.

- **Fess up.** Everyone makes mistakes, including leaders. When you can acknowledge your slip-ups as well as your successes, people will admire your honesty and forgive you for them. Owning up to your mistakes makes you more human and encourages others to be open about sharing their bloopers too, rather than trying to mask them.

- **Learn fast.** Check progress at each stage of an innovation project as well as at the end. Celebrate the things that are working and fix the parts that can be done better as you go along. If you monitor projects closely, problems can be quickly spotted and taken care of before things spiral out of control.

Make play a priority

Like daydreaming, most people look down on play in the workplace. They see it as childish, time-wasting and frivolous. There's a general attitude that if you're playing then you're not getting down to the real business of working. This is a real shame because play is synonymous with fun – and fun is one of the most powerful idea generators around. It's by fooling about that you get to try out different options, figure out what works and what doesn't. Through play you can rearrange things, turn them inside out and upside down; you can look for hidden analogies and challenge your assumptions. People who are enjoying themselves will always come up with more ideas than those who take themselves too seriously.

I'm not saying you shouldn't ever be serious during the creative process. Being level-headed has its value when you're ready to take your ideas and lessons, evaluate them and make them workable in reality. Play and practicality aren't mutually exclusive concepts – they both have a role to play when you're innovating; but play comes first! In the early stages of creativity, it's vital for ideas to flourish. You're not really creating when you're carrying out a pre-set strategy, hammering through your to-do list or worrying about the cost of this or that, are you?

Letting go of a serious-minded attitude and having fun isn't always as easy as it sounds. It's something that I see people really struggle with during my workshops on creative thinking and applied innovation. Sometimes the problem isn't necessarily with you as an individual, it's with your environment. In a profit-driven workplace (and most are), there's usually little time for random experiential processes that may or may not benefit the bottom line. A study by staffing firm Robert Half International (2012) revealed that a surplus of red tape is holding businesses back from being more innovative. Of the 1,400 chief financial officers interviewed, 24 per cent blamed excessive bureaucracy as the top creativity killer, and 20 per cent said being bogged down with daily tasks and putting out fires is holding them back from coming up with new concepts. Yet creativity thrives in an atmosphere that's free from such pressure. If you're a business owner or manager, you're in an excellent position to look at ways of establishing a more creativity-friendly work environment.

The fun factor

A psychological study at the University of Western Ontario found that upbeat work environments can spur creativity (Nadler, Rabi and Minda, 2010). The researchers manipulated happy and sad moods with help from music and video clips. They discovered that those in a positive frame of mind were more flexible in their thinking and had wider perspectives, fuelling their ability to tackle tricky problems creatively. Researcher Ruby Nadler says, 'Generally, a positive mood has been found to enhance creative problem-solving and flexible, yet careful thinking'. So, people who watch funny videos on the internet at work aren't necessarily wasting time. This is great news for employers who want to stimulate non-stop creativity in their workplace.

Be honest with yourself – do you go out of your way to encourage fun, humour and play within your team, or do you crush it? To have fun with your team, you'll need to relax and lower your guard a bit. Many leaders find this difficult, preferring to keep a distance. However, you won't lose respect by introducing a bit of play into the creative process; if anything, your team will respect you more and the brilliant ideas that come of it will be well worth it. Take inspiration from leaders such as Anita Roddick, who in 2003 announced to her Body Shop financial investors, 'Well, I think we're not going to grow next year. We just want to have more fun' (Csikszentmihalyi, 2003). It's not about being childish but 'childlike'. The most highly creative people are children after all.

CASE STUDY   'Serious fun' at Virgin

Fun is a key vehicle through which the imagination can be geared up and explored. When you're inspired and happy, your brain is free from the temporary niggly concerns that hold back fresh ideas, and it becomes easier to take risks. No one is more aware of this than Richard Branson, founder of the Virgin Group and acclaimed business magnate. He rarely wears the conventional suit and tie, he organizes outrageous launch events, and even goes as far as to perform risky stunts for the media. As *Time Magazine* wrote, 'Branson seems hell-bent on making sure that everybody, but everybody, is having as much fun as he is' (Branson, 2011). Branson goes to great lengths to make sure his colleagues are enjoying themselves. He regularly writes people letters to tell them what's going on and encourages them to send him their own ideas. He also builds fun into things such as product launches, celebrations and meetings. On Virgin Atlantic's first flight, the plane was filled with conjurors and entertainers, and champagne flowed abundantly. People danced in the aisles to the latest hits. The film *Airplane* was shown and the cabin crew started a ritual of handing out choc ices during the film. This has become a fun tradition whenever a new route is opened up, and Virgin workers clamour to be part of it (Armstrong, 2008). The Virgin Group's passion for play is how they set their parameters for working together and giving great customer service, and they've successfully carried it into a jumble of radically unrelated industries.

Practical play

People love to work hard when they get to play hard too. This may especially be the case with younger workers; the results from a survey of 2,000 UK employees carried out by online HR specialists BrightHR in collaboration with psychological wellbeing consultants Robertson Cooper indicate that more millennials expect fun to be an integral part of their lives at work than any other demographic (BrightHR and Robertson Cooper, 2015). In addition, people who took part in fun workplace activities had much higher mean scores for creativity (55) than those who had not taken part in a fun activity in the past six months (33), regardless of their age. The following tactics are great for injecting more fun into your work environment.

Have a laugh together

Humour bolsters creative output. Why? First, getting into a humorous frame of mind loosens you up so you can widen your thinking. The release of tension triggered by humour produces enkephalin flow in the brain, and this sets you up to be open to new and sudden mental shifts and ideas. Second, it allows you to take things less seriously. This is key. If you can poke fun at something, you're much more likely to test assumptions and break the rules that uphold it. And by doing this, you can find more and better alternatives. Lastly, it triggers the brain's associative capability so you can make new and unexpected connections between existing ideas. This leads to those 'Aha' moments that you get when you suddenly see things from a new and surprising perspective.

One exercise you can use to loosen and stir up people's thinking at the beginning of a brainstorming session is to have them make up funny or cheeky mottos for their products and organizations. This is an exercise that creativity author Roger von Oech (2008) likes to do to start his seminars and conferences. Some of the examples he quotes in his book *A Whack on the Side of the Head: How You Can Be More Creative* include:

'Where you're not alone until you want a loan.'

– For an international bank

'We put the "cuss" in customer.'

– For a large retailer

'Good people, good medicine, good luck.'

– For a health insurance company

'A leader in technology whether the customer needs it or not.'

– For a large computer company

'Customer service is our number one priority: please leave your complaint at the beep.'

– For a major airline

Try this as a warm-up exercise next time you have an ideation meeting and see what bold and humorous lines your team come up with. It's just the trick to get everyone's creative juices flowing. Other ways to think humorously:

- Break up the intensity of your creative sessions with funny five-minute video clips.
- Attend a comedy club with your team or watch slapstick films.
- Make a note of the funny things that happen to people in the office and share them for laughs (with people's permission, of course!).

Invite play into the office

The physical space where people work can be a powerful instigator of creativity. Children feel most free to play and create when they are in a comfortable and stimulating environment, and so do adults. It's important to create spaces where workers can take time away from the seriousness of the day and have full permission to play without being judged. Creative companies get this and offer breakout zones, fun outings and recreational activities to help people feel young at heart and foster playful creativity. Google has led the way with its bright, sunny offices around the globe being likened to play parks. There are scavenger hunts, gaming rooms, in-office slides, aquariums, beach volleyball courts, tropical jungle huts, climbing walls, massive dinosaur skeletons, free all-you-can-eat cafeterias and more. Facebook has its arcade games, free bikes, DJ mixing facilities, pool tables, hackathons and woodworking shops, while Groupon boasts an enchanted forest for people to chill out and create in.

The challenge for companies is to encourage play without seeming insincere. Don't just copy Google – the funky office-as-playground approach works for them, but you need to do what fits with your own culture and physical infrastructure. Put out a few feelers to determine what kinds of playful solutions would be appreciated by your team. Ping pong tables and bean bags are mainstream when it comes to playful design and help to get people away from their desks. But you can take it a notch further by installing swings, putting greens, hammocks, dartboards, ball pits or any other activity station where people can go to break the monotony of the daily routine. Cultivating creativity isn't just about manipulating the office layout or décor, however; you can introduce play through, for example, karaoke competitions, nerf gun wars, silly dress-up days, laughter workshops, spy-themed adventure games, clown hire, gingerbread-house decorating contests or fun exercise classes such as trampolining.

Innovate with optimism

One of the biggest reasons that innovation efforts fail is that they are often killed by corporate dinosaurs who are pessimistic and resist the challenges being made to the status quo. Do you recognize any of these statements? (See Figure 12.1.)

Figure 12.1   Dinosaur speak

As a change architect, you will undoubtedly run into opposition and misgivings about the new ideas being implemented. This is sometimes known as the status quo bias, which inclines people to (James, 2009):

- Keep things the way they are, even if they didn't originally choose their current position.

- Avoid the risks generated by change, even when the risks are far less than if they were to make no change.

If you want to make enemies, try to change something.

WOODROW WILSON, 28TH President of the United States, Address to the World's Salesmanship Congress, Detroit (July 1916)

The best way to combat negative dinosaur speak and the status quo bias is optimism. Optimism is massively underrated in business, and yet study after study has found it to be an indispensable quality in leaders that others want to follow. It is important in a general sense, but it is even more vital when attempting to drive real innovative growth. Making any type of change requires marshalling a great deal of energy, and optimism is the fuel that powers us along with the hope that we are making things better.

Positive growth

Optimism begets positive action and mental resilience, which are necessary for growth and flourishing. Linked to this is research undertaken by Stanford psychology professor Carol Dweck (2006) on the differences between people with fixed and growth mindsets. Looking at her findings from a leadership perspective, we learn that bosses with a fixed mindset operate from a philosophy that people's basic qualities (such as personality, intelligence and talents) are carved in stone. They're of the mind that you make do with what you're born with and have little belief that they or others can change. Unsurprisingly, developing people's creativity and inventiveness is not a priority for these immutable types. However, leaders with a growth mindset assume people's basic qualities can be developed with work and determination. They place great value on learning, are open to feedback, and are confident in their ability to cultivate their own and others' creative talents. These bosses seek out constructive ways to praise, empower and motivate their workers and are resilient in the face of setbacks. There's no way around it. If you want to be a leader who helps people 'grow' their creativity and fulfil their potential, you have to be optimistic about it.

Cheerfulness is a creative choice

Optimism feeds positive emotions and engagement, which are antecedents of creativity (Emerald Group, 2015). Barbara Frederickson's (2004) work on the study of positive emotions led her to develop the Broaden and Build Theory, the substance of which is that positive emotions, such as joy, interest and gratitude, do much more than cause happiness and contentment in the moments we experience them. They also broaden behaviours such as play, awareness, discovery and inquisitiveness. When we experience positive emotions, our minds open up to new possibilities, actions and ideas, and we become more flexible and creative in the way we work. As you apply optimism as a leader and allow people to enjoy what they're doing, you will find that in time they will be more inclined to experiment and show initiative. How can you be a more optimistic influence to your team? Here are some quick pointers you can put to the test:

- **Be positive, no matter what.** First off, practise being positive and upbeat every day. Don't fall into the trap of only being positive when something good or momentous happens; it's easier to maintain a positive attitude on an ongoing basis than it is to regain it once you've succumbed to negativity.

- **Embrace newness.** When a new idea is introduced, get behind it fully and make sure you encourage everyone to 'give it their best shot'. Be positive about changes to new products, processes or procedures. Lukewarm initiatives are unlikely to become roaring successes. Some failure is OK, but if teams see innovations flop time and time again, they won't be inspired to keep creating.

- **Master your strengths.** Focus on what you and others do well and build from there. Commit to your professional development. Your journey to mastery will bring confidence and a growing capability to succeed. Be on the lookout for victories and celebrate them along the way. By ritually fuelling the growth of your team, you'll be hardwiring yourself to be a more optimistic and innovative leader.

- **Take in inspirational material on a daily basis.** I like to watch TED videos on entrepreneurship and innovation and read about the latest cognitive research. Others might prefer daily quotations, motivational tapes or reading biographies of successful people. What can you read/watch/listen to/play to get a jolt of optimism and good feeling each day?

- **See the silver lining.** We can all learn to reframe our thoughts to look for the hidden positives in any negative situation – the 90 per cent we still have rather than the 10 per cent we have lost. That bit of bad news or bad luck won't last for ever. Shift your attitude to being helpful, not helpless. What can you do right now to alleviate the situation? Is there an opportunity hidden here somewhere? If there's nothing you can do, don't dwell on it.

- **Expect people to succeed.** One of the most powerful gifts you can give someone is to believe in their potential. This is the key to helping them accomplish more and more. Even when a member of your team fails to achieve what they set out to do, don't wallow with them. Give them encouragement instead so that they feel energized to tackle the next challenge: 'Never mind. I know you'll do better next time.'

Supportive systems

What if you were to put creativity at the heart of each and every process and project? Innovation in organizations doesn't just happen – it needs some support. First off, it begins with leadership. If you're an entrepreneur or manager, you're in the best place to commit to and capitalize on this extraordinary resource through the systems and structure of your organization. How can you make creative exploration easy for everyone? Can you adapt current systems to include innovation? Small organizations are usually better at innovating collectively than large ones because they have fewer barriers and more flexible conditions. Decision-making processes in larger organizations can be painfully slow and people are less likely to see their ideas being considered seriously. Leaders who focus on innovation and remove obstacles can bring about fast changes with effective initiatives, such as letting people make decisions, investing in their growth, sharing information and data, trusting them to do the right thing, giving them opportunities to collaborate and be socially active, and allowing them to take risks without fearing a backlash if they make a mistake.

If your role is less leader and more 'small cog', you can still make an impact in your immediate team or work section. Initially, try concentrating on the areas that you can directly influence and that don't require authorization, such as improving your personal creativity, collecting insights for the department and making incremental changes to processes. For bigger initiatives, find managers or mentors who can support you in making change happen. Or get a group of like-minded innovators together to extend your clout. Have patience and stick with it because it won't happen overnight – it's best to take small steps to get others on board bit by bit.

Collaboration station

For innovation to occur you need an atmosphere of trust and collaboration. In what's fast becoming a virtual world where people are tied to their desks and devices, consider how you can set up your offices in ways that encourage real face-to-face conversations. Create 'water cooler opportunities' where people can bump into colleagues from different areas of the business or visitors from outside. These serendipitous encounters facilitate the exchange of ideas and information that can help a company progress. They are also a great way to form trusted partnerships of people who can challenge and support each other.

Think about how you can design greater movement into your environment, so people feel free to roam – strategic coffee machines, flexible seating, printers in the middle of the office, moveable walls, a central atrium/lobby. Assemble social spaces for people to mingle and hold meetings in unforced circumstances, such as lounges, cafeterias, huddle spots and breakout areas. At its new US headquarters, Samsung introduced huge outdoor areas sandwiched between floors to entice engineers and salespeople to mix with each other. Install idea boards or interactive touch screens in common areas. LinkedIn has 'whiteboard walls' everywhere to provide a canvas for capturing ideas as they come, keeping them visible for others to see and expand on. But before you go tearing down all cubicles and closed spaces, spare a thought for the introverts in your organization who might be intimidated by so many accidental interactions. Give them their private space with walled-off workstations, which can also double up as bases for one-on-one discussions.

Inclusive innovation

Other than formal brainstorming, there are innumerable ways to encourage ideas from workers, customers or the wider community. For instance, by running competitions, hosting workshops/events or through collaborative web platforms (crowdsourcing). Three times a year, former Disney CEO Michael Eisner would hold a Gong Show for his workers to keep fresh ideas coming in. Eisner and a few of his executives would devote a day listening to anyone who wanted to pitch an idea, from set designers to secretaries to theme park attendants (Tucker, nd). Usually up to 40 people were allowed to present their ideas, no matter how outrageous. Although most ideas were gonged, the process succeeded in creating an atmosphere where people felt safe to speak up. Most of Disney's animated feature movies began life in these sessions, such as *The Little Mermaid* and *Pocahontas*, as did the idea for Disney's retail stores.

Some companies keep the pipeline of innovation going by making it easy for workers to make suggestions for improvement and development on a routine basis – and benefit tremendously from it. Leading Japanese car manufacturer Toyota implements over one million employee ideas every year, 95 per cent of them within 10 days of being submitted (Lindegaard, 2011). On average, each Toyota employee submits 100 ideas per year, quickly adding up to several million suggestions. Most of them are incremental ideas that help the company improve piece by piece, rather than radical, far-reaching ones; but the important thing is the culture in which this innovative mindset is nurtured. Ideas and suggestions made by team members are part of the Toyota Way and a cornerstone of its success in the global market. Thanks to collaborative technologies, it's never been easier to enable your team to come forward with ideas. Even though you won't implement every idea, the innovative spirit you'll create will be priceless.

Other companies choose to look outside for new options in order to break free from company-centric perspectives. For instance, Cisco runs an annual global innovation competition to help identify new business ideas, with a $250,000 grand prize for the winning team. In some cases, Cisco goes on to invest in the winning idea, but the main goal is to build innovative relationships and partnerships. Take note: the opportunities for promoting innovation in your business are as endless as innovation itself.

Key takeaways

For creativity to flow through an organization, it has to be led enthusiastically from the top. Leaders must learn to think of innovation as a core capability. This chapter offers practical insights to make creativity and innovation part of your company DNA.

- **Focus on the end game.** Creative leadership is essentially about creating, having and sharing a purposeful mission and vision – providing the passionate 'why' and 'where' that mobilizes teams into action.

- **Don't be afraid to fail.** Fear causes us to shy away from the unknown and hold back from taking chances in case we fail. To become better innovators, we need to fight the knee-jerk emotional reaction of fear, focus on the opportunities available, and take calculated risks. Of course, no one likes to make mistakes, but if you do, welcome them as a form of learning – heed the lesson, change your direction and move on.

- **Engage in play.** Not being able to have fun at work dulls your creative instincts and causes the whole work environment to suffer too. You can play and still be practical. Play can take many forms – bring more fun (and less seriousness) into the workplace with humour to engage the happy side of people's brains. Consider how you can set up the work environment to provide fun stimuli for unconventional ideas, and the free time to find them.

- **Optimism.** Be a source of positive energy. Avoid pessimistic thinking and see the good in everything – even bad situations or solutions. Communicate in ways that lift people up and help them overcome feelings of self-doubt. Seek out positives everywhere! Good vibes keep the place buzzing.

- **Set up supportive systems.** Innovate from the bottom up through deliberative practices and open networks that allow people to share ideas and information wherever they are in the hierarchy. Structuring the office environment for collaboration and movement helps to increase the creative connections between teams, while suggestion schemes and competitions can elicit new ideas from people inside and outside the organization.

References

3M (2018) [accessed 20 August 2018] Who is 3M? [Online] http://www.3m.co.uk/intl/uk/aad/index.html

Allen, P (2014) [accessed 24 July 2018] The biggest failures of successful people (and how they got back up), *Lifehacker*, 7 October [Online] http://lifehacker.com/the-biggest-failures-of-successful-people-and-how-they-1642858952

Amazon (nd) [accessed 20 August 2018] Earth's Biggest Selection [Online] https://www.amazon.jobs/team-category/retail

American Express (2017) [accessed 23 July 2018] Redefining the C-Suite: Business the Millennial Way [Online] https://www.americanexpress.com/uk/content/pdf/AmexBusinesstheMillennialWay.pdf

Armstrong, J (2008) *Unleashing Your Creativity: Breaking new ground... without breaking the bank*, A & C Black, London

Branson, R (2011) *Losing My Virginity: How I've survived, had fun, and made a fortune doing business my way*, Crown Business, New York

Bright HR and Robertson Cooper (2015) [accessed 26 July 2018] It Pays to Play [Online] https://pages.brighthr.com/rs/217-MIC-854/images/itpaystoplay.pdf

Csikszentmihalyi, M (2003) *Good Business: Leadership, flow, and the making of meaning*, Penguin Books, New York

de Geus, A (1997) [accessed 26 July 2018] The Living Company, *Harvard Business Review*, March/April [Online] https://hbr.org/1997/03/the-living-company

de Geus, A (1999) *The Living Company: Growth, learning and longevity in Business*, Nicholas Brealey, London

Dweck, C (2006) *Mindset: The new psychology of success*, Random House, New York

Emerald Group (2015) *New Perspectives in Employee Engagement in Human Resources*, Emerald Group, Bingley

Frederickson, BL (2004) The broaden-and-build theory of positive emotions, *Philosophical Transactions of the Royal Society B*, **359** (1449), pp 1367–78

Google (nd) [accessed 20 August 2018] Our Company [Online] https://www.google.com/about/our-company/

Gower, L (2015) *The Innovation Workout: The 10 tried-and-tested steps that will build your creativity and innovation skills*, Pearson, Harlow

Graham, DT (2015) [accessed 25 July 2018] Pixar Co-founder: You Have to Embrace Failure to Succeed, *Daily Herald*, 6 August [Online] https://www.dailyherald.com/article/20150806/news/150809323/

James, R (2009) [accessed 28 July 2018] Status Quo Bias: Avoiding Action, Avoiding Change [Online] Available from: https://www.slideshare.net/rnja8c/status-quo-bias

LEGO (2012) [accessed 20 August 2018] Mission and Vision, 18 January [Online] https://www.lego.com/en-gb/aboutus/lego-group/mission-and-vision

Lindegaard, S (2011) *Making Open Innovation Work*, CreateSpace, North Charleston, SC

Mühlfeit, J and Costi, M (2017) *The Positive Leader: How energy and happiness fuel top-performing teams*, Pearson, Harlow

Nadler, RT, Rabi, R and Minda, JP (2010) Better mood and better performance: learning rule-described categories is enhanced by positive mood, *Psychological Science*, **21** (12), pp 1770–76

Petersen, DE (2007) [accessed 20 August 2018] At Ford, Quality Was Our Motto in the 80s, *Wall Street Journal*, 22 June. [Online] https://www.wsj.com/articles/SB118247749692744393

Robert Half International (2012) [accessed 26 July 2018] Robert Half Survey: Lack of New Ideas, Red Tape Greatest Barriers to Innovation, 4 April [Online] http://rh-us.mediaroom.com/news_releases?item=1418

Tucker, RB (nd) [accessed 28 July 2018] Effective Idea Selection is Critical to Systematic Innovation, *Innovation Management* [Online] http://www.innovationmanagement.se/imtool-articles/effective-idea-selection-is-critical-to-systematic-innovation/

Virgin (nd) [accessed 20 August 2018] Our Purpose and Values [Online] https://www.virgin.com/virgin-management-limited/careers/OurPurposeandValues

von Oech, R (2008) *A Whack on the Side of the Head: How you can be more creative*, Business Plus, New York

Conclusion

Where do you go from here?

Creativity is not a talent, it's a way of operating.
— JOHN CLEESE, British actor and comedian

Well, you've reached the end of the book but, as ever, 'the end is just the beginning' and this marks the start of your own creative success story. While reading can inspire you to learn and gives you the tools you need to become a more creative decision maker, nothing beats getting out there and being creative for real. We've covered a lot of ground together and I'd like to leave you with some final words of encouragement as you apply the methods in this book. Creative thinking is in some ways very simple, and in other ways very complex. Despite the teachings being common sense, I know how tough it can be to break the shoddy thinking habits and biases that are cramping your innovative style. You might be fired up to erase assumptions, run properly structured brainstorming sessions, build stronger ideas and be more proactive, but then what happens? You catch yourself doing what you've always done.

We believe we're open-minded and immune to slip-ups in our thinking, and yet statistically we fall prey to the same selective, reactive and assumptive faults as the next person. The bottom line is that most brainstorming sessions don't work. And that's not because there's anything wrong with brainstorming (if it's done by the book with a good strategy, of course. *See Chapter 7*) – but because it's badly managed and rife with people's thinking errors. The good news is you've read the book and have learnt some powerful ways to run your own brain.

Decisions, decisions

Our decisions affect everything we do. Choosing to change is potentially one of the most difficult decisions we will ever make. But it's also one of the most important. Creative change is needed to shape the future and do things better than we did before. Old ideas are no longer enough. We should constantly be seeking out innovations, improvements and updates in all our work practices and offerings, even if our only reason for doing so is to keep pace in a competitive environment. If you don't innovate, the rest of the world moves on and you are left behind. It may well be time for you to make some brave but necessary decisions to meet new challenges and help your company thrive, not just survive.

Innovation doesn't just happen in an organization. You need to create the right environment and atmosphere in which you can facilitate new ideas and make them useful. Any time you need to define a problem, source new possibilities, evaluate potential alternatives or implement that epic new idea, dip into this book. Apply the four-step Solution Finder process to brainstorm effectively without restrictions and extend your creative power beyond what you previously thought possible:

Step 1. Understanding – Define the challenge.
Step 2. Ideation – Generate ideas.
Step 3. Analysis – Evaluate ideas.
Step 4. Direction – Implement the solution.

The Solution Finder won't make you a perfect thinker all of a sudden, but it will keep your reasoning and nasty habits in line so they don't mess things up. The tools and techniques I've included in each chapter will amplify your and your team's ability to tackle things clearly, creatively and constructively. From changing perspectives, to reverse brainstorming, to heart vs head evaluation: you have lots of methods at your disposal here, helping to trigger masses of ideas and make sense of all the data available for analysis. Many of them counteract more than one thinking error at a time, so you can kill two (or more!) birds with one stone.

In today's fast-moving business world, we often have to make decisions at high speed, without enough time to systematically go through all the above steps of the Solution Finder. In these situations, the most effective decision-making strategy is to keep an eye on your goals and then let your gut instinct suggest the right direction to follow. This approach dominated much of Steve Jobs' decision making at Apple. Remember, do nothing and nothing happens!

Stick at it

The creative process is not without its challenges and it's likely that you will encounter setbacks along the way. Don't be disheartened if you do; instead, learn from them and ensure that you always celebrate your successes. With the help of this book and periodic revisits of the Decision Radar, you will grow in confidence as you make better decisions and these decisions turn new ideas into successes. Stop doing the things that keep you stuck or slow you down, and start doing those that will take you somewhere different – both mentally and physically. Ask yourself, 'How good can it get?'

Thank you for reading. The world needs more inspiration and innovation. I wish you every success as you bring your awesome new ideas to life.

Chris Griffiths

APPENDIX: ACTIVITY ANSWERS

Months of the year (page 2)

April

August

December

February

January

July

June

March

May

November

October

September

The equation (page 18)

Most people are inclined to see this as a numerical problem, but the answer demands that you approach it more visually and imaginatively.

With one straight line $2 + 7 - 118 = 129$ can become:

Figure A.1   The equation answer

$2\ 4\ 7 - 118 = 129$

Now it's correct!

Other possible ways to answer this question include:

Putting a strike through the equals sign so that it reads: $2 + 7 - 118 \neq 129$

Modifying the equals sign to make: $2 + 7 - 118 \geq 129$

Drop the block (page 28)

The answer is that it depends on where the person is and the environment they are in:

1 If the person is on Earth....

Figure A.2 The block drops *down* to the ground

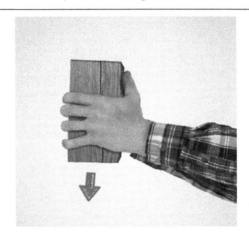

The block of wood will drop *down* to the ground because it is drawn to earth by gravity.

2 If the person is under water...

Figure A.3 The block floats *up*

The block of wood will float *up* to the surface of the water because it's less dense than water.

3 If the person is in space...

Figure A.4 The block will *not move*

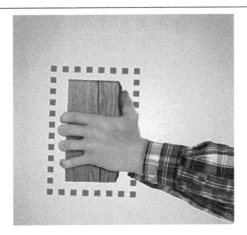

The block of wood will *not move* because there are no overall forces in any direction.

SOURCE: Brainstorming.co.uk (2011) Creative thinking puzzle 2 – the 'drop the block' problem, Infinite Innovations Ltd, [Online] http://www.brainstorming.co.uk/puzzles/dropblock.html

Scrambled letters (page 45)

1 With a bit of focus and filtering, you can weed out the extraneous letters to reveal this common word:

SUPERMARKET

2 This problem is a bit trickier. To solve it, you need to interpret it more literally. Instead of crossing out six letters, you first cross out the 'S', then the 'I', then the 'X', the 'L', the 'E', the 'T', and so on, until you have crossed out 'S I X L E T T E R S'. You will be left with the word:

BANANA

Assumption-busting questions (page 56)

1 He was a skywriter whose plane crashed into another plane.

2 Draw a longer line next to it, so the original line is shorter than the new line.

The tricky grid (page 58)

Flip the grid upside down. The number 6 becomes a 9. Circle the numbers 1, 9, 1 and 1 as shown below.

Figure A.5 The tricky grid answer

INDEX